# WORLDLY AFTERLIVES

## HISTORIES OF ECONOMIC LIFE

*Jeremy Adelman, Sunil Amrith, Emma Rothschild, and Francesca Trivellato, Series Editors*

*Worldly Afterlives: Tracing Family Trails Between India and Empire* by Julia Stephens

*The Crowd in the Early Middle Ages* by Shane Bobrycki

*A Third Path: Corporatism in Brazil and Portugal* by Melissa Teixeira

*Power and Possession in the Russian Revolution* by Anne O'Donnell

*Toward a Free Economy: Swatantra and Opposition Politics in Democratic India* by Aditya Balasubramanian

*No Return: Jews, Christian Usurers, and the Spread of Mass Expulsion in Medieval Europe* by Rowan Dorin

*Desert Edens: Colonial Climate Engineering in the Age of Anxiety* by Philipp Lehmann

*Distant Shores: Colonial Encounters on China's Maritime Frontier* by Melissa Macauley

*A Velvet Empire: French Informal Imperialism in the Nineteenth Century* by David Todd

*Making It Count: Statistics and Statecraft in the Early People's Republic of China* by Arunabh Ghosh

*Empires of Vice: The Rise of Opium Prohibition across Southeast Asia* by Diana S. Kim

*Pirates and Publishers: A Social History of Copyright in Modern China* by Fei-Hsien Wang

*Sorting Out the Mixed Economy: The Rise and Fall of Welfare and Developmental States in the Americas* by Amy C. Offner

*Red Meat Republic: A Hoof-to-Table History of How Beef Changed America* by Joshua Specht

*The Promise and Peril of Credit: What a Forgotten Legend about Jews and Finance Tells Us about the Making of European Commercial Society* by Francesca Trivellato

*A People's Constitution: The Everyday Life of Law in the Indian Republic* by Rohit De

*A Local History of Global Capital: Jute and Peasant Life in the Bengal Delta* by Tariq Omar Ali

# Worldly Afterlives

## TRACING FAMILY TRAILS BETWEEN INDIA AND EMPIRE

JULIA STEPHENS

PRINCETON UNIVERSITY PRESS
PRINCETON & OXFORD

Published by Princeton University Press
41 William Street, Princeton, New Jersey 08540
99 Banbury Road, Oxford OX2 6JX
press.princeton.edu

GPSR Authorized Representative: Easy Access System Europe - Mustamäe tee 50, 10621 Tallinn, Estonia, gpsr.requests@easproject.com



ISBN 978-0-691-20545-8
ISBN (e-book) 978-0-691-27780-6

Library of Congress Control Number: 2025939942

British Library Cataloging-in-Publication Data is available

Editorial: Priya Nelson and Emma Wagh
Production Editorial: Kathleen Cioffi
Jacket Design: Karl Spurzem
Production: Danielle Amatucci
Publicity: William Pagdatoon and Kathryn Stevens

Jacket Credit: Renluka Maharaj, *Susie, Sero, and Bebe.* Archival photograph printed on canvas, acrylic paint, acrylic markers, colored pencils, rhinestones, plastic leaves and paper flowers, 30 × 40 × 2 inches, 2020.

This book has been composed in Arno

Printed in the United States of America

10 9 8 7 6 5 4 3 2 1

MIX
Paper
FSC® C183721

# CONTENTS

# Introduction

## WORLDLY AFTERLIVES

*GOWSEE SHUFFLED his feet while waiting with several dozen other Indian laborers outside a small building. Heat radiated from the building—the sun beat down on the tin roof, and the windows were closed, blocking relief from the cooling sea breezes. He was told that the conditions were necessary so an officer could take a picture of his face—they called it a photograph. Gowsee was unsure what to make of this bizarre procedure. He had traveled miles on foot to reach the Immigration Depot, a formidable space filled with painful memories. He thought back to the day several years earlier in 1873 when he had first entered the depot on arrival in Mauritius from India. They had taken his name and given him a number in return, 361788, which British officials would use to amass a bureaucratic record of his life. On that fateful day, he tried to appear calm to reassure his wife, three sons, and daughter-in-law, who traveled with him. Internally, he was less confident. Had the family made the right decision to leave their home in Ghazipur? Was he wrong to trust the sweet-talking agent who had convinced him that Mauritius was a land where chili trees bore gold? He laughed now to think how gullible he had once been. He never could have imagined the terrible sea sickness and the endless hours of back-breaking labor that awaited them on the plantation.*

*They survived, but the immigration depot was not done with them. His employer explained that now that they had completed their first term of indenture, Gowsee and his sons must return to the depot to have their photographs taken. The picture would be affixed to an "Old Immigrant Ticket," which they would be required to carry to prove their residence and ongoing employment. Gowsee had seen other Indians return after such trips, carrying their tickets, bearing their ghostly grey faces, in government-issued tin boxes strung around their necks. They were the most hideous jewelry Gowsee had ever seen! But their bearers told him they must keep the papers safe from the elements and prying hands, which the boxes helped ensure. If an officer interrogated them on the road, and they failed to produce these documents, they would be dragged off to jail and charged as vagrants.*

*Suddenly, the officer's assistants pushed Gowsee into the sweltering building, filled with strange chemical smells. In front of him, the officer manipulated a peculiar wooden box with two menacing glass eyes that stared back at him. The assistant told him that the camera had traveled all the way from England. He had heard that the wealthy* goras, *as the Indians called the Europeans, paid princely sums to have their pictures taken in studios in Port Louis but also that criminals were made to sit for these pictures so that the police could keep their images locked away in their cabinets forever.*

*Later, the assistant handed him his "Old Immigrant Ticket" with a warning to guard it with his life. Attached to the paper was his picture, about a finger-length in size. He stared mesmerized at his face and his bald head—nearly five decades of work and worry had taken its toll—but he noted with pride that his flowing white beard made him look like an elder of authority. His sons were staring with wonder at their photographs, but he ordered them to put them away—who knew when and where they might need these strange images in the future?*[1]

Today, Gowsee's photograph hangs in a simple white frame alongside pictures of his son, grandson, great-grandson, great-great-grandson, and great-great-great-grandson in a home in the United Kingdom.[2] The nineteenth-century photographs traveled there from the Mahatma Gandhi Institute's archives in Mauritius, which holds approximately 175,000 ID photographs that were taken of indentured immigrants between 1864 and 1914, likely the earliest large-scale use of photographic identification for a non-criminal population.[3] Copies of the photographs of Gowsee and his sons were retrieved by Caitlin Golaup, who married into the family. She later shared them with another roots researcher who also married into the family, Kyriaki Anagnostopoulou, who had the pictures framed as a gift for her father-in-law, Gowsee's great-grandson. This image inspired Caitlin to make another collage of photographs that included women relations, which she posted to a Facebook Group, "Gowsee Udhin and Rosunnee Emamboccus' descendants."[4] Gowsee's photograph has thus traveled many routes. As Kyriaki explained: "When Mauritian family come to visit, they will often take pictures of it. . . . So the pictures have become pictures that others are now showing to their own descendants. It's taken on a life of its own. . . . Even though it was originally a means of documenting indenture and technically showing that this is my slave, it has now become a family album and possibly an heirloom in the future."

Caitlin and Kyriaki are serious family researchers who have traced their families' Mauritian roots, as well as Ukrainian-Jewish, Polish, Trinidadian, American, Austrian, Greek, Italian, Irish, Scottish, and English ancestors. I found their profiles on Ancestry.com and MyHeritage.com. When I reached out to them, Caitlin and Kyriaki explained that their investigations had been met with curiosity, but also puzzlement, from other family members. Why were the White foreigners who married into the family researching their Indian and African roots? As another White foreigner who married into a family that traces its roots through Kerala and the Gulf, I could sympathize with this feeling of being an insider-outsider to family histories. (Caitlin also told me that she thinks that some of her Mauritian in-laws are puzzled that she would be so interested in the past since they want to "look forwards rather than backward.") Resisting the narrow boxes in which heritage is often framed, Kyriaki described her son, Gowsee's fifth-generation descendant, as a "citizen of the world."

Could Gowsee have imagined that his photograph and family would have such worldly afterlives? We can never know—the opening paragraphs of this book are my fictionalized account of his experience being photographed. But my account is not conjured from nothing, nor does it seek to recuperate a past otherwise lost.[5] Instead, it draws on the vast archives that British colonial officials amassed to track the over thirty million Indians who left the Subcontinent between the middle of the nineteenth and the middle of the twentieth century, of which the collection of indenture photographs in Mauritius is but one example.[6] The book collages materials from these archives with vestiges of the past that migrants and their descendants passed from generation to generation—albums, stories, material, and immaterial inheritances—of property and heirlooms, of habits of mind and body, and of memories of what was lost. I am especially concerned with the creative possibilities that open up when we travel between these different means of collecting and making sense of the past.

While many of the family stories I trace stretch back even further, I pick them up in the following pages as they intersect with the heyday of British imperial power in the Indian Ocean. This "Age of Empire" saw the consolidation of Crown government in India after the Rebellion of 1857 alongside the rapid expansion of the British Empire across Asia and Africa.[7] The economic extractions of British colonialism pushed Indians out of India while propelling them towards other parts of the empire. Famines devastated India, forcing many to seek livelihoods elsewhere. These crises were set in motion by disruptive El Niño weather patterns, leading to devastating droughts in the 1870s and 1890s, but British policies greatly exacerbated them. Peasant households increasingly produced raw materials for industrializing economies elsewhere rather than food to feed their families. Growing cotton, indigo, rice, and jute in good times could net Indian farmers profits, but when a crop failed or prices crashed, they were left with nothing to eat. Miserly British relief programs, cloaked in Malthusian doctrines that cast famine as a "natural" check on overpopulation, left millions of Indians dead. Millions of others left their homes in search of something better.[8]

Some found their way to recruiters, selling stories of the riches that could be reaped abroad. Most famously, over a million Indians were contracted as indentured laborers to replace enslaved Africans on plantations in the Caribbean and Africa. Others, who violently resisted empire, traveled in chains to Britain's penal colonies.[9] Yet numerically, these migrants constituted only a fraction of overall migration from the Subcontinent. Some signed other types of contracts to defend and expand the British Empire as soldiers, sailors, and police.[10] Many others took loans from a *kangani*, the Tamil word for a recruiter, to help their families financially in exchange for joining a gang of workers traveling to Malaya, Ceylon, and Burma, the closest and most popular destinations for colonial-era Indian migrants.[11] Having traded along the coasts of the Indian Ocean for centuries, Indians plied much of its transregional trade, even as they were pushed into subordinate positions by European businesses backed by colonial governments.[12] New cadres of graduates from English-medium colleges, who often struggled to secure gainful employment at home, set out to work in colonial offices and courtrooms across Asia and Africa. Others pursued innumerable other pathways abroad as nannies to British families, circus performers, and students.[13] Most eventually returned to India, but others remained abroad, forming a vast global diaspora.[14]

The descendants of these migrants, alongside many more recent migrants from the Indian Subcontinent, today are part of what many describe as the "Indian" or "South Asian" diaspora, one of the world's largest.[15] But stories such as Gowsee's, Caitlin's, and Kyriaki's suggest how family trails unsettle national, ethnic, and regional labels, as well as the distinction between labor and merchant diasporas, which many academic studies adopt. Instead, they point to histories in which different forms of mobility were entangled: physical migration, intermarriage/cohabitation, conversion, socio-economic ascent and descent. They suggest diasporas flowing into each other during an era when colonialism, global capitalism, world wars, and post-colonial nationalism set many different peoples adrift. The resulting families often describe their diasporic identities as a bequest of worldly habits, of being "citizens of the world," and of being descendants of empire. For many families, these legacies outweigh conventional definitions of diaspora that center on ancestral homeland or ethno-religious identity—categories that divide their own kin.

Just as these families complicate geographically bounded frames for studying diaspora, they also unsettle historical temporalities that divide past and present migrations. Gowsee's photograph now exists in many places and inhabits multiple historical moments. I have imagined what it might have felt like as a pendant hanging around his neck. At that moment, it was a talisman, at once subjecting him to surveillance and preventing his arrest as a vagrant—a symbol of the limbo he inhabited between the enslaved and the free. Today, sitting in an archive, it takes on a different life as a memorial meant to educate the public about the history of indenture. In this reincarnation, Gowsee is both present and absent—he is visually present in the photograph but marked by its faded monotone and delicate condition as long since dead. Digitized copies of the picture have traveled even further and taken on other relationships with the present, disembodied into megabytes before being reembodied as framed family heirlooms. They arrive in descendants' inboxes as the first glimpse of a relation about whom stories have been passed down but whose face they had never seen. The initial surprise that such an image exists in a distant archive quickly transforms into a sense of recognition—an inherited nose or chin.

This tendency to shape-shift between absence and presence, embodied and disembodied forms, allows these objects to bring the past into the present in unexpected ways. In the book, I engage with these presences through a framework of haunting. Borrowing from Avery Gordon's *Ghostly Matters*, I recognize haunting as "that which makes its mark by being there and not there at the same time."[16] I noticed this ghostly aura in other objects (and memories of objects) through which families connected with the past. It was the absence/presence of the remembered, but now missing, trophies that haunted the armoire of a family in Kuala Lumpur. Whether touched or conjured as memories, these objects invite an intimate connection with the past that stirs the senses differently than a historian's carefully constructed argument. When families affix a modern photograph to a century-old one and gently caress the assemblage, the past is hauntingly close and yet not quite touchable; the dead are present but also painfully absent. Thinking with ghosts challenges historians to question the linear chronologies that undergird our analysis, which assume the pastness of the past and its separation from the present. Haunting also opens space for considering how our emotions are at play in our work, shaping our analysis in ways that are obscured through disciplinary norms that often still discourage historians from writing themselves into their scholarship.[17]

My interest in these haunting presences may seem strange to professional historians. We are meant to read sources, not caress them. But I suspect that my encounters with ghosts will feel less odd to descendants (a position which historians, too, might assume). Family roots researchers and historians often sit side-by-side in archives but less frequently acknowledge each other's presence. Professional historians often view roots researchers as hobbyists who might benefit from reading our work but have little to teach us. My many encounters with families inside and outside archives have convinced me otherwise. Families have pushed me to use new sources and methods, leading me outside the archive to albums and curio cabinets. They have challenged me to think about what it means to ethically engage with the past when the lines between the living and dead blur. I have also tried to reciprocate. I have shared archival materials with descendants and suggested how my own frames of gendered analysis might enable them to reexamine family stories, often framed as histories of founding patriarchs, to recognize the influence of women. In the process, our collective understanding of diaspora and family shifted, showing how historians and descendants have much to learn from each other, even when we might not always agree.

## "I Am Diaspora": Diaspora and Empire

One such transformation was how working alongside families and descendants pushed me to rethink conventional academic approaches to diaspora. Academic studies of diaspora typically frame it through national, regional, or religious modifiers, referring to the Indian, South Asian, Sikh, or Tamil diasporas. In contrast, I found that outside of academia and in the borderlands where it interfaces with other creative fields, the descendants of migrants who traveled the Indian Ocean during the heyday of the British Empire were approaching diaspora in more fluid and mobile ways. Esha Pillay, who runs an Instagram account called "Coolie Returns," captured how diaspora, particularly when used without a modifier, opened possibilities for engaging with the intergenerational legacies of migrations that defy political borders and identarian categories. The descendant of indentured migrants, she explained that she was uncomfortable identifying as "a Fijian" or even "an indo Fijian in Fiji." She felt a deep connection to Britain, and when she traveled as a young adult to the UK, she described feeling that she had arrived in the "Motherland." This connection, however, did not inspire diasporic patriotism but rather a feeling of intergenerational trauma that Britain was "responsible for my family's displacement." Summing up her refusal of a narrow definition of belonging, Pillay proclaimed: "I am diaspora."[18]

Similar themes ran through a collective conversation between the writer-academic María del Pilar Kaladeen, architect Sumayya Vally, poet Gitan Djeli, and artist Shivanjani Lal, who also trace their family histories through journeys of indenture. Kaladeen noted that although she has used the phrase "'indentured labor diaspora' . . . I don't think it adequately represents the way that it can sometimes feel as though we are all family to each other." Vally ruminated that "To be hybrid is a position of power. The ability to absorb, intuit and resonate across geography and cultural conditions is itself a language of imagination and empathy." Djeli elaborated that although the contributors shared common bonds, their ancestors "did not travel with the same caste, social, educational, and economic background." Instead, she pointed to "this ocean journey that connects us to each other, but also to the diaspora of the last five hundred years of colonization."[19]

These five ruminations on diasporic family pasts from individuals working in different creative fields provide a template for rethinking what it means to be diasporic. All invoke the idea of being diasporic without a modifier—gesturing at a relationship to being diasporic that exceeds categorization as "Indian," "South Asian," or "Indo-Fijian." While all think deeply about the legacies of indenture, Kaladeen even finds the label "indentured labor diaspora" limiting. Instead, they frame diaspora, family, and empire as deeply entangled in ways that push us to rethink each. They speak of bonds rooted in shared experiences of oceanic journeys and the violence of being subject to imperial power as more formative than ties to an ancestral homeland or an adopted host land. As a "Motherland," Britain becomes part of a family saga in which the intimacy of connection makes the violence of abuse even more painful. The children and grandchildren of this colonial diaspora share a kinship beyond those limited to heteronormative couplings and biological reproduction. It is these family trails that the book traces.

Following these trails requires rethinking the who, what, where, and when of how we study diaspora, family, and empire. I start by considering why I find the concept of diaspora useful despite the many questions scholars have raised about its applicability to Indian Ocean migration.[20] Following family trails has meant traveling to nearly every region of the globe, so the book is not geographically limited to the Indian Ocean. Still, it is profoundly shaped by insights and methods from this field. Most of the family trails I traced were journeys between different regions of Asia and between Asia and Africa. For scholars who foreground such South-South migrations, the term diaspora can seem an awkward fit. Its original association with Jewish biblical exile and the predominance of South-North migrations within diasporic studies, including Atlantic slavery, have linked diaspora to forced separation, extended exile, and longing for return to an ancestral homeland. Many of these characteristics map awkwardly onto the geographies and temporalities of migration in the Indian Ocean during the Age of Empire. Migrations between South and Southeast Asia and between Asia and Africa were often temporary, with migrants returning home permanently or for periodic visits, muting for some the experience of exile that has been so central to other diasporic experiences. As Isabel Hofmeyr has argued, "the Indian Ocean has been home to failed diasporas, notably people who move but do not embark on projects of cultural memory and constructing homelands."[21]

In other cases, migrations were more extended but multi-sited, blurring the distinction between homeland and destination. For example, amongst the records of indentured Indians who migrated from Calcutta and Madras to

Natal, South Africa, I found references to migrants who had previously spent time in Mauritius, Guiana, Trinidad, St. Lucia, St. Vincent, Reunion, Jamaica, Suriname, and Guadeloupe, suggesting that they served out one term of indenture, returned to India, and signed up for an additional term of indenture in a new locale.[22] These itineraries extended even further in future generations. I traced how one family's journey from India to Natal in the early twentieth century now shapes how they think about their twenty-first-century migration from South Africa to Qatar. Natal functioned as an adopted host land for this family in one generation, and South Africa has become a remembered homeland in another. Just as Natal became part of South Africa after 1910, shifting political borders meant that migrants moved through landscapes that were themselves mobile, including during the seismic partitions of the Subcontinent in 1947 and again in 1971. The economic disruptions of the Great Depression, followed by World War II, and then the decolonization of Asia and Africa in subsequent decades saw families who had moved for generations around the Indian Ocean caught, as Kalyani Ramnath elegantly puts it, between "borders arbitrarily drawn and mobilities ignored."[23] Uncomfortable in new nations and citizenship regimes that sought to equate territory with racial, religious, and linguistic belonging, many kept moving, as I found when I reached out to the descendants of colonial-era migrants. Many were themselves also migrants interested in learning more about their ancestors as a means of reflecting on their own journeys. Such repeated, circuitous migrations are not unique to the Indian Ocean, but subsequent waves of colonialism, global depression, world wars, and post-colonial nation building have made for particularly complex journeys.

While these circuits have led some scholars of the region to avoid the concept of diaspora altogether, others consider it valuable in particular contexts. For example, Sunil Amrith writes, "The term is more useful, however, when it draws our attention specifically to the kinds of connections migrants maintain with their homelands and with others of shared origin dispersed around the world."[24] In this framing, scholars use diaspora to describe groups that self-consciously cultivated homeland-oriented imaginaries and ethno-linguistic patriotisms, such as Engseng Ho's exploration of the role of ancestral graves in Tarim in anchoring the Hadhrami diaspora, or Amrith's own study of the rise of a Tamil public sphere in British Malaya.[25] The idea of diaspora has also been usefully deployed to study political projects of expatriate nationalism, as in Sana Aiyar's study of Indians in Kenya.[26] Many scholars of the region, however, remain wary. Rachel Leow has recently offered a particularly pointed critique, arguing that diaspora may be an "inescapably arboreal concept" that elevates "biological models of race," "territorialized loyalty," and "patrilineage and patriarchies."[27]

I echo Leow's call to rethink diasporic histories in non-essentialist terms, including by centering women. Rather than abandoning the idea of diasporic roots, however, I try to reimagine them outside of what Leow identifies as the limits of "arboreal" thinking. As conventionally imagined, the family tree presupposes a permanent and stationary attachment to land, and a linear logic of growth, rooted in the past and branching into the present. But actual nature is far more creative. In the following pages, I trace diasporic roots not just vertically as they became embedded in a particular patch of soil but also horizontally across fluid landscapes in which water and earth intermingled.[28] Drawing on my experience as an amateur gardener, I think with perennial roots, which, unlike trees, must be periodically divided and transplanted to thrive. Like perennials, diasporic families spread their roots through movement rather than attachment to a single place. I also think of mangrove trees, which thrive not on land but in salty water. While away from my garden, researching in Abu Dhabi, I took pleasure in observing its mangroves. I learned to think with their roots, which sometimes rise out of the water and turn upwards like branches, as the past haunts the present.

In trying to rethink diaspora, I also look to the borderlands where academia interfaces with art and literature as offering possibilities for thinking about mobility, rather than essentializing categories of identity, as a thread linking diasporic histories. Within academia, diaspora studies are deeply shaped by methodological nationalism, or the tendency to take nations as the default unit of analysis, even as the field reflects a broader embrace of transregional research. The almost ubiquitous use of modifiers, whether "Indian" or ethnolinguistic or religious categories such as "Tamil" or "Sikh," treats diasporas as bounded communities. They function akin to de-territorialized nation states that are geographically dispersed but nonetheless defined by identarian boundaries. Yet the artists and writers cited earlier engage diaspora more fluidly. On Instagram, a platform where I found many creative efforts to document migrant pasts, the hashtag #diaspora has over a million posts, far outnumbering references to specific regionally, ethnically, or religiously defined diasporas.[29] Academics sometimes complain that diaspora has become too mobile a concept, a diaspora of diasporas, which threatens to vacate the term of any meaning.[30] But I embrace this mobility as resonating deeply with how the families that populate the coming pages talked about the past and its relationship to their present. These cultural memories focus less on origin than the legacies of repeated movement. They are the mindset of worldliness that Kyriaki Anagnostopoulou attributed to her son, and the hybridity that Sumayya Vally invoked as "a language of imagination and empathy."

If these soaring imaginaries speak to the power of oceanic journeying in fostering diasporic memory, I also came to see how the legacies of empire weighed them down. In Chapter 2, I explore how a family who repeatedly litigated their affairs in colonial courts in Bombay and Zanzibar passed the resulting habits of litigiousness from generation to generation long after the assets they disputed were exhausted. The recent flourishing of legal history in Indian Ocean contexts suggests that they were joined by many similarly litigious Parsi, Hadhrami, and Chettyar families, who made fortunes arbitraging between Asian, African, and global markets, and lost these same fortunes litigating in colonial courts.[31] Colonial legal logics became woven into the warp and weft of these families' most intimate affairs. Colonialism also imparted other habits. In Chapter 3, I speak with a family about how their vexed relationship with South African settler colonialism lives on in the family's compulsive desire to invest in real estate. They speak to how settler colonialism affected groups, including Asians in Africa, who do not typically feature in studies that oppose White settlement to indigenous displacement.[32]

That such migrants and their descendants are rarely considered part of a British imperial diaspora shows how essentialized notions of race and territorial nationalism continue to undergird much scholarship on diaspora. Work on the British diaspora and empire thus typically foregrounds the dispersion of White migrants from Britain across the empire and the resulting Anglophone and settler-colonial cultures that emerged.[33] Conversely, studies of the South Asian diaspora have emphasized the role of dispersed Indians in anticolonial movements, inspiring diasporic patriotism that resisted empire.[34] Studies of how migrants from India identified with empire, however, are limited, perhaps because they represent a potentially problematic false consciousness—a sense that such Indians overlooked imperial racism and violence.[35] This is the case, however, only when diasporic identification is understood primarily as a feeling of patriotic belonging—hallmarks of an approach shaped by methodological nationalism. Thinking diaspora through family, in contrast, opens avenues for exploring how colonial-era migrants and their descendants identified with empire without endorsing it, including through inheritances of traumatic displacement. Empire reshaped family relations. Many also experienced empire as akin to a family relationship. Thus, in Chapter 3, I consider the case of an Indian-South African matriarch who wore a pendant with the image of Queen Victoria on her breast even as she protested against White racism. She used embodied intimacy, literally wearing the Queen as one might a familial relation, to stake her own claims to imperial motherhood.[36] As these examples suggest, studying diaspora through the intersection of family and empire unsettles ancestral homeland and ethnoreligious identity as the central lens through which we think about the legacies of migration. It foregrounds the intimate, also often violent and traumatic, inheritances of mobility and empire.

## Feminist Family Histories

Studying diasporic families in this way requires unsettling who we consider family and how we study them. The book works at the intersection of two fields: critical histories of gender and sexuality and biographical family histories. The former has shown how governing intimate relations, just as much as territory, was central to European empires.[37] Imperial regimes restructured conjugal and inter-generational relations by applying new systems of family law to marriage and inheritance. Policing the family, particularly those that crossed borders, was central to instituting racialized regimes of governance. Hiving off domestic from market relations also birthed new economies that masculinized market relations. These insights have defamiliarized structures often treated as timeless and rooted in biology, including definitions of family that prioritize legal and conjugal relations over other forms of kinship, as well as racial and religious identities.

These insights have percolated more slowly through the scholarly literature on diaspora, which often still centers on mobile men as key figures in ethnonationally or religious-regionally defined diasporic communities. According to official migration statistics, which measured movement across political boundaries, men significantly outnumbered women in the great wave of Asian migration that stretched from the middle of the nineteenth to the middle of the twentieth century.[38] But this one rubric for measuring the relationship between gender and migration has spawned a scholarship that is decidedly patriarchal in orientation. Thus, Indian Ocean studies has privileged the perspective of masculine merchants, scholars, seamen, and laborers, who are described as scattering their seed along its coasts. While this scholarship acknowledges the influence of women's wombs and local soils in shaping diasporas, they chart genealogies organized around masculine lineages.[39] These accounts, as Chie Ikeya pointedly critiques, relegate women to minor roles, "domesticating and nourishing what have been sown, spun, and propagated by men."[40] This is beginning to change, but much work remains.[41] Patriarchal frames also dominate public histories of diasporic communities, which often center hagiographies of great men.[42] Roots researchers understandably often begin their explorations with such patriarchal norms and identarian categories baked in. Yet, as I found out when I spoke to them, many also sensed that their families' pasts were more complicated.

The simple but still radical *feminist* move of asking about the women in such families is the first step towards excavating these more complex histories. I began my research for Chapters 1 and 2 looking for the histories of two great men and their families, Thamboosamy Pillai and Tharia Topan, who are frequently cast as the progenitors of the Tamil-Hindu diaspora in Malaysia and the Gujarati-Khoja diaspora in Zanzibar. When I connected with their descendants, they, too, were primed by previous conversations with other scholars and journalists to tell me about their fathers and grandfathers. But when we began speaking about women in their families, particularly Thamboosamy's and Tharia's wives, Alamaloo and Janbai, we together unearthed alternative histories: from the critical role of widowed matriarchs in managing family businesses to transnational networks that bound women to women through overlapping habits of cosmopolitan consumption rather than via shared blood or identity. When we foreground women in studies of diaspora—from mothers who anchored households of migrant men, to the daughters of mixed couples (married or not), to women who undertook shorter or temporary journeys that were excluded from official measures of migration—the very idea of what it means to be diasporic necessarily shifts. The legacies of repeated mobility come into focus as one of the key features of what it means to be diasporic.

Yet historians who study family and empire also have much to learn from descendants and roots researchers. In engaging deeply with family stories, the book borrows from historians who have used the lens of a particular family to navigate imperial and global geographies.[43] I have also learned from scholars who have written about their own families—projects that challenge academic norms that cast the historian as an objective, outside observer of others' pasts.[44] Yet these works rarely grapple deeply with how historians and roots researchers engage with the past in different ways.[45]

In thinking through this question, I have been inspired by scholars studying the Black Atlantic. Since at least 1976, when Alex Haley published his seminal *Roots*, scholars and lay people have looked to family history to grapple with the legacies of slavery. As a result, scholars working on Black diasporas have engaged deeply with family archives and memories to recover histories obscured in official sources. My work has been enriched by such engagements, from Tina Campt's work on family portraits and albums to Tiya Miles's retelling of family journeys through textiles.[46] In Chapter 5, I also draw inspiration from Alondra Nelson's analysis of DNA genealogy, which, while attuned to its many problems, shows the surprising ways African Americans have used it to fight for reparations and restorative justice.[47]

While inspired by work on the Black Atlantic, the book explores the different land and seascapes through which historians and roots researchers travel in the Indian Ocean. Historians of African slavery have struggled with the problem of humanizing subjects who were often recorded as nameless inventory.[48] While I have similarly encountered silences and dehumanization while tracing families through archives, I also grappled with invasive detail and excesses of information. After abolition, British officials sought to prove that the

Indian laborers who replaced enslaved Africans did so voluntarily and that indenture promoted family ties, in contrast to enslaved mothers who were separated from their children at auctions. Creating dossiers of consent and kinship was thus crucial to veiling the continuities between the two systems. Similarly, documenting the belongings of migrants was essential to depicting them as owners of property, rather than the enslaved property of others. British officials recorded the contents of even minuscule estates when migrants died abroad—such as the leather saddlebag of Said Tasselm, a *fakir* or wandering holy man, who died in Alexandria, Egypt, and the crumpled IOUs found in the pockets of Narang Singh, a watchman for the Shanghai Nanking Railway.[49] These records provide remarkable tools for tracing family trails. But some contain family secrets that migrants or their descendants might have wished to hide, necessitating delicate ethical maneuvers.

## Haunted Collages

Working with families, paging through photo albums and caressing delicate heirlooms together, taught me to engage with the past through feeling ghostly presences rather than just reading texts and analyzing arguments.[50] Concretely, this involved incorporating visual and material sources into my work alongside textual documents. These alternative archives, which are central to how many families engage with the past, are crucial to writing inclusive histories of migration in the Indian Ocean, even as they remain peripheral to much historical research.[51] According to the 1911 census of India, only 5 percent of Indians were literate and only 1 percent of Indian women.[52] Given that literacy rates were low and highly gendered, images and objects are essential to writing histories that look beyond the migration experiences of elite men.

Yet this shift required more than incorporating photographs and objects as sources. It entailed learning to *feel* sources, as I feel my grandmother's ring rub against my finger. It required finding ways to weave into my staid scholarly prose the haunting intimacy with the past that this touch conjures. It meant thinking of history not as an abstract inheritance but as an heirloom, derived from the Middle English *lome* or implement—a tool from the past that only gains value in the present when we use it to weave something new.[53] Approaching history as heirloom necessitated taking seriously the skills passed from one generation of women to the next as methods of interpreting the past. It meant finding inspiration for my work in unexpected sources, such as the art of Suchitra Mattai. Mattai uses vintage needlework (depicting historical scenes of women, enslaved/indentured people, and colonial settings), sari scraps gifted from her mother, and sewing skills inherited from her Indo-Guyanese grandmothers to construct multi-layered woven sculptures that reimagine time and space.[54] Her art helped me to see roots as also threads that could be salvaged from one garment and sewn into something new.

As I made this shift in my thinking, I came to notice things that I had previously ignored, like the images of my own fingers in the digital photographs of documents I collected from archives. In this way, it equally transformed how I interacted with textual documents as well as objects and images. Migrants, many of whom were illiterate, *felt* the power of texts. They literally *touched* the documents that sealed their fate—placing their thumbprint on a labor contract. But documents were not just tools of official control. Letters, sometimes with snapshots enclosed, allowed migrants to connect with distant kin. Here, again, touch was crucial—I encountered many examples of letters that were carried in migrant's pockets, a form of intimacy potentially more powerful than hearing words that were often written and read by others.[55] As I imagined how touching these letters and photographs transported migrants and their relations across continental distances, I also came to understand why, when I touched them, I felt *haunted* by a past that felt more intimately present.

The book deploys haunting as a method to explore how a focus on feeling, particularly the intersection of physical touch and emotional connection, destabilizes dominant historical methods and temporalities. In both the humanities and social sciences, texts reign supreme as sources and as method—so much so that scholars read many things as "texts" that are not even written documents. As Clifford Geertz famously argued: "The culture of a people is an ensemble of texts, themselves ensembles, which the anthropologist strains to read over the shoulders of those to whom they properly belong."[56] In contrast, families made me see that not everything is a text waiting for scholars to read. They taught me that the past can be seen, touched, and felt—by viewing photographs, wearing family heirlooms, retelling stories, and sifting through archives.

In conceptualizing how these practices might work as alternatives to "reading" the past, I have been inspired by practices of artistic collage, particularly the work of artist Renluka Maharaj, whose artwork graces the cover. Maharaj's ancestors migrated from India to Trinidad and Tobago as indentured laborers, and today she uses her training in photography and painting to create arresting visual reinterpretations of that past. Maharaj's recent work was sparked by a series of postcard photographs of indentured Indian women. The photographs were taken by French photographer Felix Morin, who ran a studio in Port of Spain, Trinidad from 1869 until the late 1890s. In a series that came to be known as "Coolie Belles," Morin adorned Indian women with elaborate jewelry before taking their photographs, which he sold to tourists.[57] The photographs, in Maharaj's words, were "objectifying, exoticising and, thereby, othering these women." As she explained of the mixed-media collages that she subsequently created: "It became important that I lift them out of these archives and re-present

FIGURE 0.1. Renluka Maharaj (Trinidad and Tobago, b. 1966), *Lillah (Pelting Mangoes series)*, 2020, found photograph, acrylic paint, rhinestones on canvas, 2022.4.3. Courtesy of the Flaten Art Museum, St. Olaf College, Northfield, MN. Purchased by the Flaten Art Museum at St. Olaf College with support from the Dreyfus Foundation and Brenda Berkman '73. Selected by the 2022 students of ART 280: Art Now Critical Issues in Contemporary Art taught by Assistant Professor of Art and Art History Hannah Ryan: Emily Barta (staff), Lily Braafladt '22, Sophie Call '24, Zoe Golden '22, Emma Haren '22, Marcus Hauck '24, Cris Hernandez '23, Elias Ravn Iversen '25, Lauren Jacobson '24, Manaw Kyar Phyu '25, Jessenia Mia Prado '24, Lauren Schilling '25, Martha Slaven '24, Charlotte Smith '24, Han Timm '22, Kira Vega '24. Photography by Cy Hennings '26.

them in a respectful, beautiful, engaging and confronting way. Given my fragmented history, any one of these women could be a relative and I felt it was my responsibility to protect them."[58] In the works exhibited as part of the traveling exhibit "Pelting Mangoes" (2020–2021), Maharaj overlaid colonial-era photographs with vivid hues and embellished them with beads, rhinestones, glitter, and gold leaf (see Figure 0.1). In 2022 and 2023, she expanded on these themes in a multi-media exhibit, "Bhumi's Daughters," in which additional collaged photographs were introduced with a film, "March for the Ancestors," which Maharaj also produced. In the film, members of the Indian-Caribbean diaspora in New York paid homage to their forebearers by marching through Little Guyana (Richmond Hill) and carrying fabric banners bearing photographs of family members. Maharaj also incorporated objects that evoked memories of her childhood home in Trinidad, including a vintage dresser painted a vivid neon green and swings that hung from the ceiling. Visitors could view the photographs while sitting on the swings, literally setting the images in motion.[59] Harkening back to the framed family portrait of Gowsee and his descendants, Maharaj's work was reminiscent of strategies that I had seen families use to transform documents of objectification and surveillance into intimate keepsakes.

Drawing inspiration from Maharaj's multi-media collages, I adapt these techniques by thinking deeply about how working across different archives and mediums, including texts, images, and objects, produces multi-dimensional, tactile views of the past. I also borrow from Maharaj and other descendants a sensitivity to the power of moving documents originally produced and archived in colonial contexts into new assemblages. By handling such materials in ways that seek to dignify their subjects, we cannot undo, but might mitigate, the legacies of violent touches. Thus, Maharaj seeks to "protect" the women in her collages from the invasions of the photographer Morin, who may have manhandled their bodies as he clothed and bejeweled them for consumptive display. The opening page of each chapter features a different kind of source or combination of sources that were crucial to my research with that family—a map, photograph and bracelet, a genealogical tree, an album, and an Instagram post—but each chapter also weaves across multiple archives and mediums to create new assemblages. These haunted collages blur the distinction between lives in the past and creative possibilities in the present—akin to the vivid hues that Maharaj layers on top of black-and-white photographs.

In repeatedly moving between institutional archives, family collections, and oral histories, I also grapple with conflicting views of the past, including cases where my analysis diverged from how families understood their ancestors. Rather than minimizing such moments of dissidence, I allow myself to be haunted by them. Often, while working on the book, I woke in the middle of the night, trembling with the knowledge that however I reconstructed a family's past, someone, dead or alive, would find my version wanting. But eventually, I learned to embrace rather than resolve the inevitable rips, seams, and patches in the narratives I was assembling, just as a collage exposes rather than hides its imperfect, assembled form.

For me, encounters with photographs were particularly productive in pushing me towards ideas of haunting and collage. The philosopher Jacques Derrida saw photography as sharing a particular affinity with "ghosts and phantoms," writing, "The spectral is the essence of photography."[60] Photography unsettles our notions of reality and fantasy, toying with the genre's simultaneous claims to capture reality, including through its entanglement with regimes of surveillance and identification, while also being clearly fabricated. Similarly, when we view a portrait photograph, we feel that the subject is both there and not there, a ghostly presence. This aura is even more powerful when a photograph's black-and-white coloring and delicate condition signal the pastness of the reality it displays. Yet when we pick up and handle it, the border between past and present blurs. Photographs are also not just static visual images—they are embodied and disembodied objects that we enlarge, convert between physical and digital forms, wear, and assemble into albums, a form of collage that I discuss in more depth in Chapter 4.

An early archival encounter was influential in shaping my thinking about the haunting power of photographs. The encounter involved a file from the British consulates in China, dated April 22, 1919, titled "Will of Sher Dilkhan in favour of his son Ussuf Khan (born July 15, 1919)." When I requested the file, I received a sealed envelope indicating that Sher Dilkhan deposited it with the consulate, but it was never opened, perhaps because he had left China. The text of the will suggested that he was one of the many Indian men who temporarily worked as policemen and private security guards in China and Southeast Asia during the nineteenth and twentieth centuries.[61] Not wanting to disturb the integrity of the archive, I asked an archivist for assistance, who unceremoniously slit open the envelope, as I considered how the file was henceforth forever altered. I then extracted an Urdu will and gasped in surprise when a photograph tumbled out (see Figure 0.2). Staring back at me was a middle-aged, portly man with an elegant handlebar mustache, wearing a suitcoat and vest—presumably the author of the will, Sher Dilkhan. In my surprise, I felt a ghost spring from the archives.[62]

Here was truly a haunted collage—an assemblage of text and image, which conjured ghosts as it tumbled into my hands and swirled through my imagination. In the will, Sher Dilkhan indicated that all his property should pass to his son, whose date of birth was listed several months *after* he composed the will. Did he imagine that if he died before his son was born, he would at least know

FIGURE 0.2. Installation of *Bhumi's Daughter*, October 1, 2022–January 21, 2023, Project for Empty Space, Newark, NJ. Courtesy of Renluka Maharaj.

his father's face? What did Sher Dilkhan think, instead, of encountering me staring back at him? But I was haunted not just by the sight of Sher Dilkhan, but also the absent presence I keenly felt—the woman in the story. By bequeathing his property to an unborn son (who he probably did not know was a boy), Sher Dilkhan obscured the living, breathing woman carrying the fetus. In my encounter with the file, I sensed that historical time was "out of joint," to borrow from Hamlet's exclamation on seeing his father's ghost.[63] The past and present collapsed as my demand to open the envelop unsealed the past, revealing Sher Dilkhan shuddering at my intrusive desire to write about a woman whom he wished to conceal, abetted by the serpentine logics of British bureaucracy. Would his descendants want to know about this past I had unsealed?

Imagining Sher Dilkhan's disapproval, and the possible reaction of his descendants, is part of entering archives as haunted spaces. Historians are not taught to ask permission of the dead, nor did I conjure a séance to ask his consent to write about his intimate affairs. While I found many descendants of subjects whom I first encountered in archives, I was not able to trace Sher Dilkhan's kin. But imagining what they might think of my work opens a different ethical stance towards historical research. Working with families, who often view the relations between the living and dead in more permeable ways, has meant embracing haunting as a means of ethically engaging with the past, as well as a research method. It has

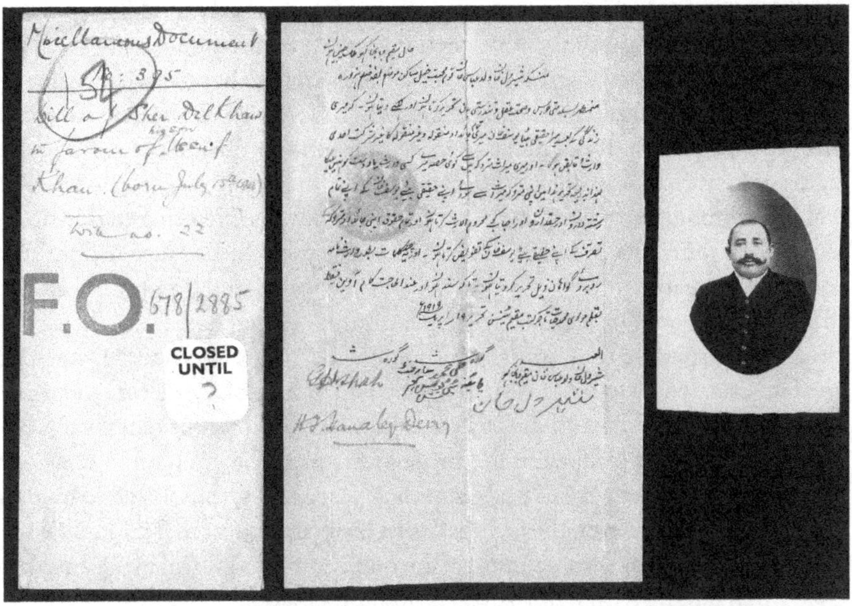


FIGURE 0.3. Will of Sher DilKhan with enclosed photograph, deposited in British Consulate, Jientsin, China, 1919, FO 678/2885. Courtesy of The National Archives (UK).

meant grappling with difficult, sometimes unresolvable, dilemmas of responsibility, privacy, and consent. I have had to look beyond official policies, which for many archives include open access to records after a typical lifespan (often 100 years) has passed since their creation, in theory ensuring that people mentioned in the records are dead. While such closure policies are convenient for archives that are custodians of thousands of documents, they overlook how documents can still impact living descendants. Historians who read documents in much more depth are potentially in a better position to consider such complex issues. However, they often receive little training in ethics and, thus, frequently, by default, outsource questions about privacy and consent to archives. Yet archival policies can often feel decidedly ad hoc. The records of one legal case I used for the book were open to researchers at the British Library, while duplicate copies were closed until 2030 at the British National Archives.[64] Given that history is increasingly entangled with public debates about social justice, the idea that historians can outsource ethics to archives is untenable.

Yet at universities in the United States, where I am based, institutional structures further reinforce the idea that ethics is primarily relevant to research on living subjects and constituted through following bureaucratic and legalistic protocols. Unlike many social scientists in the United States, most historians do not submit their research for review by their university's federal Institutional Review Board (IRB), which is officially charged with ensuring that researchers follow ethical guidelines when working with human subjects. The growing popularity of oral history led to some confusion concerning the status of historical research and IRB protocols. In 2017, however, the US federal government issued a final ruling that officially clarified that oral history, along with journalism, is not subject to IRB oversight because it does not constitute research under its protocols. The critical distinction for the IRB is that historians are not engaged in "generalizable" research because their conclusions are specific to their particular subjects.[65] This decision has been of great practical relief to oral historians, who had previously sometimes clashed with IRB panels over whether they were required to anonymize their subjects, a practice that is at odds with the profession's norms, which often consider naming subjects as crucial to understanding past agency, causality, and human individuality.[66] However, the fact that most historical research falls outside the purview of IRB review can minimize the often complex ethical questions that arise when talking with living subjects about the past.

For families, revelations about dead relations—bequests to concubines and illegitimate children, information about their religious or ethnic background, and details of their property—can feel like information about themselves. Families chose to share or not share such information with me, but what about the information I gleaned from public archival records? As I grappled with such instances, some colleagues suggested anonymizing my subjects to minimize the potential risk of exposing "private" information. However, some of my subjects or their relations were well-known historical figures. Anonymizing them would obscure how my work intersected with historical scholarship and popular memory. I worried that anonymizing subjects when writing family history also reified the notion that these were "private" stories hived off from broader "public" histories, of politics and economy, nation and empire.

I learned long ago the folly of this approach. I began researching this book working on inheritance cases, in which the past is literally proportioned into private parcels of property. This research inspired my broader interest in how, for families, the past often haunts the present through inheritances—of receiving (or losing) bequests of property, handling heirlooms, or remaking memories in light of one's own life circumstances. But, working on legal disputes over estates made me deeply suspicious of the ethics of engaging the past through frameworks rooted in property law. Courts often failed to resolve family disputes, even over property, much less over memory. No one owns the past, and ethical frames built on conceptions of privacy, with its deep ties to private property, fail as guides to navigating contested histories.

Most critically, I found that most of the people I interviewed did not want their words or the histories of their ancestors to be anonymized, even if there was some information they did not want to be public. Many had spent years tracing their family history and wanted credit for their research. Professional standards dictate that I cite my fellow scholars by name when incorporating their findings. Why should I not give similar credit to family researchers, even if doing so opened the possibility of recognizing that our views of the past might diverge? Naming subjects encourages the circulation of historical knowledge between academia and broader publics. It also makes scholars more accountable to those who populate their studies—including empowering them to challenge our work.

Ultimately, I have cobbled together solutions to these ethical dilemmas on a case-by-case basis. Drawing on guidelines published by the Oral History Association and informal guidance from IRB administrators, who agreed to offer counsel even though they deemed my work outside their official ambit, I have used consent forms when conducting interviews. However, I found that these protocols often reduced ethics to law—protecting scholars and universities from being sued—rather than training scholars to grapple with the complexities of weighing complex, sometimes competing, responsibilities to our research subjects, those who read our work, and uncomfortable truths. Throughout, I have tried to respect the desire of families to shape how their pasts are presented, but sometimes honoring the wishes of one relation meant offending another. The dead also have a stake in how their histories are narrated although I was often unsure about what they would want told. I worried about revealing their secrets, and about hiding their pasts because today their descendants find them troubling. Balancing these different perspectives seemed to require sometimes writing about controversial pasts and sometimes omitting them—choices that I have tried to make as transparent as possible even as I feel haunted by what often felt like imperfect solutions. In the coming pages, I do not claim the authority implied by having *heard* the voices of ghosts speaking the secrets of their past. But I do know that I *felt* their presence. This feeling did not deliver the certainty of knowledge that I craved as a historian, but it did create a profound, if sometimes troubling, sense of obligation to handle their legacies with care.

## "Public" Histories in the Digital Diaspora

The early inspiration for this book came from the realization that many of the researchers who occupied the desks beside me in archives, from London to Pietermaritzburg, were tracing their roots. Much family research, however, now occurs online. Many popular genealogy websites, including Ancestry.com and Familysearch.org, are of limited use for families whose roots traverse Indian Ocean geographies, although I encountered some who were creatively repurposing these platforms. The families I worked with often used other tools, which also became critical to my research. I received tips on Facebook groups and traded WhatsApp messages with descendants who crowd-sourced information from distant relations through group chats. The importance of such digital platforms exploded during the COVID-19 pandemic. I could not physically travel to archives, and I was overwhelmed caring for my own family. Burned-out but bored, late at night, I found myself exploring new landscapes of diasporic heritage that flowered when people looked online for the social connections put on hold in person. Diasporic households were already adept at forging such bonds—embracing digital tools to extend kinship networks they had long maintained with letters and photographs. Yet, as many lost older relations to COVID, family histories seemed more precious and fragile. During late-night scrolling sessions, many were re-imagining how to engage with the past through digital archives that featured family photographs and heirlooms.

The importance of such digital spaces for public engagement with the past in the Global South and Indian Ocean region, particularly around themes such as migration and family, has received scant attention. Public historians have long recognized the importance of family history and acknowledged roots researchers' pioneering role as early adopters of digital history.[67] A rich literature on "digital diasporas'" has also amply documented how migrants creatively use digital media to remap the relationship between space, community, and intimacy.[68] Yet minimal scholarship has engaged with the dynamic intersection between these two areas—the particular importance of digital media for imagining alternative diasporic pasts. This is surprising given the enormous popularity of projects such as the Instagram account and Substack "Brown History." The account has a remarkable 700,000 followers (and counting) and crowd-sources content from across the globe.[69] One of its most popular features is the hashtag #brownhistoryphotoalbum, which includes family photographs and oral histories of migration.

The scant academic attention that scholars have paid to such forums (although many are avid followers) reflects the deep biases in how "Public History" has been studied. The ambitions of Public History are vast, with many scholars now embracing a broad definition: "History for the public, about the public, and by the public."[70] Yet Public History as a subfield still bears the imprint of its early development in the United States in the 1970s, and its investment in institution building, including degree programs that created an employment pipeline to museums, heritage sites, archives, public policy, and corporations looking to document their history. Recent efforts to "internationalize" the field have primarily looked to overlapping initiatives in Europe or countries such as Australia, Canada, and South Africa, with large-scale public and private investments in heritage and overlapping legacies of White-settler colonialism.[71]

Even when scholars further diversify geographically, they often assume that Public History necessarily plays out in national or local contexts. For example, the editors of the volume *What is Public History Globally?* claim that "Like culture, public history comes from somewhere: it is local; it is from 'around here'—a locality, region, state or nation."[72] I find this a jarring statement as a scholar of the Indian Ocean, a rich laboratory of mobile cultural forms, such as the unique genres of music that developed on board the region's *dhows* (sailing ships).[73] Yet, because many formal heritage projects depend on funding from states, which prioritize national or regional narratives, or universities and foundations, there is a strong bias towards location-based research.[74] This often limits "global" frameworks to comparisons between national contexts. Thus, while rich studies of heritage projects and public memory exist for many parts of Asia and Africa, only a handful of scholars truly pursue such work across Indian Ocean contexts.[75] Fewer still consider their dynamic interface with family history and digital media.

Yet public histories need not be tethered to one place, as quickly becomes apparent when we look to more expansive vistas of engagement outside projects that enjoy state or institutional backing. I signal this shift in perspective by thinking about "public" versus "Public" history. In the following chapters, I look for evidence of such public engagements across spaces and mediums—a hidden grave and garlanded statue in Kuala Lumpur, a bracelet that traveled from Zanzibar to a museum collection in Salem, Massachusetts, and photographs of Asian seamen featured in outreach programs sponsored by the British National Archives. While I find traces of diasporic pasts in all these sites of public heritage, I also analyze how official narratives, as promoted by states, newspapers, and museums, frame these histories through identarian categories that prioritize migrants' attachments to specific homelands and adopted host lands rather than the experiences of repeated mobility that I often heard families emphasize.

In contrast, I found that digital spaces sometimes (although certainly not always) provided more fluid landscapes for pursuing diasporic trails that flowed against compartmentalizing logics. The low start-up (although often labor-intensive) costs for creating accounts and pages on Facebook or Instagram reduce the need for state sponsorship or institutional backing. At the same time, their inherent placelessness encourages thinking across borders. The name "Brown History" reflects such efforts. While widely understood as a forum featuring diasporic South Asian perspectives, the account self-consciously resists a binary divide between those inside and outside the region, looking also at migrations during Partition. The name "Brown History" also emphasizes connections with other areas of the Global South, including by featuring mixed family relations.[76] In Chapter 5, I look in depth at another Instagram account, "Gulf ⇄ South Asia," which is even more radical. It pushes back against the disproportionate emphasis in studies of diaspora on migrations between the Global North and South to instead feature content that emphasizes the alternative temporalities, including temporary migration, and spatial routes that link these two regions. While the founders and users of these platforms struggle with their profit-seeking algorithms, the accounts show how digital spaces are creative vistas for reimagining what might constitute public history.

---

The following chapters follow the arc of an afterlife, as the living passed into the realm of the dead, became the subjects of recent memory, and then more distant history. It opens with a funeral and proceeds to the division of a deceased's estate. It then turns to the retelling of migrants' stories by future generations and their incorporation into public histories of nations and diasporas. Each chapter narrates a stage in the unfolding of an afterlife through the story of a different family moving across the Indian Ocean and the British Empire. We begin with the funeral of Thamboosamy, a colonial bureaucrat-turned-business tycoon who traced his roots to South India but was born in Singapore and rose to prominence in Kuala Lumpur in British Malaya. This chapter considers how cosmopolitan legacies accumulate and erode in an urban geography reshaped by shifting regimes of ethnic, religious, and national categorization. Chapter 2 takes up the next stage of the deceased's afterlife: the division of assets, in this case, a process that unfolded in colonial courtrooms in Zanzibar and Bombay. It pivots around the story of Janbai, the matriarch of an Indian Ocean family firm. The chapter triangulates between legal records, a manuscript family biography, photographs, and jewelry, both present and absent, to consider how multi-media collages reveal suppressed histories of gendered mobility.

Chapter 3 shifts forward in time to examine how subsequent generations have attempted to reconstruct their ancestors' migrations from colonial documents, inherited family stories, and online genealogy platforms. It follows the trail of Angamma, who, as an eight-year-old girl, traveled from Madras to Natal to work on a coffee plantation. The chapter shows how the multi-generational trauma of indenture led to selective remembering, erasure, and recovery, including a recent flowering of interest in the stories of indentured women.

Chapter 4 turns to what happens when family histories become public patrimony. It looks at the different ways in which public histories of Asian seamen might be visualized by constructing an album of John/Jan Mohamed using photographs scattered across archives in the US and UK. Unable to track down descendants, the chapter considers how strategies borrowed from family history, including album making, can contribute to public engagements with diasporic histories that move beyond national frames. Chapter 5 explores rapidly evolving digital genealogy landscapes to show how they open new possibilities for doing public history in Indian Ocean contexts. I also reflect on my own experience researching the chapter while living as a temporary migrant in the United Arab Emirates, which in recent years has hosted the largest number of Indian migrants of any country.[77]

This book is not a history of my family. But my conversations with others about their ancestors often circled back to my roots. Those sharing their stories with me also wanted to know my own. My early interest in history was sparked by listening to my grandmother narrate how her family fled anti-Jewish pogroms in a town then in Russia, now in Ukraine. I grew up in a mixed-faith household and now share my life with my husband, whose family has moved between Madras (now amended as Chennai in his passport), Bombay, Riyadh, New York, and Hong Kong. I hope this book will one day help me explain to my daughter her sprawling roots, even as it hopefully aids other families like ours in tracing their diasporic trails.

# 1

# Cosmopolitan Graves

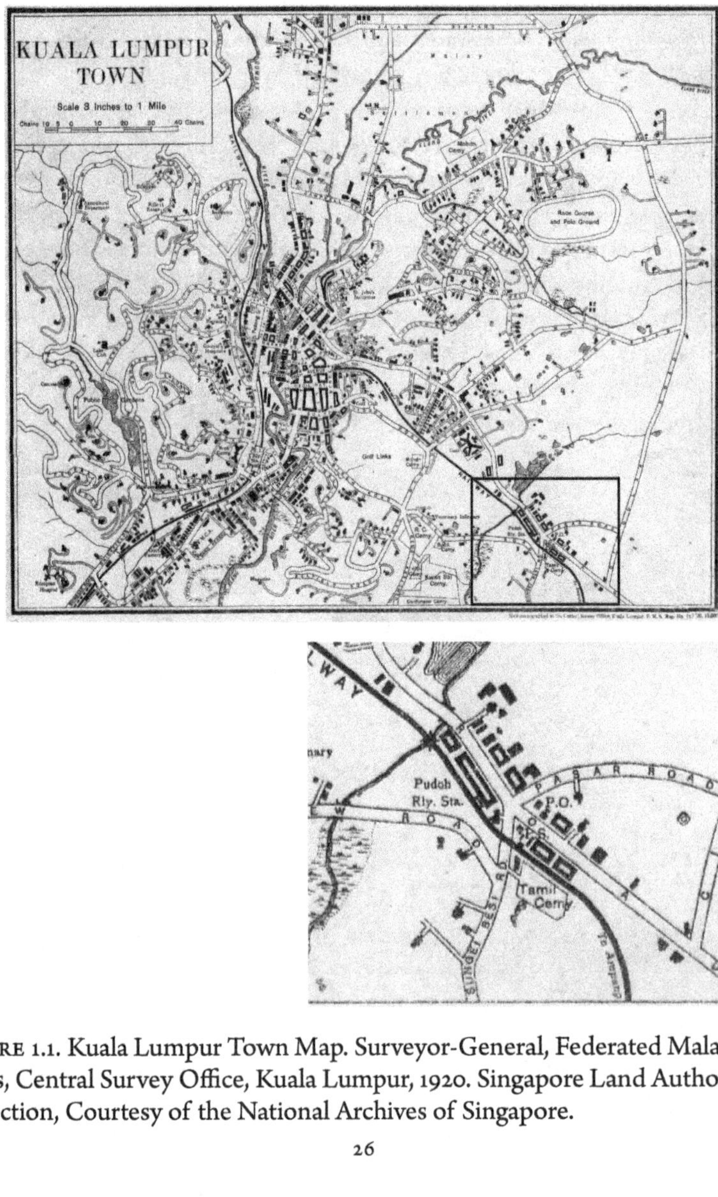


FIGURE 1.1. Kuala Lumpur Town Map. Surveyor-General, Federated Malay States, Central Survey Office, Kuala Lumpur, 1920. Singapore Land Authority Collection, Courtesy of the National Archives of Singapore.

THE SHAPING of an afterlife often started even before death, and as the following chapters trace, it proceeded through the funeral of the deceased and the division of their estate, tussles in which the desires of the newly departed competed with the demands of the living. As the years passed, descendants told shifting stories about the dead, adapting to changing family circumstances and broader geopolitical transformations. The lives of migrants were also sometimes incorporated into new national histories, marshaled in service of identities that they may have barely recognized. These complex processes, however, almost always began with an immediate imperative: what should be done with the body? The physical problem of disposing of the body was governed by pragmatic concerns—what to do with decomposing flesh—and symbolic performance. Funerals were liminal events, straddling the living and the dead, spiritual and material, private and public.

The kin and associates of Thamboosamy Pillai embarked on these complex negotiations on the morning of July 24, 1902, when the prominent Indian businessman, community leader, labor recruiter, and one-time colonial official passed away in Singapore.[1] Thamboosamy had been ailing for months and traveled to India to consult medical specialists before returning to Malaya. Unfortunately, these efforts were to no avail, and he passed away at fifty-two. After his death was announced, speculation immediately began about his funeral. The local press in Singapore initially reported that he would be buried in the Tamil cemetery there. Several days later, however, the press announced that William Treacher, the British Resident-General of the Federated Malay States, had dispatched the government's official yacht to carry Thamboosamy's embalmed body back to Kuala Lumpur.[2]

On Sunday, August 3, Thamboosamy's body was buried in the Tamil cemetery on Cheras Road in Kuala Lumpur with much pomp and a diverse audience in attendance. His corpse, housed in an elegant coffin decorated with silver adornments, was carried on a bier to the gravesite, accompanied by a band playing Handel's "Dead March" and displays of Chinese fireworks. The music and the coffin were nods to European sensibilities—Hindu bodies were traditionally only wrapped in cloth to ease the departure of the soul from the body.[3] But Tamil and Hindu funerary elements also abounded, a mixture that continues to be a feature of Indian diasporic funerals in Southeast Asia today. In describing Thamboosamy's funeral, the press noted that Tamil attendees carried long blades of grass, shielding the living from the polluting presence of the corpse.[4] At the gravesite, a barber shaved the head of Thamboosamy's eldest son, who then threw a handful of rice and coins on a cloth covering the body, an act replicated by Thamboosamy's other relatives and close friends. The barber then gathered the cloth, presumably collecting the enclosed coins as payment for his participation. Afterward, the coffin was covered with more coins and earth. The eldest son then commenced a ritual in which each of Thamboosamy's four sons held a clay pitcher punctured with a small sickle and proceeded to circle his father's grave as the water poured out. After this ceremony had been repeated several times and the pitcher was empty, it was flung to the ground and broken. The press reported that the ritual was "symbolical [sic] of life and death."[5]

Despite the extensive reporting of Thamboosamy's funeral in the press in both Singapore and Kuala Lumpur, the coverage commented little on several decisions about the proceedings that I found particularly notable. Thamboosamy's body was transported back to the city where he made his fortune, rather than an ancestral homeland in India, and buried rather than cremated. Cremation was increasingly favored by some local Hindus (and Sikhs) as more orthodox, but Thamboosamy and his family did not follow this pattern.[6] The ritual care and public memorialization of his body mapped different diasporic imaginaries. Seminal works by David Arnold and Engseng Ho have explored how the memorialization of the dead was critical to cultivating religiously bounded and homeland-rooted diasporic identities. Arnold explores the globalization of cremation as a marker of Hindu identity. Ho traces the gravitational pull of the ancestral graves of dead men, the *sayyid* saints of Tarim, the genealogical center for a sprawling Hadhrami diaspora (now in Yemen).[7] In contrast, Thamboosamy's burial in an adopted city, whose terrain was in a ceaseless flux of urban development and shifting identarian boundaries, embodies the alternative modes of being diasporic that this book pursues through multi-gendered family trails.

Captivated by the interplay between the funeral's cosmopolitan cultural repertoire and the burial's rootedness in fluid urban geography, this chapter braids archival and family history with excavations of Kuala Lumpur's haunted landscapes.[8] While I set out in search of Thamboosamy's grave, I found his afterlives in other landmarks, from road signs to statues to family armoires. Crucially, I also heard from Thamboosamy's descendants about the bodily remains of mothers and grandmothers—showing how tracing familial lineages through women further unsettles identarian approaches to diasporic pasts. These excavations unfolded in archives, where I traced Thamboosamy's signatures across city plans, land deeds, petitions, and tax records that charted Kuala Lumpur's growth into the hub of British Malaya's booming mining and plantation economy. On historical maps, I located the schools, clubs, temples, graveyards, and cremation grounds he helped establish. These demarcated a civic landscape, both increasingly segregated along ethnic and religious lines while also governed by a multi-ethnic elite bound together in mutual pursuit of wealth and ruthless exploitation of working-class laborers.[9] Crossing the city in Ubers that crawled through dense traffic, I tried to match modern addresses with early twentieth-century references as I sought out tumbling-down graveyards in the shadows of gravity-defying skyscrapers.

I also discovered more intimate landmarks, such as Thamboosamy's glass-doored armoire, now in the home of his great-grandson and filled with miscellaneous tchotchkes but haunted by the memories of the horse-racing trophies it once housed. Together, these excavations reveal how, for diasporic families, legacies of mobility and cosmopolitanism exert subterranean influences beneath the surface of bounded national, regional, and religious identities.

To understand this layered landscape, I use both terrestrial and aquatic analytics, reflecting the city's deep ties to the Indian Ocean.[10] Thamboosamy's body was embalmed before it was buried—a funerary preparation necessitated by its seabound journey through the Strait of Malacca and a symbol of how the pulls of water and earth mingled in the riverine landscapes of Kuala Lumpur. Drawing inspiration from Nurfadzilah Yahaya's use of fluidity as a vehicle for attending to entangled histories of water, land, and fluctuating regimes of law and bureaucracy, the chapter probes how Thamboosamy's life and legacies were repeatedly reshaped by the currents of mobile urban geography.[11] Shifting roadways and monuments mapped fluctuations in the ethnic and religious categories through which the colonial and later post-colonial governments divided its populations.

Born into a family already migrating between South and Southeast Asia in earlier generations, Thamboosamy's life trajectory was propelled by the undertows of an older oceanic cosmopolis flowing beneath the currents of ascendant colonial power. The Malay peninsula and the archipelago of islands to its east drew in and propelled outwards to Arabia, India, and Africa a whirling population who traded, intermarried, and blended religious, linguistic, and cultural customs.[12] These currents created deeply mixed family legacies, sometimes with patrilineal genealogies that emphasized ties to specific regions and religions, but whose wider family lives, when accounting for women, were deeply cosmopolitan. In the nineteenth century, the currents of this older cosmopolitanism met the tsunami of European imperial expansion and capitalism.

Religious and ethnic categorizations were the new canals that the colonial regime built to contain the Indian Ocean's cosmopolitan flows. During Thamboosamy's lifetime, structures of "in-direct" rule through which the British governed Malaya bound Malay identity more closely to being Muslim. Critical to this process was how the authority of its regional sultans was increasingly circumscribed to religious law and customary practices marked as

Islamic.[13] Efforts to link Malay and Muslim identity also affected other groups. Efforts by some Indians to secure cremation grounds suggest how non-Muslims also sought new forms of orthodoxy, sometimes by distancing themselves from customs associated with Muslims. Meanwhile, from the 1870s, colonial census takers began dividing the population of the Malay peninsula according to various regimes of ethnic, linguistic, national, and racial categorization.[14]

However, the labels and boxes they used constantly shifted, reflecting the difficulty of applying such divisions to internally diverse and deeply intermingled groups.[15] In the decades leading up to and following independence, these categories crystalized into the common formula of dividing Malaysians and Singaporeans into separate ethnic groups of Malay, Chinese, Indian, and Other. Across the decades, however, the boundaries around these categories have continued to morph as nationalist movements, post-colonial governance, and Islamism have emphasized different relationships between ethnicity, language, religion, indigeneity, and cultural practices.[16] Indian Ocean currents have repeatedly overflowed colonial and post-colonial canals.

When I traveled to Kuala Lumpur, the different stories I heard about Thamboosamy's legacies suggest that the competing flows of cosmopolitanism and the channeling effects of categorization continue to shape the city and its inhabitants today. When learning of my interest, many Indian Malaysians lamented that Thamboosamy is not given a more significant role in national textbooks, crediting this to the official privileging of Muslim-Malay historical contributions. These concerns map onto the struggle between ethnonationalism and ethno-pluralism and their late twentieth-century fusion with opposing programs of Islamism and secularism, through which contemporary Malaysian politics and society are often analyzed. Some of these interlocutors found my interest in searching for Thamboosamy's grave odd. I sensed that they felt that given that most Tamil Hindus today are cremated, this dimension of his afterlife was irrelevant or even unsettling. Linking diasporic pasts to arguments for pluralism in the present often relies on fitting historical figures into boxes that resemble contemporary identarian categories while suppressing other dimensions of their legacies. This is a pattern I have repeatedly seen in public histories, not just in Malaysia but also in South Asian American and British Indian heritage projects, which I examine in Chapter 4. Yet conversations with Thamboosamy's family suggest other ways of engaging such legacies. For his great-granddaughter, my interest in his grave elicited stories about how cosmopolitan habits remain vital today—as an ongoing inheritance of migration, intermarriage, and broad-mindedness passed from one diasporic generation to the next.

## Thamboosamy and the Cosmopolitan Geographies of Colonial Kuala Lumpur

Thamboosamy's rise began in Singapore, where he was born in 1850 and grew up among an elite group of Indians who enjoyed strong connections to ascendant British power brokers. He may have been a relative of Naraina Pillai, a Tamil merchant who traveled from Penang to Singapore in 1819 with Stamford Raffles, often referred to as the founder of modern Singapore.[17] Recognizing Singapore's potential as a hub of British trade, Raffles orchestrated the island's purchase in 1824 from the Sultan of Johor, one of nine independent Malay rulers who would come under increasing British control as the century progressed. Along with the ports of Penang and Malacca, Singapore formed the Straits Settlement, which was governed as part of British India until 1867. Later, as British control over the Malay peninsula coalesced, they expanded their regional influence through a system of protectorates, in which the Malay sultanates became British vassal states of the Federated and Unfederated Malay States. Yet Singapore remained a rugged outpost for the first several decades of its existence. The Indian convicts who were tasked with clearing the jungle and building roads were routinely dispatched to hunt tigers that roamed the island.[18] Men like Naraina, however, were already laying the foundations for the city's urban tapestry. Naraina initially worked in the colonial treasury but quickly built an independent portfolio of business interests. Anticipating the city's growth, he recruited bricklayers and carpenters from Penang and founded a brick kiln, leading him to be remembered as "Singapore's first building contractor."[19] He also laid the foundation for the Sri Maha Mariamman Temple, Singapore's oldest Hindu temple.

The younger Pillai's biography followed a similar trajectory while unfolding against the backdrop of accelerating British colonial power. Thamboosamy was educated at the elite Raffles Institution, a school which Raffles set up in 1823 to educate local and European boys and promote the study of Asian languages and literature.[20] The school would ultimately produce a cadre of young men who staffed the city's colonial bureaucracy, law, and business firms. As one of these young men, Thamboosamy began his professional career as a clerk at Singapore's oldest law firm, Rodyk and Davidson, gaining legal expertise that he would draw on throughout his life. Like the many elite diasporic South Asians drawn to careers in law, Thamboosamy's ability to navigate new colonial legal cultures proved to be an essential engine of his upward mobility. Legal expertise allowed men like Thamboosamy to secure employment in colonial offices in different parts of the British Empire or set up shop as lawyers for diasporic merchants, as Gandhi did in South Africa.[21] Engagements with the law, however, often proved bittersweet as many of these same families would find themselves embroiled in lawsuits involving their business and personal matters—a pattern that was true of Thamboosamy's descendants and, as we will see, also the family of Tharia Topan and Janbai, who are the focus of the next chapter.

In his early twenties, Thamboosamy leveraged his legal skills and relations with elite Britons to position himself within Malaya's expanding colonial power structures. The opening of the Suez Canal in 1868 dramatically increased Singapore's importance as a hub of trade between Europe and Asia. At the same time, Britain began extending its influence over the Malay hinterland through structures of informal colonialism, which left its various sultanates in place but under British control. The first British residents arrived in the sultanates of Perak, Selangor, and Negri Sembilan in the mid-1870s, harbingers of the dual system of rule. When J. G. Davidson, Thamboosamy's boss, was deputed to serve in this capacity in Selangor, Thamboosamy accompanied him. In the coming years, Thamboosamy would adopt Kuala Lumpur as his home base and root himself in a city that was both a hub of diasporic Asian investment, having been founded by Chinese merchants in the 1850s, and of colonial administration, becoming the capital of not just Selangor but also the Federated Malay States (which included the sultanates of Selangor, Negeri Sembilan, Perak, and Pahang) in 1895.

Thamboosamy first navigated these landscapes from a perch in the British Residency's Treasury Department, where he served as chief clerk. His title belied the influence he rapidly amassed—during several periods in which the treasurer himself was absent, Thamboosamy assumed his duties.[22] The position strategically placed Thamboosamy to gain knowledge of, and influence over, Malaya's rapidly developing economy. He evaluated loan applications from merchants hoping to open new tin mines, paid contractors to pave roads, audited customs and tax accounts, and prosecuted opium shopkeepers for license violations.[23]

Thamboosamy simultaneously set the foundations for his own business empire, often investing in areas where he was also involved through his government work. In March 1884, he applied for permission to purchase government lands to set up a plantation to cultivate pepper and "Indian Cereals and Condiments," noting that if his application were approved, he would "send an agent to India and Singapore to make arrangements to procure Coolies."[24] In April 1884, he advised the British Resident that the government should develop toddy (palm wine) and *bhang* (marijuana) farms since the region's growing population of coolie laborers would create a demand for these products.[25] In 1887, Thamboosamy traveled to Negapatam (now known as Nagapattinam) in southeastern India, where he had family ties, to recruit five hundred laborers to work for the Public Works Department, and he would later employ similar laborers on his own plantations.[26] He thus proved critical in tying Kuala Lumpur's urban development and its emerging hinterland economies to the transregional flow of labor between Malaya and south India. In the twentieth century, these connections propelled the mass movement of labor to supply Malaya's booming rubber plantations.[27]

Thamboosamy was thus concurrently building infrastructure for Indian labor recruitment, ensuring that the government was invested in its success, and setting up his own businesses, first in plantations and later construction and mining, that would profit from the flow of cheap labor from southern India to Malaya. When Thamboosamy left government service in 1889, the British Resident noted with regret that "his ability as an accountant, his acquittance with the customs of the country and his intimate knowledge of the people will be much missed in my office."[28] Some of his European associates, however, felt uncomfortable with the amount of power that Thamboosamy had amassed. The Treasurer argued in favor of appointing a European, with a higher salary and the rank of Assistant Treasurer, to take over Thamboosamy's duties.[29]

While preceded by a period of ill health, Thamboosamy's exit from his government position accelerated his commercial ascent. During his years as a subordinate to British officials, he amassed a staggering knowledge about the region's economy and far-reaching connections to those instrumental to its development, both within the colonial government and beyond. Expanding his involvement in labor recruitment, Thamboosamy secured a contract to supply coolies to load and unload goods from the Selangor Government Railway in 1893. The official evaluating the bids noted that while Thamboosamy's was somewhat higher than his competitors, he was confident that Thamboosamy could meet the government's "requirements," suggesting that officials were keen on working with him as someone they already knew and trusted.[30]

While leveraging his ties to colonial power centers, Thamboosamy also networked well beyond British elites, benefiting from relations he cultivated with members of the Arab and Chinese diaspora in Southeast Asia. Just a year after leaving his post as chief clerk, Thamboosamy was corresponding with the government as the acting attorney for Syed Mohamed Alsagoff (originally Al-Saqqaf in Arabic). Alsagoff was a leading Arab merchant based in Singapore whose family traced their roots to Hadhramaut but who made their fortune trading in spices in Singapore. Alsagoff likely hoped that Thamboosamy's prior connections to the colonial administration would prove beneficial in navigating a complex claim involving compensation for land that the government had purchased from his late father.[31]

Thamboosamy's growing ties to the Chinese community in Malaya were even more critical. The Chinese diaspora fueled Singapore's and Kuala

Lumpur's economic development and represented a numerical majority of the population in both cities.[32] While tin had been mined in the Malay peninsula from at least the ninth century, Chinese merchants pioneered the industrial development of Malaya's tin mines and their links to modern global supply chains in the early nineteenth century.[33] Seeking to tap into these lucrative ventures, Thamboosamy partnered with three Chinese merchants, including the famous Cantonese capitalist Loke Yew, to develop a significant tin mine, with a joint capital of $10,000 and employing Tamil and Chinese laborers. In approving their joint proposal, the Inspector of Mines noted that the "applicants form a powerful coterie."[34] The Inspector's comments proved correct; the company would become the first to use electricity in their mines, kickstarting the broader electrification of Kuala Lumpur.[35] Thamboosamy benefited from Chinese mining expertise, but men like Loke Yew also profited from access to Thamboosamy's networks. He connected them to South Indian Chettiar financiers, who gained a reputation throughout Asia for providing capital for non-White investors who faced discrimination from European banks.[36] His Chinese partners surely also valued his ongoing links to the colonial administration, including via Thamboosamy's influence as a member of the Sanitary Board, which advised the government on matters from urban planning to taxation. At his appointment in 1894, the Resident noted that Thamboosamy's fluency in both English and Malay would be especially advantageous.[37]

Thamboosamy knew how to "play the game," to borrow language from one of his obituaries, and in Malaya that meant solidifying professional and business relations through an active social calendar.[38] His "curry tiffins" were popular among the city's colonial elite, which was dominated by Europeans but also incorporated wealthy Chinese, Indians, and Malays.[39] In India, the word "tiffin" connotes a light meal served at lunch or teatime, which originated as an Anglo-Indian modification of the English colloquial "tiffing" or sipping. But in British Malaya, tiffins were elaborate feasts drawing on the region's diverse food cultures. A typical spread might include rice, meat and fish curries, dozens of *sambals* (pickles, chutneys, and side dishes), 100-year-old eggs (preserved duck eggs that were a Chinese specialty), and Malay sweets such as *gula melaka,* a combination of palm sugar and sago pudding.[40] In addition to hosting gatherings at his home, Thamboosamy was also a fixture of the region's racing scene, owning several prize-winning horses. He was one of the first men in Kuala Lumpur to own a gharry, a horse buggy pulled by specially bred ponies, which wealthy residents raced along the city's thoroughfares. According to local legend, he had a fierce rivalry with another Tamil merchant, who bested Thamboosamy by purchasing a Sandalwood pony from Indonesia "that would knock spots" off "Tamboosamy's Deli pony."[41] Thamboosamy was also an honored guest at the nuptials of the region's elite. *The Selangor Journal* reported in detail on these celebrations and noted that Thamboosamy gifted two gold rings to the Malay couple, Inche Halimah and Said Abdul Rahman Al Jafri, in August 1895.[42] The following April, he attended the wedding of the British couple, Mr. D. J. Highet and Miss F. L. Carpmael, gifting them a set of fish knives and forks.[43] While weddings and funerals have often been studied as religious rituals that helped solidify communitarian identities, the presence of a wide range of guests shows how Kuala Lumpur's cosmopolitan elite valued the presence of others at these seminal celebrations. The care with which Thamboosamy gifted culturally appropriate items to couples of different backgrounds further demonstrates the centrality of material practices to how different diasporic communities forged links that at once recognized, but also bridged, their differences.

Geographically, the influence of this multi-ethnic elite was mapped onto the city's emerging streetscapes through the construction of elite schools and clubs. The Victoria Institute, which resembled Thamboosamy's alma mater, the Raffles Institute, was founded by the Sultan of Selangor and members of the city's business elites, including Thamboosamy, in celebration of Queen Victoria's Golden Jubilee. It remains a prestigious presence in the city today, and its students fondly embrace the motto: "Once a Victorian, always a Victorian."[44] The persistence of this seemingly anachronistic slogan suggests how certain forms of colonial cosmopolitanism have enjoyed surprisingly long afterlives in cities like Kuala Lumpur, particularly among diasporic elites who have felt more marginalized in post-colonial Malaysia.

While a prominent member of Kuala Lumpur's multi-ethnic elite, Thamboosamy also shows how the city was developing more compartmentalized social spaces. He would be remembered most prominently for his contributions to two of Malaya's most famous Hindu sites, the Sri Maha Mariamman Temple in Kuala Lumpur and the shrine to Lord Murugan at Batu Caves. The latter would become the epicenter of the annual celebration of the Thaipusam festival in Southeast Asia, the region's largest Hindu pilgrimage, which was particularly popular with working-class Tamils. Thamboosamy's workers, who used the caves to store road-making materials, may have been the first to set up makeshift shrines at the site. Yet the popularity of the cave with Chinese devotees, who likewise considered them sacred, shows how working-class social worlds in Malaya were also deeply cosmopolitan.[45] In appealing across classes and tapping multi-stranded sacred traditions, Batu Caves suggest how even religious spaces that were increasingly marked as tied to a particular group often remained cosmopolitan in practice. Even today, the Thaipusam celebrations at Batu Caves, one of Malaysia's most well-known festivals, attract diverse devotees and tourists.

Public accounts of Thamboosamy's life foregrounded his connections to influential British and Chinese power players in Malaya even as he became a recognized leader of the Tamil-Hindu (sometimes alternatively understood as the

Indian) community. At home, however, he seems to have shared intimate connections with a Muslim-Malay woman, Tipah binte Alli. We know of this connection because Thamboosamy made provisions for her in a codicil, or amendment, he added to his will in 1899. In the process, he left a clue to her existence in colonial archives, even as she went unmentioned in public sources such as newspaper obituaries. When I met his descendants, they also seemed to know little about her, indicating how, at times, colonial records can prove to be crucial in unearthing otherwise hidden subaltern pasts.[46] In the will, he specified that Tipah should be allowed to live in the house he rented for her after his death. He also provided her a monthly stipend of $15, but only if she remained "single and chaste." While ensuring that she escaped poverty, this was a paltry sum given Thamboosamy's wealth—little more than the average monthly salary of a houseboy or cook in Selangor in 1900.[47] Yet, in an act of cross-religious recognition, Thamboosamy made a provision for Tipah to pursue her spiritual obligations, specifying that she should be given $750 to travel to Mecca if she wished. Thamboosamy also set aside funds for her funeral. However, he did not mention provisions for any children the couple might have had.[48]

In writing about Asian entrepreneurs like Thamboosamy, who built their fortunes during the Age of Empire, historians of the Indian Ocean often differentiate between colonial and bazaar economies. The former was dominated by European capital and global in scale while the latter provided an intermediate sphere connecting local economies in Asia and Africa to intermediate transregional markets in which non-European traders continued to flourish.[49] Rich new scholarship on the Indian Ocean, however, has emphasized that colonial cities were built and Asian fortunes made at the interface between the colonial and the bazaar. Thamboosamy embodied this pattern. It was men like Thamboosamy who made it possible for the British to recruit cheap labor to build colonial Malaya's public infrastructure, tin mines, and rubber plantations.[50] But while helping to build British power, they also used the knowledge they gained about colonial markets and legal bureaucracy to amass personal fortunes by arbitraging between the colonial and the bazaar.[51] Some scholars approach these diasporic merchants through the lens of vernacular capitalism, framing their role as brokers between the colonial and bazaar as akin to translators moving between different languages.[52] In Thamboosamy's case, I find cosmopolitanism more helpful in capturing not only his facility in translating across languages and lingos, including Malay and British law, but even more critically, leveraging truly hybrid practices to amass vast financial and social capital—as was so vividly on display at his funeral. A low-paid clerk could do the work of translation; building a business empire, as Thamboosamy did, required more.

Thamboosamy's life shows how cosmopolitanism, as a framework that emphasizes qualities of worldliness born of mixing and hybridity, complements the book's centering of mobility as a critical feature of diasporic family legacies. Migrants like Thamboosamy did not just travel from one fixed place to another. They produced new worlds in the process. The predominantly material means through which Thamboosamy built such worlds also push Indian Ocean scholarship to look beyond the analytics of linguistic translation and archives of literary and intellectual texts, which have been the primary lenses through which many have engaged the concept of cosmopolitanism.[53]

Thamboosamy's worldliness was forged less in the realm of texts and ideas and more through economic, spatial, and embodied practices—in the ways that he inhabited diverse social worlds, both professionally and intimately, and exhibited social capital in registers legible to multiple audiences. Compared to many of the other migrants I studied while researching this book, Thamboosamy left quite extensive textual trails—in the archives of the colonial bureaucracy where he worked, in relationship to the properties he bequeathed to temples, and in papers kept by his family. But these texts were overwhelmingly about Thamboosamy's finances, not his ideas about political subjecthood or moral philosophy. They offer a portrait of a man equally at ease in a Tamil temple and at a European racecourse, whom both British officials and Chinese investors trusted, and who founded sites of Hindu worship and was concerned about providing funds for his Muslim mistress to travel on *hajj* after his death. Thamboosamy's worldliness was at once rooted in his family's ties to older Indian Ocean circuits, deeply entangled with British colonialism, and constitutive of something new, spatially manifest in Kuala Lumpur's emerging urban landscapes. Cosmopolitanism in this formulation remains tinged with the European dominance in which it was historically produced, both as a concept rooted in Enlightenment philosophy and in material contexts shaped by imperial hierarchies. But it also recognizes that migrants like Thamboosamy became global as much through their interactions with non-Europeans as Europeans, and the circuits they traveled between India and Empire were routed through Asia, which was by far the most common destination for Indian migrants.

I have found such forms of cosmopolitanism, material and embodied rather than textual or intellectual, to be highly relevant to understanding diasporic families. Only a minority of migrants in the nineteenth century were literate, and those who were, often had little time to read, let alone write philosophical treatises. Instead, they spent much of their lives figuring out how to live comfortably, or at least tolerably, in new climates, make familiar flavors out of foreign produce, and forge households with partners from different backgrounds. When they could scrape together some savings, or in Thamboosamy's case, a sizeable fortune, they had to figure out how to invest in new industries and work with foreign business partners. They, like Thamboosamy, more often tried to turn colonial and capitalist systems to their own ends than to resist them, although some joined anti-colonial and communist movements. They were everyday cosmopolitans—not idealistic proponents of world brotherhood but deeply creative in their own ways. They formed their own global communities in miniature out of the wide-ranging relations required to survive in places where they lived alongside others—not just locals but also migrants from different places.

Such diasporic cosmopolitanisms also rarely manifest as utopic visions of universalism or equality, ideas central to Enlightenment cosmopolitanism but also deeply belied by the realities of European colonialism and capitalism. Thamboosamy's cosmopolitanism was forged not in literary exchanges or coffee-house debates but in markets and within his household. These spaces were unapologetically ordered through deeply unequal relations—of class, gender, and colonizers versus the colonized. Markets and households also depended on coercion, both economic and physical. They were nonetheless generative of critical intermixing of cultures and classes. Even the colonial-official-turned-historian John Sydenham Furnivall, whose writings are often cited as exemplifying colonial ideologies of ethnic and religious compartmentalization, recognized the market as a space of mixing. He wrote that the peoples of Southeast Asia are "in the strictest sense a medley, for they mix but do not combine. Each group holds by its own religion, its own culture and language, its own ideas and ways. As individuals they meet, but only in the market-place, in buying and selling."[54] For Furnivall, the market was distinct from religion, culture, language, and conjugal relations. Thamboosamy's life suggests otherwise. Making deals in colonial Kuala Lumpur required socializing across its diverse populations, skills at which Thamboosamy was adept. Thamboosamy used his political connections with British officials, financial ties to Chinese merchants, and his mixed household relations to amass the necessary capital—social and financial—to profit off the labor of his less fortunate fellow migrants. Studied through such material and embodied manifestations, cosmopolitanism thus loses its rose-tinted idealism. The cosmopolitan relationship that Thamboosamy forged with his Muslim mistress was an assertion of gendered, economic, and racialized power. It also appears to have entailed elements of mutual recognition. Reframing cosmopolitanism as shot through with hierarchy and coercion, rather than showing its limits, deepens its power for analyzing the actualities of modern global relations.

## Funerary Geographies

Having spent the years before his death setting the foundation for his posthumous afterlife, Thamboosamy surely also saw his physical afterlives as critical to securing his future reputation. While there is little direct evidence of why he and his family chose to bury his body in the city, contemporary debates about funerary practices and landscapes suggest that this choice was deliberate and part of broader efforts to map different visions of diaspora through the spatial allocation of cremation grounds and graveyards.

Discussions in Kuala Lumpur about where and how dead bodies should be disposed of unfolded in conversation with regional and global trends. In the nineteenth century, managing dead bodies became a key site for realizing new visions of modernity. Emerging understandings of sanitation and public health fueled new concerns about the proximity of dead bodies to living inhabitants. Religious reform movements across faiths targeted popular funerary rituals that were deemed to lack scriptural authority while also imposing bourgeois notions of propriety about what constituted appropriate sensorial displays of mourning.[55] In British Malaya, these battles played out across a colonial landscape where European and Asian investors competed to control urban real estate. As scholarship on Singapore has documented, these concerns spurred early efforts to regulate burial grounds, particularly Chinese cemeteries, which colonial officials saw as preventing European development in valuable suburbs. The Chinese community fiercely pushed back, temporarily curtailing proposed limits on their funerary practices that would later be more thoroughly imposed by the post-colonial state.[56] Yet, while these debates played out in communal terms, the realities of urban development were often quite different. One Chinese correspondent in Singapore surmised: "the English golfer daily drives the flying ball through a Chinese cemetery, and makes his putting grounds and teeing places among the Mongolian dead."[57]

Although several decades behind Singapore in its urban development, Kuala Lumpur was also caught up in campaigns to regulate funerary geographies that saw similar tensions between compartmentalizing pressures and cosmopolitan flows. These dynamics shaped discussions among Indians in Kuala Lumpur about how best to dispose of their dead. Members of the Sikh community, many of whom served in the police force in Kuala Lumpur, had been cremating their dead since at least the 1880s, and the government allocated the community a plot of land for the purpose in 1893.[58] A few years later, in 1896, members of the Jaffna Tamil community, citing the precedent set by the Sikh community, petitioned for their own cremation grounds. While tracing their origins to south India, the Jaffna Tamils had settled in Ceylon before migrating to Malaya, where many worked as staff in government offices. In their petition, the Jaffna Tamils noted that when the community in Kuala Lumpur was still small, the prohibition on cremation did not "weigh very much on their minds." But now that the community had grown, the petitioners described their inability to perform the religious rite of cremation in stark terms: "To bury their corpses is not only a direct violation of a Religious Commandment [that] they are bound to obey on pain of forfeiting eternal benefit to their souls, but it is also considered a lasting curse and shame to surviving families of [the] deceased for generations!"[59] By referencing the codifying logic of a "Religious Commandment," a term evoking a Christian-legal imaginary, the petitioners echoed broader pressures to present religious communities as distinct and reducible to the commensurable epistemologies of "World Religions."[60] Dated a mere two days after the petition from the Jaffna Tamils, the Chettiar community, mentioned above as prominent South Indian moneylenders, also petitioned the government for a cremation ground.[61]

As a member of the Sanitary Board and considered by many British officials the unofficial head of the Indian community, Thamboosamy was asked to weigh in on creating new cremation grounds. His response was tepid, noting that "any Hindu can be cremated on the Sikh cremation ground." If additional land was set aside for cremation, he preferred that it be managed by the Hindu cemetery, over which he presided. Neither the Sikh community nor the Jaffna Tamils and Chettiars, however, liked the idea of a joint cremation ground.[62] Eventually, the government struck a compromise, setting aside a new cremation ground to be used by all Indians but with distinct sections for Sikhs and the Jaffna Tamils. This plan, however, was later revised to make the second plot accessible to Hindus in general, and Thamboosamy was initially listed as the custodian. But in 1901, the responsibility for managing the Hindu section reverted to the Jaffna Tamils, who had submitted the original petition. The committee permitted other Hindus to burn their dead on the grounds but charged non-Jaffna Tamils a fee, drawing further complaints.[63] As these complex negotiations demonstrate, the Tamil-Hindu community in Kuala Lumpur (not to mention the Indian community) was highly diverse, incorporating groups from different Tamil sub-regions and professional castes as well as communities whose multi-stepped migrations, such as the Jaffna Tamils, gave them a distinct identity. While some sought to amalgamate these groups into larger categories, perhaps due to the greater political leverage they could achieve as a larger collective, others focused on more narrow affiliations, rooted in region, religion, language, and profession. Such competing claims to community complicated the formation of stable boundaries between different groups. Even those who sought to draw distinctions between communities often did so by adopting strategies they observed others deploying.

These dynamics also shaped efforts to "reform" funerary customs. While organizing into associations divided along ethnic and religious lines, elite members of different groups pursued overlapping programs that targeted lower-class spirituality and urban consumption customs. In their place, reformers advocated distinctly bourgeois practices, including orderly processions that would not interfere with traffic, solemn music that did not interrupt the work of others, and the use of discreet coffins that did not draw attention to dead bodies. The Selangor Chinese Funeral Association, for example, advised its members to avoid engaging the services of "Tamil big drummers," who played tunes such as "Marching Through Georgia" and "Carry Me Back to Old Kentucky." The association deemed such displays of working-class cosmopolitanism entirely unsuitable for such solemn occasions. The president advised instead that Chinese orchestras should be engaged.[64] Chinese reformers, however, were not alone in their concern that popular Tamil bands were transforming funerals into urban spectacles that clashed with bourgeois conceptions of solemnity. Indian reformers in Singapore also complained about the practice of "engaging Indian music in funeral processions."[65] Such complaints were directed at "the lower strata of Hindu society," whom middle-class reformers criticized for making "deafening noises."[66]

In the cosmopolitan spaces of urban Malaya, such efforts rarely solidified into what David Arnold has referred to as "defiantly militant, Hindu nationalism" that helped globalize Hindu cremation.[67] While some embraced the logic of purification, they did so alongside efforts to defend hybrid practices that were seen as essential to co-existence with other communities. For example, in 1906, Indians in Singapore engaged in a heated exchange in the local press after one Sergeant Ramasamy, a member of the Singapore Police Force, arranged for his sister-in-law's corpse to be transported in a coffin and hearse. While he faced pushback for what some described as a "Semi-Christian funeral," others leaped to his defense, calling his critics "bigotted."[68] His allies insisted on the importance of a "decent method of removal of the remains" to maintain the community's dignity amongst "the many and varied nationalities that inhabit this part of the world."[69]

Thamboosamy would have likely concurred with these sentiments. His funeral broadcast his status in a dizzying array of different cultural idioms. His family and associates went to great lengths to have his body returned from Singapore to be buried in Kuala Lumpur. They secured transport on the official yacht of the British Resident of the Federated Malay States. Retracing Thamboosamy's route as a young man, his posthumous journey publicly celebrated the imperial geographies through which he had mapped his ascent. After arriving in Kuala Lumpur, the body was then elaborately transported to the cemetery at Cheras Road in a silver-encrusted coffin, which was set on top of a bier. The display of his body echoed the figure he cut in life—known for sporting a European suit with a colorful turban.[70] Once the funeral commenced, his family members cast handfuls of coins into his grave—a use of currency in burial rituals that would have also resonated with the Chinese present. Onlookers could also not help but think of the vast wealth that Thamboosamy had amassed during his life as the coins piled up on his grave. One of his descendants also told me stories about fireworks being set off during his funeral procession, apparently a nod to the Chinese belief that they warded off evil spirits, even as Tamil attendees carried long blades of grass to accomplish a similar end.[71]

Holding Thamboosamy's funeral in Kuala Lumpur meant delaying his burial for over a week. During that time, his corpse might begin to decay in the tropical heat and moist environs of its watery journey. The stench of carrying an already decomposing body within the hold of the imperial yacht may have also been a concern. The body was, therefore, embalmed, a process with little antecedent in Tamil tradition. Yet wealthy Chinese in Malaya, like their counterparts in other places with large Chinese overseas communities, frequently embalmed their dead to enable their bodies to be sent home to China. (Less wealthy members of the community sometimes instead buried their dead and then exhumed the body and sent the bones of the deceased back to China.[72]) It is, therefore, possible that the professionals who handled Thamboosamy's body deployed techniques with Chinese influence. When the Sultan of the Malay state of Johor passed away in London in 1895, his corpse was embalmed by a French specialist using the latest European techniques of arterial injection. The French doctor, however, noted that he had first removed the organs to cleanse them, a practice which he deemed "not necessary . . . not scientific" but was "according to Eastern ideas the only decorous thing."[73] Given that embalming is not a traditional Islamic technique (Muslims generally bury their dead as quickly as possible), what "Eastern" traditions the doctor referred to was unclear. But his comment hints at cosmopolitan modes of handling the dead, which had been honed through centuries of Asian mobility and reinterpreted through colonial circulations.

While in the decades after Thamboosamy's death cremation emerged as the predominant funerary practice for Hindus, elements of the hybrid practices on display at his funeral remained. A quick perusal of the names of leading mortuary service providers in Singapore and Malaysia today reveals firms with names such as Hindu Casket Services, Shiva Casket Company, Little India Casket Services, and Selayang Indian Casket.[74] While most of these companies specialize in cremation, the inclusion of "casket" in their names and as a standard feature of their funeral packages documents their ongoing reliance on hybrid practices. While Hindus and Sikhs in India often consider the use of a coffin or casket as an impediment to the release of the deceased's soul, beliefs in the diaspora have adapted to different sensibilities concerning the public display of dead bodies.

While members of the Indian diaspora have thus used funerary practices to mark their specific religious and regional identities, they have also embraced accommodations that reflect their cosmopolitan surroundings. These sentiments were captured in an oral interview with Valuppillai (b. 1912), a Ceylonese-Tamil who served as a government bureaucrat in Singapore (similar to the Jaffna Tamils mentioned earlier). When asked about Hindu funeral rites, he responded that ideally, the body would be cremated (or, in some cases, buried) within one day. In rare cases, when a close relative wished to come from abroad, such as "Ceylon or London or Australia," the body would be embalmed. The interviewer then asked whether the embalmer would need to be Ceylonese or Hindu, to which Mr. Pillai replied: "No, not necessarily . . . once a person is gone, there's no difference between all these people of (different) religions. He knows no bounds of race and religion. . . . It is only when we are alive, we talk about different race and language and all that. Once we closed [sic] our eyes . . . all go into the same ocean like that—ocean of life."[75]

## Mapping Thamboosamy's Legacies Across Fluid Logics of Compartmentalization

During Thamboosamy's lifetime, greater religious and ethnic compartmentalization was already shaping the city's geography. Pressure to replace Thamboosamy with a European after his resignation from the Treasury Department and his emerging role as a spokesperson for "Indian" opinion reflected these logics. Yet in the 1890s, colonial officials still cited his fluency in Malay as a reason for appointing him to the Sanitary Board, suggesting that the assumed overlap between ethnic, linguistic, and religious identities remained fluid. Compartmentalizing logics strengthened during the early twentieth century even as the relationship between national origin, language, and religion took on different configurations. During this period, elite Indians increasingly positioned themselves as the natural representatives of the rapidly growing population of plantation workers in Malaya, mostly Tamil speakers from South India. These elites turned to Tamil newspapers and publications to solidify this new public, a shift that emphasized language's importance as a communal identity marker. At the same time, colonial policies of indirect rule circumscribed the authority of the Malay sultans to religion and customs. As a result, an emerging Malay public initially foregrounded shared Muslim identity rather than ethnicity.[76] During the early decades of the twentieth century, Muslims of Indian, Chinese, and Arab heritage played vital roles in the emergence of Malay print culture and social reform movements. Inversely, by the 1920s, upper-caste Hindus were coming to dominate Tamil newspapers and associations, linking a more bounded, elite Hindu tradition to Tamil identity.[77]

The crosscurrents of a global depression, which decimated the markets for Malaysian tin and rubber in the 1930s, and nationalism, which would see the formation of new post-colonial states across the region in the 1940s and 1950s, propelled a more ethnically bounded and territorially rooted Malay identity. In 1957, Article 160 of the Constitution of Federal Malaya (later adopted by Malaysia) defined a Malay as "a person who professes the religion of Islam, habitually speaks the Malay language . . . (and) conforms to Malay custom." Under the New Economic Policy introduced in the 1970s, the post-colonial state implemented affirmative-action policies aimed at uplifting groups defined as *bumiputera,* or sons of the soil, predominantly Malays, but also Orang Asli (original people), and several "native" groups of eastern Malaysia. These categorizations relied on creative inclusions as well as exclusions. Some groups who migrated to the peninsula as late as the twentieth century, including from Indonesia, were classified as Malay and *bumiputera,* reflecting both the idea of a greater Malay world stretching across the archipelago but also the centrality of Islam to who was imaginable as "Indigenous."[78] Inversely, these definitions excluded some non-Muslims who could trace their presence in the peninsula for centuries, such as the Chetti Melaka, sometimes known as Indian Peranakan (literally womb, but colloquially the progeny of mixed marriage).[79] Since the 1970s, the global rise of Islamist movements has linked the emphasis on Islam as an immutable feature of Malay identity to political-legal projects seeking to make it a constitutive feature of Malaysian political and legal institutions. These forces have made other groups feel ever more marginalized.[80] Meanwhile, linguistic nationalist movements in India, which led to the creation of the regional state of Tamil Nadu in 1956, and the power of global Hindutva in recent decades, have also contributed to the stronger assertion of Tamil-Hindu identity among some Indian-Malaysians although often unfolding in different ways than in India itself.[81] Yet despite all the forces pushing Malaysians into different boxes (albeit shifting ones), individuals and families continue to present themselves through different categories in different contexts. As Kalyani Ramnath has shown through her research on how families with ties to South and Southeast Asia navigated new regimes of citizenship and legal documentation in the post-colonial period, individuals' lives frequently defied the boundaries imposed by states.[82] They might click one box on the census, detail a different identity in claiming property in a civil dispute, and assert another identity in a newspaper editorial. As I would find, narratives about family lineage, particularly ones that center on women as well as men, have also been rich spaces for exploring cosmopolitan pasts that defy compartmentalization.

When I went in search of Thamboosamy's grave and his descendants, I found that these patterns manifested in the different ways he was remembered publicly and in family stories, and even in contrasting ways among his descendants. Before traveling to Kuala Lumpur, local contacts pointed me towards his great-granddaughter, Santa Kumarie. Santa had been interviewed by several newspapers about her family's history and given a talk in 2015 about

Thamboosamy, which was organized by the Malaysian Branch of the Royal Asiatic Society (MBRAS) and the Badan Warisan Malaysia (BWM), or Malaysian Heritage Trust.[83] When I contacted these groups, they connected me with Santa. They also suggested that I try posting to the Malaysia History and Heritage Club (MHHC) on Facebook, which is known as a space in which history buffs and those curious about looking beyond an ethno-nationalist history of Malaysia gather to exchange information and tips. When I followed up on this suggestion, I received dozens of responses, which provided little additional information about Thamboosamy's grave (although some recalled that his body had been transported aboard the Resident's yacht) but mentioned several other living relatives. As I explore in more depth in Chapter 5, digital spaces like the MHHC have opened new horizons for exploring diasporic histories but remain all but absent from most scholarship on public history.

After following up on these leads, I eventually met Santa Kumarie in January 2023 at a Punjabi café called "Big Singh" in Petaling Jaya, a satellite town west of KL city. The café served North Indian fare, although a large red Chinese lantern above our table, hung in preparation for the lunar new year, left little doubt that we were in Malaysia. Santa walked in carrying a canvas bag, and she quickly began pulling out newspaper clippings, photocopies of legal documents, and old pamphlets. These documents were part of an extensive personal archive that Santa had amassed over the years as she pieced together the history of her great-grandfather. She told me that she had been told very little about her family's history during her childhood. When I asked her why she thought that was the case, she said she suspected that her older relations felt embarrassed that the family was "not as great as they once were." She mentioned that she believed that her family had lost a lot of wealth during the Great Depression when they were forced to mortgage and eventually sell off substantial real-estate holdings.

As we talked further, however, she also told me that she suspected that the family felt self-conscious that their personal lives did not conform to what many in Malaysia expected from Tamil Hindus by the 1950s and 1960s when she was growing up. She mentioned that while the family celebrated Hindu festivals such as Deepavali (Diwali), they marked the occasion by eating *wajik* rice and *dodol*, two popular Malay sweets. She told me, "We never cooked *murukku* (a fried snack). What kind of Tamil family doesn't make *murukku*?" She also mentioned that the family spoke English and Malay at home, and many were barely conversant in Tamil. The older women in the family, including her great aunts (Thamboosamy's daughters), wore *sarong kebaya*, traditional Malay clothing, with elaborate *kerosang*, a three-piece brooch, rather than the *saris* associated with Tamil dress. She also remembered seeing photographs of her great-grandmother, Thamboosamy's wife, Alamaloo, wearing

FIGURE 1.2. Photograph of Alamaloo, undated. Courtesy of her great-grandson, Namasivayam.

similar clothing, and one of her cousins eventually found and shared a copy of a photo of Alamaloo with me (see Figure 1.2). She wore a Malay-style blouse in the picture, fastened with two brooches and Indian jewelry. Santa told me that the reasons for the family's customs were not openly discussed. Still, she remembered overhearing conversations among her older family members as a girl and thinking, "Something was not right with this family."

Santa also remembered her elders discussing in hushed tones how after her great-grandmother Alamaloo passed away and was cremated, her son (Santa's grandfather) had secretly taken her ashes to St. Anne's Church in Klang. He reportedly stored them behind an image of St. Anne and felt comforted by the thought that when devotees lit candles and offered prayers to the saint, his mother would also benefit from their blessings. Given the family's public Hindu identity, this would have been a controversial choice, although it was also around this time that some members of the family converted to Christianity.

While Santa struggled as a child to make sense of these stories, later in life, she found some papers among her father's things, which deepened her understanding that her family's background was more complex than the "Tamil-Hindu" label could fully accommodate. These included a copy of a legal case between Thamboosamy's descendants and other members of the Tamil community contesting whether the Sri Maha Mariamman temple was a private family shrine or a public temple. In the case, the name of her great-grandmother, who was among the defendants, is listed as "Alamaloo alias Noorvi (f)." Santa told me that this document offered further support for her childhood hunch that her great-grandmother might have been Malay and possibly a Muslim. The name Noorvi itself does not provide any clear indication of her identity. The use of an alias, however, perhaps resonated with Santa's sense that the women in her family had more fluid identities—she also mentioned to me that she sometimes wondered whether Thamboosamy's mother could have been Malay.

Other conversations with Thamboosamy's family yielded different narratives about his life and legacies. Thamboosamy's great-grandson, Namasivayam, generously shared family stories and mementos with me, including the photograph of Alamaloo and Thamboosamy's old trophy cabinet (see Figure 1.3). Like Santa, he emphasized the family's pride in their ancestor but also their sense of loss. The former trophy case, now populated with more quotidian mementos, including an array of Barbies dressed in Indian and European costumes, was haunted by the absence/presence of Thamboosamy's dearly remembered, but physically absent, trophies. Yet Namasivayam also expressed some doubts about Santa's recounting of the family's past. While we did not delve deeply into their diverging memories, he told me that he wondered whether suggesting that Alamaloo was Malay might upset people who looked up to Thamboosamy as a leader of the Tamil-Hindu community.

Despite Namasivayam's concerns, I felt strongly that it would be wrong to silence Santa's version of her family history. When my research for the book first expanded from archives to embrace more extensive work with families, I thought I would honor their requests about what information I published about their ancestors, even if it sometimes meant excluding materials I had found in public archival sources. However, working with families such as Thamboosamy's descendants revealed that my conceptions of privacy and consent were better geared towards working with individuals rather than families. Families often disagreed about the past and what parts they wanted to be public. I therefore asked about these preferences, but I could sometimes not implement everyone's wishes.

In the case of Thamboosamy, the version of his past that held him up as an exemplar of Tamil-Hindu identity circulates widely. Santa's more hybrid narratives have been marginalized, perhaps because of their association with the women in her family. They are thus crucial for recovering the feminist family

FIGURE 1.3. Photograph of Thamboosamy's trophy cabinet, now in the possession of his great-grandson Namasivayam, reproduced with his kind permission.

histories this book foregrounds, even when some family members would instead emphasize other dimensions of their past. Yet, in each chapter of this book, I have made slightly different calculations about what to include and exclude. Historians have always faced such choices, and the centrality of history to political debates in many parts of the world, including Malaysia, is making many more aware of their stakes. Yet ethics remains relatively marginal to most historical scholarship and disciplinary training, particularly in comparison to fields like anthropology that focus on "living" subjects. I see writing openly about how I have navigated difficult choices about which family stories to include and exclude as a critical step toward shifting these dynamics.

Sometimes, working through these dilemmas sent me back to the archives to see whether sources I had previously consulted yielded different insights in light of my conversations with descendants. After speaking with Santa, I returned to the archive to see if I could find anything else that spoke to her suggestion that Thamboosamy's mother might have been Malay. In his will, Thamboosamy made a provision for his stepmother, "Sundarum of Tambore Negepatam," suggesting that she was from and possibly still living in Negapatam, India.[84] The only possible mention I have found of his own mother is a petition that Alamaloo submitted in 1926. In the petition, she asked that plans for a Roman Catholic church and school in Klang, to the southwest of Kuala Lumpur, be modified to protect the gravesite of her children's grandmother, Thamboosamy's mother. The letter also mentioned that religious ceremonies were still conducted at the gravesite biannually. The letter protested that if the plans were "allowed to go through the body will have to be exhumed as it would be impossible for the religious ceremonies to continue within the precincts of a Roman Catholic Church."[85] In an old newspaper article Santa shared with me, her father also mentioned that Thamboosamy's mother was buried in Klang and that a Sivan (Shiva) Temple had been built on the site because "Hindus like to build their temple by the grave of a prominent person."[86] That the grave of Thamboosamy's mother was a site of Hindu worship associated with the god Shiva might seem to put to rest speculation that she was Muslim. Yet she could have converted after marrying Thamboosamy's father, so the family might have been particularly concerned about emphasizing her Hindu identity by building a temple at her grave. Moreover, the practice of building religious shrines near graves is evocative of Sufi practices, which are associated with mystical forms of Islam but often embraced by people of diverse religious backgrounds. The contestations over Thamboosamy's mother's burial site, therefore, provide no definitive answer about her ethnic or religious identity. Instead, they situate the family within the religious geographies of an older Malay cosmopolis, in which Islam was less an identity than a lingua franca, a powerful mode of expressing sacrality that operated alongside other religious traditions. In Alamaloo's concern about building a Roman Catholic church on top of her mother-in-law's grave, we see emerging strains in these cosmopolitan geographies, but not yet their definitive breakdown.

These family stories also show women's critical roles in constituting cosmopolitan worlds and navigating their reformulation under new colonial and later national regimes of categorization. Putting together archival and remembered fragments suggests that men like Thamboosamy first learned to navigate diverse social worlds as children in the care of their mothers and other women within their household, in contexts in which the existence of multiple wives and concubines of different backgrounds was the norm. While my initial search through colonial archives foregrounded masculine social worlds, family memories, particularly about household habits and sacred spaces, set me on trails where women's contributions to cosmopolitan cultures came to the fore.

## Afterlives: Missing Graves and Worldly Reincarnations

As Santa and I compared notes, it was a lot to take in. What would Alamaloo alias Noorvi think of her final resting place in a church, given her efforts to ensure that her mother-in-law's grave did not suffer a similar fate? Some of her and Thamboosamy's descendants subsequently converted to Christianity, but it is not clear whether Alamaloo herself shifted her religious beliefs later in life. Was either woman asked about her preferences for her final resting place? Moreover, how helpful is it even to ask whether Alamaloo and Thamboosamy's mother were Malay? Today to be Malay in Malaysia implies an ethnic, linguistic, and Muslim identity and a claim to be a *bumiputera*, or son of the soil. Yet, as the chapter has traced, during Thamboosamy and Alamaloo's lifetime, the alignment of ethnic, linguistic, religious, and claims to indigeneity was far more fluid, and their children and grandchildren also experienced multiple shifting regimes of categorization. Even today, Malaysians use such categories differently, particularly when speaking to subjects other than the state. Given these shifting and still fluid meanings, it is more helpful to understand family stories about Alamaloo and Thamboosamy's mother as evidence of the family's multiple modes of being cosmopolitan, including but not limited to incorporating women with different backgrounds, than to speculate about a particular ethnic or religious genealogy.

As I learned to navigate these more cosmopolitan geographies, I nursed an ongoing desire to find evidence of their persistence by locating Thamboosamy's grave. Yet my efforts to find his grave, while connecting me to his relations, were a series of dead ends. After speaking with his family yielded no new clues about his grave, I returned to the references from newspaper articles about his funeral, which described him as being buried at the Tamil Cemetery at Cheras Road. Google Maps showed a large cemetery in Kuala Lumpur known as Cheras. The cemetery included distinct areas for Christian, Muslim, and military burials and, promisingly, a small Hindu burial plot next to a modern crematorium. Family friends, who trace their roots to Kerala but have been in Malaysia for multiple generations, generously offered to accompany me on a trip to the cemetery—I think perhaps concerned that a lone foreigner would stand out. When we visited the cemetery, we first stopped at the crematorium, where one of the employees was puzzled by my inquiry but attempted to help. He was unequivocal, however, that I should not enter the Hindu graveyard as street dogs had taken it over and was unsafe. He recommended that I contact the official trustee of the cemetery, the Sri Maha Mariamman Temple, which Thamboosamy had endowed. Following his advice, I visited the temple, whose staff members were equally puzzled by my query and wanted to know where I had obtained the information that Thamboosamy was buried at Cheras Road. Although somewhat incredulous, the temple staff promised to make further inquiries. The following day, they contacted me to let me know that they had spoken to one of the temple trustees who had knowledge of the matter, and he had informed them that Thamboosamy was not buried at Cheras cemetery. Instead, they told me that his gravesite was on a plot of land that the temple had long ago donated to SMK (P) Pudu, a girl's school founded by Anglican missionaries in 1914. They assured me that there was no longer anything to visit, although they politely offered to accompany me if I wished to persist in my search. I sensed that further inquiries were not welcome.

At first, I was skeptical about the trustee's account and thought it was perhaps a polite way of diverting a noisy foreigner. However, as I dug through old city maps, I found evidence that strongly supported the trustee's account. A map from 1920, with which the chapter opens, shows a "Tamil Cemetery," located on Cheras Road, but much closer to the city than the current cemeteries known as "Cheras." A further map from 1945 shows the cemetery, now labeled "Hindu," alongside the Pudu Girls School (see Figure 1.4). A short distance away, the map also indicates Hindu and Sikh Cremation Grounds, which were the subject of debate during Thamboosamy's lifetime. (These cremation grounds continue to exist today but are known as the Malaysian Indian Ceylon Crematorium, harkening back to the Jaffna Tamils connection.) Further inquiries about the school's history also turned up anecdotes that a neighboring slum area had once been a Hindu cemetery.[87] While there appear to be no physical remains of the cemetery left, the history has also not been completely forgotten, as evidenced by the information provided by the temple trustee. That Thamboosamy's body now lies beneath a Christian school for girls also evokes the stories I heard about the graves and ashes of his women relations.

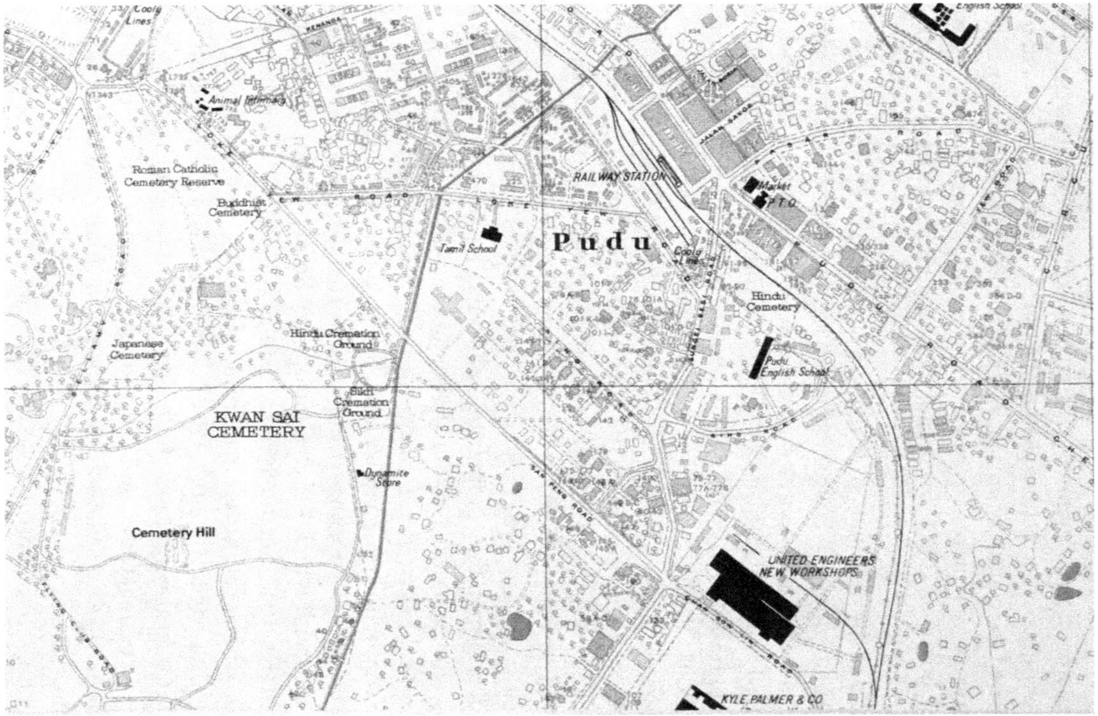


FIGURE 1.4. Location of Hindu Cemetery and Pudu Girls School from Malaya. Town Plan of Kuala Lumpur (1945). [G.S.G.S. No. 4476]. Second edition. Scale 1: 6,336. Shelfmark Maps 60010.(1.). Courtesy of the British Library archives.

FIGURE 1.5. Bust of Thamboosamy at Batu Caves, with his name obscured under yellow paint. Photograph by author.

Thamboosamy's simultaneous presence and absence in the remembered landscapes of Kuala Lumpur can also be felt in other ways. While lamenting that her great-grandfather is not more widely recognized, Santa noted that his statue at Batu Caves has recently been moved to an out-of-the-way location to the side of a newly built office building. She told me that relations between the family and temple trustees have long been tense, dating back to their legal battles in the 1920s over who would control the property. This was especially true after some members of the family became Christians. Santa also noted that the fact that some of her family were not primarily Tamil speakers clashed with the temple's public identity as a center of both a Hindu workshop and Tamil communal life. When visiting the caves, I, too, noticed this odd placement and that the Tamil and English inscriptions had been painted over. However, someone had taken the time to place a fresh floral garland around Thamboosamy's neck and leave an apple (see Figure 1.5). Where the text had been painted over, material practices lived on—which I took as a metaphor for how material forms of cosmopolitanism can persist even when new ideologies and idioms of compartmentalization dominate public discourse.

Thamboosamy's afterlife thus occupies uneasy fault lines in contemporary Kuala Lumpur. He is certainly remembered as a pioneering Indian leader whose visage is often used to represent the Indian contribution to Malaysia's multi-cultural history. But I encountered a hesitance to dig deeper, lest doing so upset the already precarious status of Indian-Malaysian belonging. As Thamboosamy's great-grandson suggested, chipping away at the box that Thamboosamy occupies as an identifiably Tamil and Hindu figure perhaps feels risky when the larger edifice supporting ethno-pluralism and secularism feels shaky. In public spaces of memorialization, Thamboosamy must fit into a bounded history, where cultures co-mingled but did not mix. If this chapter were based on archival research and conventional historical methods alone, I would probably end here with a nostalgic lament for an Indian Ocean cosmopolitanism that was once vibrant but is now largely superseded by national, religious, and regional/linguistic identities.

Yet, turning to family memories and layered landscapes suggests how cosmopolitanism continues to flow beneath the surface of the more visible struggles between ethno-nationalism and ethno-pluralism. An empty trophy case, built-over gravesite, and garlanded but nameless bust—these traces show the enduring legacies of cosmopolitanism, particularly in its material manifestations, even when built over or buried.

Yet, while graves and burial have been central to this chapter, there is also a danger in seeing this haunted past as necessarily hidden or suppressed. My conversations with Santa also suggested vibrant, living legacies of cosmopolitanism that the family has readily embraced and, when asked the right questions, is happy to share with others. After our meeting, Santa and I kept in touch via WhatsApp, as our initial conversations about Thamboosamy extended to the family matriarchs and outwards from there to his scattered descendants. Santa sent me family photos of relatives across Malaysia, Singapore, Australia, New Zealand, and Canada who have married spouses from many different backgrounds. She proudly explained to me that her family is "broadminded." She emphasized that her relations had inherited this from her great-grandfather, along with their love for animals, suggesting his passion for horse racing has evolved into new forms even as his trophies have disappeared. This facet of Thamboosamy's afterlife can be easy to miss if we approach diaspora primarily through ties to specific places or bounded ethnic or religious identities. These frames dominate official "Public" histories. But Santa's generosity in sharing her family history with me and her enthusiasm for telling the stories of her maternal as well as paternal ancestors suggests that this is not a divide between public and private histories but between capital "P" and lowercase "p" public histories. Approaching diasporic histories through family, and including the legacies of women as well as men, opens the possibility for engaging alternative pasts not just within families but as larger collectives—themes I explore in more depth by turning to another matriarch and an alternative collection of archives in the next chapter.

# 2

# In-Laws

FIGURE 2.1. Photograph of Janbai. Gift of Minnie Bachelder, 1932. Image TR2016.13. Reproduced courtesy of the Peabody Essex Museum, Salem, MA.

AS WE saw in the previous chapter, afterlives unfolded in many stages, beginning before death and stretching for years and even generations. In the last chapter, we entered this chain of events with a funeral. This chapter focuses on a later stage following the death of Sir Tharia Topan in February 1891. It explores how the division of the deceased's property was a key site for contesting diasporic legacies. In the proceeding chapter, we started the story with the family's patriarch—here, I begin instead with a matriarch.[1]

In the months after her husband passed, Janbai faced a difficult choice about whether to take the family's quarrels to court. While burying her husband and celebrating his life at the Khoja *jamat khana,* or place of religious gathering, in Bombay, she had already clashed with her stepsons. They disapproved of how much she had spent on Tharia's funeral. To her, it seemed a wise investment in asserting the family's standing even as they lost their patriarch. For her stepsons, it was a waste of resources, unbecoming to their father, who disapproved of such lavish spending. Even before Tharia's death, Janbai and her stepsons, the eldest of whom was Janbai's senior by eight years, were jockeying over who would assume control over the family. Its dealings in textiles, spices, ivory, and (before abolition) enslaved people stretched from India to Africa, Arabia, China, and the United States.[2] In anticipation of this moment, Janbai, who was then living with an ailing Tharia in Bombay, convinced him to add codicils to his will, making additional bequests of property for her and her children. Tharia had been having rather different discussions about the family firm with his sons via letters circulating between Zanzibar and Bombay. Janbai now had to decide whether to litigate their differences in court.

From the middle of the nineteenth century, British colonial courts consolidated a new body of family or "personal" laws to govern disputes involving "domestic" affairs, including divorce and inheritance, areas in which women also featured prominently. Unlike other areas of the law, including criminal and commercial cases, the outcome in matters of personal law depended on the religious identity of the litigants, with courts deciding cases according to their interpretation of religious texts and customs. As a wide range of scholarship on South Asian legal history has demonstrated, law, as a vehicle for governing the family, emerged as a critical site for consolidating newly bounded, if still highly contested, identities. In these battles, women became symbolic totems through which men consolidated new national and religious identities.[3]

The problem was that Janbai and Tharia's family defied the compartmentalizing logics of colonial personal law and identitarian categories, much as Thamboosamy defied emerging regimes of ethnic and religious categorization in Malaya. The process of consolidating new bodies of personal law was highly fraught—often entailing sprawling legal battles over competing religious interpretations. But these struggles proved particularly intense among groups that fell outside of the dominant division of Indian society into Hindus and Muslims. These included smaller religious groups such as the Parsis and minorities within religious minorities, including the Gujarati-Khoja trading caste, many of whom, like Janbai and Tharia, were Shia Ismaili followers of the

Aga Khan—terms I explain later.[4] Colonial courts attempted to decide whether Khojas and other Ismaili groups followed "orthodox" Muslim personal law or retained Hindu practices from before their conversion to Islam. These efforts were often frustrated by the reality that inheritance customs varied from family to family, and the actual divisions of estates depended on wrangling within families. Such contests did not necessarily pivot around opposing constructions of religious identity, although they might overlap.[5]

The legal battles of such minorities within minorities were also shaped by their overrepresentation among diasporic mercantile communities. Ismailis, alongside Parsis, Baghdadi Jews, and other diasporic minorities, proved particularly adept at mastering the habits of cosmopolitanism that propelled Thamboosamy's successes.[6] These same qualities made them litigious—a manifestation of their broader facility in navigating colonial bureaucracies and jargons to gain competitive advantage. Families divided by distance were also more likely to turn to courts. Dividing their estates often required moving assets across jurisdictions. Alternative modes of resolving such disputes, such as mediation by elders or community councils (such as the Khoja *jamat*), could break down when opposing parties were dispersed. Diasporic minorities like the Khoja Ismailis, therefore, often ended up in court, and, in the process, helped propel the circulations of law across the British Empire. These contests played out not just as battles over identity, which has been the focus of much scholarship on law, family, and gender in South Asia. When we approach them through the lens of diasporic family relations, we see that they were just as often contests over mobility—of how best to move assets and manage relations across space and generations. They were about reconciling different notions of law and documentary forms, including wills and letters, and whether such papers reflected the deceased's true intentions. They were also struggles over the role of different family members, in particular widows versus sons, in managing family firms that straddled continents. In these wranglings, women like Janbai played a central role, not as mere symbolic totems but as agentic movers and shakers.[7]

Yet, such litigation could be financially and emotionally costly for families. Litigation, with all the accompanying lawyers' and court fees, could decimate fortunes in a single generation. In the months after her husband's death, Janbai may have been weighing such costs while deciding whether to petition the courts to intervene. Litigation also strained family relations as kin battled kin in the public theater of colonial courtrooms. Legal proceedings were splashed across newspaper columns for neighbors and business associates to read. In cases involving families like the Topans, who split their time between eastern Africa and western India, their legal battles in the British consular court in Zanzibar were reported within days in the press in Bombay—creating a transoceanic circuit of legal gossip.[8] This was "divide and rule" enacted on the intimate terrain of family relations and with potentially severe consequences for the longevity of diasporic family businesses. The dispute over Tharia's estate would inevitably air the family's dirty laundry and could place their future fortunes at risk. However, the potential payoff for the legal victor was also high. Ultimately, the pull of the courts proved too great to resist. The family ended up litigating Tharia's estate and opposing each other in multiple additional legal disputes.[9]

Janbai's engagement with the courts and the legal records left in its wake show the promise and limits of legal history as a vehicle for recovering the agency and subjectivity of diasporic women. Viewed retrospectively, historians have demonstrated that colonial law had many detrimental impacts on women, codifying their subordination within patriarchal family structures and their marginalization from commercial markets.[10] However, for individual women, particularly women like Janbai, who were wealthy and adept at pitting different patriarchs against each other, colonial courts offered an alluring avenue to pursue their interests. In court, women sometimes won surprising victories against men.[11] Legal records also offer rich resources for tracing histories of such women, revealing their presence even when they are obscured in political and business archives.[12] In the previous chapter, another legal record, the reference to Tipah binte Alli in Thamboosamy's will, also provided critical insight into his mixed household.

Yet, while mining legal records to write alternative histories of diasporic families and gender relations, I have also become aware of their limits. All too often, even though women appear in legal records, they do so as nodes within networks governed by men—as inheritors of wealth amassed by men, through representations penned by lawyers, who were overwhelmingly men, and as subjects of legal judgments authored by judges who were also men. When I began working on this chapter, I thought Tharia, not Janbai, would be its central character.

While pouring over the records of the dispute over his estate, I also reached out to one of the couple's surviving grandchildren, Farouk Topan. Farouk is an esteemed writer and professor of Swahili literature who now lives in London. He was anxious to see the materials I had gathered about the legal dispute over his grandfather's estate. In exchange, he offered to share an unpublished biography his father had written about his father, Tharia. When we met, we thought our conversation would focus on Tharia. However, exchanging observations about the two sources, we increasingly found ourselves speaking about Janbai, not unlike my queries in the last chapter progressively shifted from Thamboosamy to Alamaloo.[13]

While that initial conversation reframed my analysis, I remained frustrated by my inability to see Janbai other than as caricatured by the men in her

FIGURE 2.2. Bracelet (unknown artist). Nineteenth-century gold. 2 ½ × 2 ¾ in. Museum purchase, 1932. Object E22365. Reproduced courtesy of the Peabody Essex Museum, Salem, MA.

life—as a grasping young wife and ignorant mother. Several years later, however, a late-night Google search revealed another trail in the most unexpected place. In the catalog of objects held by the Peabody Essex Museum in Salem, Massachusetts, I found a gold bracelet and portrait photograph that Janbai gifted to Caroline Batchelder, the wife of an American sea captain who traveled to Zanzibar (see Figures 2.1 and 2.2). The intimacy of staring at the face of a woman whom I had been researching for years but whose photograph even her grandson Farouk did not possess made me feel that I was in the presence of a ghost. It was evidence of the haunting power of visual sources to reveal modes of agency obscured in other mediums. Janbai's gifts to Caroline also suggest the spectral agency of heirlooms as objects that trace social connections beyond those dominated by elite, lettered men. The passage of the bracelet and portrait from Janbai to Caroline and from Caroline to her daughter before entering a celebrated museum collection offered a glimpse of how moving objects and images linked women to women. These relations are often obscured in global histories of law and commerce. In contrast, assembling haunted, multi-media collages reveals women's global influence within and beyond family relations.

## Indian Ocean Itineraries

Janbai and Tharia's lives defy area-studies boundaries that segment Asia, Africa, and the Middle East into distinct regions. The couple moved along circuits of economic, political, and cultural connection that knit together the Indian Ocean's coastal littorals. Both were from families that traced their origins to Kutch in Gujarat. Located on the northwestern coast of India, Gujarat has been closely connected to Indian Ocean circuits of people, goods, and ideas for millennia. Kutch was one of Gujarat's regional hubs, and from at least the eighteenth century, its merchants played a crucial role in networks linking western India, eastern Africa, and the Gulf. During this period, Kutch was ruled by an Indian princely dynasty, the Raos of Kutch, who maintained a semi-autonomous government under British suzerainty. This liminal position within British imperial geographies allowed merchants from Kutch to access new imperial infrastructure, including British courts, and to remain connected to older oceanic networks. They continued to transport their wares aboard *dhows* (smaller sailing vessels common in the Indian Ocean), offering cheaper and less closely regulated transport even after the advent of faster steam-based shipping.[14]

This geography was held together through spiritual circuits. Janbai and Tharia belonged to a caste of Khoja traders from Sindh and Gujarat, many of whom became part of a global Ismaili community during the nineteenth century. The Ismailis, a Shia sect of Islam, are followers of the Aga Khans, whom they believe to be descendants of the Prophet Muhammad and his living *imam*, or spiritual successor. Today, Ismailis, while numerically small, exercise global influence through communities spread across Asia, Africa, Europe, and the United States, known for their business prowess and contributions to education and development initiatives. According to some community histories, the Khojas converted to Islam in the fourteenth century under the influence of charismatic Ismaili *pirs,* or spiritual guides, originally from Persia. Scholarly work on the community has emphasized the Khojas' ties to broader syncretic regional traditions, which defy modern religious epistemologies dividing Hindu and Islamic practices. While some Khojas may have cultivated loose ties to Persian-Ismaili circuits, they were also deeply rooted in more local religious networks. This spiritual geography shifted considerably in the nineteenth century with the arrival in India of Hasan Ali Shah. Shah was the forty-seventh Ismaili *imam* and the first to use the title of Aga Khan. After organizing a rebellion against the Qajar Empire in Iran, he fled with a band of his followers to Afghanistan in the early 1840s, where he provided military support and intelligence for the British Army during the first Anglo-Afghan War.[15]

While this alliance proved short-lived, it looped the Aga Khan into colonial circuits of power, quickly pulling him towards India and the routes Tharia and Janbai would travel. After a brief stay in Calcutta, the Aga Khan shifted to Bombay in 1848, where he quickly recognized the importance of using colonial printing presses and law courts to manage his followers. He identified the Khojas as a core constituency, given their historical ties to Persian *pirs* and their growing power in Bombay, where many had relocated to benefit from the city's rising importance as an industrial center and preeminent Indian Ocean entrepôt. From at least the 1830s, however, some members of the Khoja community had been advocating religious reforms that pushed more orthodox Sunni and Twelver Shia practices. Some of these reformers resisted the leadership of the Aga Khan. The stakes in these fights were not just spiritual; the Aga Khan sought to claim the right to collect tithes from Khoja *jamats* or local assemblies. The colonial courts began intervening in the late 1840s when the Bombay High Court heard two cases concerning whether Khoja women's inheritance rights followed Quranic or customary practices. In 1866, the Bombay High Court issued a decision in what would become popularly known as the "Aga Khan Case," declaring Hasan Ali Shah the official head of the Khoja community. The case, however, did little to resolve disputes within the community, with some Khojas breaking away and identifying as Sunni or Twelver Shias, the dominant sect of Shias. Questions about how Khoja estates should be divided also remained unresolved.[16]

Tharia's and Janbai's lives closely tracked these intersecting economic, religious, and legal circuits. Tharia was born in 1823. According to family lore, as a teenager, he first left Kutch after mistakenly being accused of theft and fleeing on a dhow bound for Muscat, where he established an export market for his father's oil mill business. Tharia soon returned to Kutch, where he married his first wife and began a family, but this first sojourn whetted his appetite for further travel. Around the age of twenty, he joined a group of merchants recruited by the Sultan of Zanzibar via the Rao of Kutch to expand trade links between western India and Eastern Africa.[17] He arrived in Zanzibar during a period of political transition in the Western Indian Ocean. Zanzibar was ruled by a branch of the Busaidi family, an Omani dynasty who once ruled over an empire stretching from the Gulf down the coast of eastern Africa. By the latter decades of the nineteenth century, the Sultans of Zanzibar ruled over a much more limited realm consisting of a few small islands, which were critical trading entrepôts. As a result, the British exerted increasing control over Zanzibar, which became a formal British protectorate in 1890.[18]

Having already worked with Omanis in Muscat, Tharia's migration to Zanzibar represented a logical next step in this interregional network of political and trade connections. Tharia's father also had business connections with other Gujarati families trading in Zanzibar. These multi-generational ties helped propel Tharia's rapid ascent into the island's economic elite.[19] After working as an apprentice to another Indian firm, he struck out on his own, first as a trader and one of the region's most critical financiers. Tharia also purchased the contract to "farm" the customs revenue for Zanzibar in 1879, a position that put him at the epicenter of commercial and political power on the island.[20] While building his business in Zanzibar, Tharia also established a commercial office in Bombay, from which he expanded his trade links with China.[21] In addition to acting as the economic hub, Bombay was the center of Britain's sprawling legal influence in the region, under which British subjects were exempt from the jurisdiction of "native" courts and instead subject to consular jurisdiction. Thus, even before Zanzibar became a formal British protectorate, from the 1860s onwards, the local British consular court acted as the primary legal venue for civil disputes between the islands' mixed population of Swahili, Arab, and Indian merchants. The Bombay High Court heard appeals from the consular court, solidifying the link between the island and the growing cosmopolis.[22] Reflecting Bombay's centrality to the geographies they traveled, Tharia and Janbai relocated there in the 1880s, becoming neighbors of the Aga Khan, who also resided in the city.

## Legacies of a Matriarch in a World of Patriarchs

In contrast to Tharia, I have been unable to uncover much information about Janbai's life before she entered the Topan household. This silence reflects deeply gendered imbalances in both colonial archives and many families' recounting of their pasts, which often emphasize the contributions of fathers and grandfathers.

Historians, especially those interested in marginalized subjects, are accustomed to reading state archives against the grain. They use this technique to read colonial reports on peasant criminality to discover acts of political resistance and official descriptions of "Eastern" superstitions as expressions of subaltern rationalities.[23] In my experience, family collections also must be read against the grain to study women's lives. We must often first deconstruct the patriarchal packages in which memories of women were passed down before we can critically engage with them as historical subjects. Mohamed Hussein's unpublished biography of his father Tharia, now in the possession of Mohamed Hussein's son Farouk, invites such creative reading practices. Mohamed

Hussein credits Farouk's wife with urging him to write the biography. The biography is written in English and typed but is sometimes awkward in its phrasing. It also includes many seemingly tangential historical asides and ethnographic descriptions of Zanzibari customs that initially appear not immediately relevant to Tharia's life story. Farouk has periodically shared the memoir with scholars, who have used it to write about his grandfather Tharia's life and the role of Indian (male) merchants in the economic, political, and social landscapes of the Indian Ocean during the heyday of British imperialism.[24]

Mohamed Hussein was certainly outwardly more interested in the "wonderful and colourful" stories that he had heard about his father's life, but some of the seemingly tangential portions of the biography pertain to Janbai and invite critical reading. For example, Mohamed Hussein described in detail how Zanzibari women entertained each other, information he may have learned from his mother. Janbai's recurring presence in the biography may reflect that Mohamed Hussein had limited direct memories of Tharia, who passed away when he was five.[25] In contrast, he had an intimate, if often tense, relationship with his mother. He blamed her for squandering the family's resources in litigation and derisively described her as a "fanatic Ismaili," suggesting that the family was internally divided by broader religious debates in their community.[26] When we follow such tangents and read against the grain of Mohamed Hussein's criticism of his mother as grasping and ignorant, the biography proves an exceptionally rich source for studying Janbai. From its pages, a picture emerges of Janbai as a woman often able to get her way despite moving through social worlds dominated by men.

Janbai first appears in the biography as a young woman peddling her wares on the street outside the Topan family home. According to family lore, as recorded in Mohamed Hussein's biography, soon after the death of Tharia's second wife in 1863 (who was childless), Tharia's elder sons from his first marriage, who were approximately twenty and twelve at the time, initiated the search for a new bride for their father.[27] Although Tharia initially suggested the possibility of marrying a widow, his sons Moosa and Jaffer convinced him to marry Janbai, then twelve, after Moosa observed her selling fruits for her father's business. While also a Khoja, as the youngest daughter of a small business owner, Janbai was a surprising choice for such a wealthy man to marry. Moosa and Jaffer, however, believed that her family's relative poverty was an advantage. They assumed that after marrying into the family, Janbai would feel "entire satisfaction" and "not bring quarrel, trouble and unhappiness . . . as many step mother brings [sic]." Later, the brothers would lament that "this illiterate girl began to rise to her changed status" and began to interfere "in each and every work and act of her husband."[28]

A little over a decade into their marriage, Janbai had given birth to three healthy daughters, Jainab, Fatmabai, and Khadija, but had lost four infant sons.[29] Desperate for sons, Janbai convinced Tharia to make a pilgrimage to visit the Aga Khan in India in 1875 to ask for his intercession on their behalf, a practice that Tharia might have felt was not in line with his more modernist religious orientation. Yet Janbai prevailed, and during their visit, the Aga Khan "closed his eyes and waited in that condition for [a] couple of minutes," after which he reassured the couple that Janbai would give birth to three healthy sons. In exchange, the Aga Khan instructed Janbai and Tharia to take the boys on a pilgrimage to Karbala and to shave their heads as an act of thanksgiving. Soon after returning to Zanzibar, Janbai gave birth to her first son, Mohamed Medi, followed by another son, Mohamed Ali, four years later. After the birth of their second son in 1881, Tharia and Janbai, along with their young sons, traveled to Mecca and Karbala to fulfill their vow. (Mohamed Hussein, the couple's third and youngest son, was born in 1886.) Echoing broader schisms within the Khoja community, in recounting these events in the biography, Mohamed Hussein cast them as the product of his mother's "fanatic" religious devotion, which he associated with her lack of education. In contrast, Mohamed Hussein held up Tharia as a rational and doctrinally correct Muslim who believed that the Aga Khan was the "rightful owner of the throne of Imamat (spiritual leadership) and not beyond that." He also noted that, as the father of two adult sons, Tharia was less concerned than his third wife about producing male progeny.[30]

In this anecdote, Janbai navigated multiple intersecting spheres of masculine authority. While Tharia may not have entirely approved of his wife's devotional orientation nor been as concerned about producing additional male heirs, he apparently chose not to block her from appealing directly to the Aga Khan, the ultimate patriarchal figure for Ismailis. She thus pitted the religious hierarchies of the Ismaili community against the patriarchal structures of her family to assert her ambition for male progeny—who would provide her with yet another nexus of masculine power to leverage. Janbai's ability to play different patriarchies against one another to advance her ends increased as she aged and gave birth to additional children. According to Mohamed Hussein, by the time Janbai was in her thirties, she had assumed the rank of the "highest commanding officer or her super ladyship" within the Topan household. While Mohamed Hussein may have somewhat overstated Janbai's relative power in the family, she won crucial victories as the couple struggled over diverging ideas about how to build their household's power. In addition to their different religious practices, Janbai and Tharia differed in their approaches to managing their increasing wealth. Janbai pushed the family towards more conspicuous consumption, including household adornments and gifts. Tharia preferred business investments and colonially sanctioned philanthropy, including plans to construct a hospital in Zanzibar to celebrate Queen Victoria's Jubilee.[31]

Janbai's contrasting approach was apparent in the arrangements for the marriage of two of their daughters, Fatma and Khadija, in 1882. Their eldest daughter, Jainab, was married in a simple ceremony several years earlier. The family's rising position and Janbai's growing influence led to far more elaborate preparations for their younger daughters' joint wedding. This time around, it was Janbai, rather than Tharia, who selected the grooms, despite objections from some members of the community to one of the matches. Janbai also gained the upper hand in managing the expenses for the wedding; the family ordered elaborate jewelry and embroidered clothing from Bombay and arranged for a famous dancer to travel from Egypt to entertain the guests. With plans for festivities lasting nearly three weeks, Janbai was determined that the Sultan of Zanzibar should attend the wedding. When Tharia visited the Sultan to invite him, the Sultan explained that he did not attend any marriages, even of his own relations, to spare his subjects the extra expense of his attendance. Tharia accepted the Sultan's explanation. Janbai did not. She promptly visited the palace herself and leveraged the ruler's paternal instincts to get her way. She asked the Sultan whose daughters Fatima and Khadija were, to which he replied, "My daughters." She then asked how the marriage could take place without the presence of their "father." According to Mohamed Hussein's biography, "Sayyid Bargash knew very well Janbai was not a[n] easy nut to crack like Tharia" and promptly agreed to attend.[32]

To underline the spectacle of the Sultan's attendance, the royal guests were led along carpets from the palace to the family's residence on the night of the wedding. After welcoming the Sultan and his family into their home, Tharia and Janbai presented him with a specially carved wooden chair covered with a thin layer of silver. The Topans commissioned the chair from a workshop of Ceylonese artisans who had recently set up shop in Zanzibar to meet the island's growing demand for luxury furnishings. Two large trays of silver *riyal* coins were also presented to the Sultan on the brides' behalf. In return, the Sultan and his wife gave the brides double-stranded pearl necklaces and diamond rings set with ruby and emerald accents. While in the biography, Mohamed Hussein described the details of the wedding as one more example of his mother's domineering personality and her extravagant tastes, Janbai likely saw the lavish celebrations as an investment, just as Thamboosamy's family viewed his funeral as a crucial opportunity to cement his cosmopolitan influence. The wedding took place as Tharia was consolidating his power as one of the preeminent Indian merchants in Zanzibar, and the Sultan's attendance broadcast the family's ascendance—encouraging new alliances and warning those who might consider getting in Tharia's, or Janbai's, way. At a minimum, the celebrations left a lasting impression. As Mohamed Hussein himself acknowledged, locals who observed the wedding continued to tell stories about the celebrations even decades later—evidence that expenditures on ceremonial celebrations could contribute to long-lasting reputational legacies, not unlike the dividends yielded by other financial investments.[33]

A few years after the wedding, Tharia and Janbai shifted their household to Bombay, traveling with their four daughters and two sons. Their youngest daughter, Beuba, was a mere infant at the time. It was the second time Janbai undertook an oceanic journey soon after giving birth, the first to Karbala to fulfill her vow to the Aga Khan after the birth of her sons.[34] Tragically, the couple's eldest daughter, Jainab, died en route, and the family was forced to bury her in Aden. The move to Bombay seems to have initially been intended as temporary, at least for Janbai. She left stores of jewelry locked in safes in the family home in Zanzibar, and the couple also transferred the deed for their home in Zanzibar to her name. Tharia's eldest son, Moosa, was already in Bombay. (He would later return to east Africa to join his brother Jaffer in tending to the family's business interests in their father's absence.) In Bombay, the Topans purchased a large home a few houses away from the residence of the Aga Khan.[35] Tharia also engaged the services of Rahimtulla Mahomed Sayani, one of the top lawyers in Bombay and later president of the Indian National Congress, to draft his will, which Tharia signed in January of 1886. The text of the will set the scene for an extended legal battle between Janbai and her stepsons over who would control the family's wealth after Tharia's death.

## Bringing Family Feuds to Court

As Tharia's health deteriorated, Janbai must have wondered what her life would look like as a widow. Perhaps she feared that she would be marginalized by her elder stepsons, who disapproved of the elevated position she had achieved in the Topan household. Just as she had once traveled to press her case for sons directly to the Aga Khan, Janbai looked to the colonial courts as an alternative nexus of patriarchal authority, which she could use as a counterweight against her diminishing power within her household. Janbai's decision to turn to colonial law raises broader questions about its role in reshaping gender and family relations. The ensuing battle over Tharia's estate points to the opportunities courts offered to some elite women and the considerable costs of litigating. Asking whether colonial law helped or hurt women like Janbai overall requires an impossible calculation of net benefit and harm. Instead, it is more productive to understand how colonial courts reshaped family relations in complex ways. For families such as the Topans, colonial law was increasingly interwoven with their most intimate relations as they turned again and again to the courts to manage their affairs, producing an inheritance of litigiousness that persisted even as the family's wealth diminished.

Even before Tharia's death, Janbai sought to shore up her position in the family and viewed law as a crucial resource. Between 1886 and 1891, when Tharia passed away, Janbai waged a persistent campaign to increase her and her children's share of the estate, crucially pushing Tharia to alter the text of his will to her benefit. While she was illiterate, Janbai thus clearly understood the power of the written word under a colonial legal regime that valued textual over oral evidence. During these deliberations, Tharia was torn between what he understood to be his obligations to Janbai under religious law versus family custom, and he was undoubtedly also aware of contemporary debates and litigation within the Khoja community. In his will, he noted, "According to the Mahomedan law, my wife Bai Janbai should have an eighth share. . . . But I have not done so. The reason thereof is that there is no such custom prevailing in my house (family)."[36] In the original version of his will, he therefore bequeathed Janbai not a specific fraction of the estate but the family's home in Zanzibar and the income from a group of rented properties.

For the couple, the question of Janbai's degree of control over the properties seems to have been as crucial as its overall value. It is difficult to ascertain from the will whether the value of the properties Janbai was supposed to receive amounted to more or less than an eighth of the estate. Significantly, however, the original will specified that Janbai could not sell or mortgage the properties, positioning her as merely a custodian for properties that would pass to Tharia's male heirs after her death. This condition would have significantly limited her ability to leverage the property to pursue other commercial pursuits.[37] Given that even during Tharia's lifetime, Janbai was engaged in independent trade deals, these limits must have been grating. They might also have struck her as incompatible with Islamic concepts of women's contractual agency. Islamic law provided for married women to independently own and dispose of property during a period in which most European women were still legally in a state of "coverture," becoming economic dependents of their husbands who took control of their property after marriage. In a letter to his son, Tharia reported that Janbai would insist: "Give me in writing what I am entitled to according to the Mahomedan law."[38] In contrast to Mohamed Hussein's portrayal of Janbai's religious devotion as a reflection of her unlettered ignorance, this statement suggests that she was knowledgeable about colonial and Islamic law.

In court, Janbai would deny making this statement or otherwise pressuring her husband. Tharia nonetheless added five additional codicils to his will, increasing the bequests to Janbai and her children and crucially removing the limits on Janbai's control over the property she inherited. Janbai turned to the courts to enforce these bequests, but her elder stepsons were also adept at advancing their claims through the courts. Moosa and Jaffer argued that Tharia had effectively been forced to sign the codicils, submitting as evidence correspondence in which Tharia complained of Janbai's "zulum (oppression)," including her "high style (of living)," which made Tharia's heart "burn."[39]

As a matter of law, the case revolved around whether Tharia acted as a "free agent" when making various provisions for Janbai and her children or whether she had extracted these concessions through pressure that met a legal standard of "undue influence." This entailed a public debate about the appropriate balance of power within the Topan's marriage as the judges pondered whether a man of Tharia's standing was at the mercy of his wife. In 1893, the lower court rejected the validity of the codicils. The judge was troubled by what he viewed as an inversion of gender roles within the Topan household, describing Tharia's bequests to Janbai as "unbusinesslike" and "alarming."[40] In contrast, the judges who heard the case on appeal, first in the Bombay High Court and subsequently in the Privy Council, found the logic of the lower court's decision uncompelling. For them, Tharia's status as "a good man of business" created a strong presumption that he acted as a free agent.[41] As one of the judges explained: "the tester when importuned by his wife was capable of reasoning calmly with her and explaining his intentions to her and had no idea of being led by her wishes on the matter of the disposition of his property."[42] In contrast, concerning his intimate dealings with Janbai, the judges emphasized that his religion and race made him susceptible to bursts of passion. They could thus dismiss the complaints that Tharia wrote in letters to his elder sons about Janbai's oppressions "as the momentary expression, in Mahomedan fashion of his annoyance."[43]

This split reading of Tharia—as a rational (racially unmarked) businessman and as an overreactive (Muslim) husband—allowed the judges to view Tharia as a free agent while also rebuking him, as the Privy Council would later concur, for "exaggerated and unjust complaints against his wife."[44] Just as Janbai had convinced the Aga Khan and Sultan to weigh in on her behalf when her husband wavered in endorsing her favored plan, she convinced the British judges to throw their patriarchal weight behind her claims.[45] She thus leveraged what legal historian Mitra Sharafi has called a pattern of "chivalric imperialism" among British Indian judges who regularly positioned the courts as protecting Indian women from Indian men. The Privy Council thus largely rejected the argument that she exercised "undue influence." They only invalidated the final codicil, which Tharia had signed a mere three days before his death, based on testimony from his doctors that he was incapacitated at the time.[46]

For Janbai, this outcome was a substantial, if partial, victory. It seems to have encouraged her to pursue other fights via the colonial courts, including suing Tharia Topan's *moonim* (business manager) and the firm's cashier for criminal breach of trust the following year. Janbai, however, lost this case.[47] Meanwhile, Janbai's eldest son Mohamed Mehdi had begun borrowing money against the expectation that he would receive a large settlement from his father's estate, quickly amassing staggering debts due to lavish spending and the high interest rates moneylenders required to make such advances. Apparently, he inherited his mother's expensive tastes but not her business savvy, falling prey to others' financial scheming.

In the coming years, the family's legal troubles rapidly piled up. While Tharia's estate was still being litigated, Janbai and Mohamed Mehdi, then eighteen, brought a case in 1895 against his former tutor and his sister Fatma's husband for criminal breach of trust and appropriation. Mohamed Mehdi accused the two men of convincing him to buy expensive jewelry to use as collateral to raise loans from Marwari moneylenders. In a remarkable parallel with the language and logic of the case that his elder stepbrothers were pressing against his mother, Mohamed Mehdi argued that "the accused were in the habit of exercising undue influence on him owing to his youth."[48] It is unclear whether the criminal case was successful since the decision was not reported. Still, *The Times of India* published a story about a simultaneous civil suit between the two men soon after. In that case, Mohamed Mehdi agreed to pay his former tutor the total amount he owed.[49] It is possible that Mohamed Mehdi instigated the earlier criminal charges to pressure his tutor into forgiving the debt, a strategy that failed.

Yet just a year later, Mohamed Mehdi was again trying to use the courts to settle his affairs, this time concerning his marriage. In 1894, he married Sakinabai, but the marriage quickly descended into acrimony, and she left him after two years. Mohamed Mehdi sued her for restitution of conjugal rights, a particular colonial legal remedy that allowed Indian husbands to ask colonial courts to intervene to "restore" their wives. Sakinabai refused to return, and she would later testify in court that Mohamed Mehdi was cruel to her and pressured her father to give money to Janbai. At the time, Mohamed Mehdi did not pursue the restitution suit, which lapsed under the statute of limitations after two years. Remarkably, however, after the colonial legislature revised the statute of limitations in 1908, Mohamed Medhi sent a fresh notice for restitution of conjugal rights to Sakinabai in 1911—a decade and a half after she had left him! The suit was dismissed when the couple appeared in court the following year. In the meantime, the Ismaili *jamat* also dissolved the marriage on the grounds that Mohamed Mehdi had ceased to be an Ismaili and instead became a Twelver Shia.[50]

Like his older brother, Mohamed Hussein also became entangled in litigation, including a case that pitted him against his mother. The dispute originated in a divorce settlement between Mohamed Hussein and his former wife,

Bibi Abadi, who sued him for payment of her *mahr*, or the sum provided for in their marriage contract in the case of their subsequent divorce. Although the contract set the *mahr* at Rs. 25,000, Bibi Abadi agreed to accept Rs. 3,000 in payment provided Janbai stood as surety and entered as a party in the suit. When Janbai subsequently requested that Mohamed Hussein pay her back with interest, he refused, claiming that she had taken his place in the suit "out of natural love and affection for him" and that he should, therefore, not be required to pay her back. He also insisted that it was she who owed him Rs. 61,000, based on a settlement they had reached in a prior case in 1909. When Mohamed Hussain offered a Gujarati document as evidence, Janbai responded that her signature was obtained by "fraud and misrepresentation," having been told that the document was a power-of-attorney enabling her son to conduct business on her behalf. Given that she could not read or write and had not been accurately informed of the document's contents, she insisted that "the writing is void and not binding on her."[51] Janbai clearly understood the power of documents. She also knew how to strategically yield her illiteracy in a setting in which colonial judges were predisposed to viewing Indian women as vulnerable to masculine extortion.

The mounting number of cases involving the Topans shows how once families entered colonial courts, they often remained embroiled in litigation, with one case spiraling into another. While part of the appeal of colonial law was that it seemed to offer a definitive judgment backed up by state enforcement, these cases suggest that this promise was often undermined in practice. The Topan's repeated engagements with the courts took an emotional toll on the family, as Mohamed Hussein's complex relationship with his mother suggests. Having regularly advised the consular court in Zanzibar, Tharia was aware of the damaging effects such cases often had on families. He had pleaded with his elder sons and wife in his will that "the Court shall not be resorted to."[52] As his family defied his wishes, he must have been rolling over in his grave.

Yet despite the costs, Janbai may not have taken such a negative view of the litigation. Her interests, and those of her family, were not necessarily the same. She retained control over critical assets through extended legal battles even as the family's overall financial position suffered. In fact, at the time of Janbai's death in 1934, Mohamed Hussein was mainly living off his mother's property, including the Topan home in Zanzibar, and rents from a large plot of land in Zanzibar, housing over a thousand tenants.[53] Even as the men in her family blamed Janbai for entangling them in litigation that consumed more than 80 percent of the estate (by Mohamed Hussein's estimate), she thus achieved some level of economic security despite her sons' poor financial judgment. Acknowledging that Janbai used colonial courts at least partially to her advantage does not mean buying into colonial ideologies of chivalric imperialism.

Instead, viewed against the backdrop of Janbai's wider triangulations between masculine familial, religious, and political authorities, it shows how women who had long pitted different patriarchies against each other treated colonial law as another tool to manipulate.[54] Yet legal records alone can often obscure the high costs that came with these strategies, both in terms of the financial burden of using courts and the emotional and physical retaliation women faced in the aftermath of legal victories—costs sometimes tallied instead in family papers and oral histories.

## Portraits and Jewelry as Women's Alternative Legacies

Even when read together, the legal records and family biography provide a partial view of Janbai. We see her within the frame of her interactions with men—maneuvering across patriarchal familial structures, religious movements, and courtly politics. Yet Janbai also built influence through her relations with women. The biography mentions her visits to the homes of elite Indian and Arab women in Zanzibar and her dominance over a large household of dependents, including women Mohamed Hussein described as "slave girls."[55] Still, it lacks the vivid anecdotes about her ties to other women that it provides of Janbai's interactions with men.

The objects in the Peabody Essex Museum's collection opened new pathways for studying how Janbai cultivated networks of women. The photograph (Figure 2.1) and bracelet (Figure 2.2) were gifted to the museum by Minnie Batchelder, the daughter of Captain Nathan A. Batchelder and his wife Caroline (née Parbuck). Caroline visited Zanzibar in the early 1880s, traveling on board the "Taria Topan," which the American merchant Captain John Bertram named in honor of Tharia.[56] The pairing of the photograph and bracelet in the PEM's collection is another example of the power of images and objects to create alternative connections with the past, particularly as combinations I term haunted collages. Unfortunately, the Batchelder family lore surrounding the objects was not recorded when Minnie transferred them to the museum.[57] One can imagine, though, that Minnie treasured the bracelet. Perhaps it reminded her of her adventurous origins; she was born at sea in 1860 during another of her parents' oceanic voyages. Yet, the fact that Minnie gifted Janbai's photograph to the museum along with the bracelet suggests that for the Batchelder women Janbai's memory haunted the bracelet in ways that made it important to keep the photograph and bracelet together. The bracelet itself also tells its own stories about Janbai—its diminutive size, measuring just two-and-half inches across, creates an enchanting juxtaposition against the visual weight of its Gujarati-styled metalwork. It testifies to the enduring legacies of Janbai's excellent taste.[58]

Today, Salem is a sleepy New England town best known for its infamous role in putting local women on trial for witchcraft in the seventeenth century. However, during the nineteenth century, the city was a hub of maritime networks that connected the United States to eastern Africa. Ships from Salem ferried unbleached cotton cloth, known in Swahili as *merekani* (or American), from New England textile mills to the Swahili coast, alongside an array of consumer goods, amongst which clocks and watches were especially popular. The ships returned to Salem laden with leather hides, gum copal used for varnishing furniture, and ivory made into piano keys, combs, and billiard balls.[59] Women like Janbai and Caroline have yet to feature prominently in historical scholarship on these trade networks, which has relied heavily on letters exchanged between merchant men as sources. However, the objects in the PEM collection suggest that women were also crucial in cultivating these ties, and they did so in ways that were particularly attuned to the power of display in navigating cosmopolitan social worlds. The bracelet, far more than written letters, traveled across linguistic borders and remained a treasured object for multiple generations.[60] In many ways the importance of women like Janbai and Caroline to forging global commercial networks is unsurprising, even if historians have neglected it. The trade encouraged and depended on new habits of domestic consumption, both in Africa and the Americas, with households adorning their bodies and abodes with a proliferation of new objects imported from across the globe. Women played an outsized role in shaping these new domestic tastes—or at least this was the case in the Topan household, with Janbai carefully curating the household's clothing and furnishings. Meanwhile, Tharia reputedly only changed his clothing sporadically.[61] While Janbai's stepsons felt that she was demanding more than her fair share of the family's wealth, following the global travels of the bracelet suggests that from her perspective, she was only asking for her rightful dues as a wife and a business partner.

The portrait of Janbai that accompanied the bracelet proved even more helpful in understanding how she exerted influence within a global network of mobile women. But it took me a longer time to figure out how to look at it in a way that yielded these insights. When I first discovered the photograph, I was simultaneously overjoyed and frustrated. Staring at Janbai's face created a haunting sense of connection to the women I had already traced through archives for multiple years but had never seen. I nonetheless found myself struggling to articulate what new evidence the image provided. The photograph seemed frustratingly opaque—I did not initially see anything in Janbai's expression or the staging of the picture that pointed to new insights into her biography or personality.[62] Rather, the book on the table beside her seemed distinctly at odds with Janbai's inability to read—a clue instead to the image's fabrication. The obvious staging and lack of individuality in the photograph is quite common for portraits taken in the late nineteenth and early twentieth century, which required that subjects sit still for long periods and for which studios often provided a set menu of props.

Yet, as I began exploring the rich body of scholarship on photographs as "social" objects in India and Africa, I found that the image yielded richer insights once I viewed it alongside other contemporary photos.[63] In its style and staging, the photograph resembles a *carte de visite*, a popular genre of commercial portrait photography commonly traded among acquaintances in the late nineteenth century. The photograph was likely taken in Zanzibar, although it is possible that Janbai commissioned it during a visit to Bombay, where the family stopped en route to perform *hajj* in 1881. Both places were early hubs for the development of photography in the Indian Ocean region. As early as 1847, only a few years after the invention of the daguerreotype, the governor of Zanzibar and members of his family, including his seven-year-old niece and two Abyssinian concubines, were photographed by the French explorer Captain Charles Guillain.[64] In 1875, the Sultan of Zanzibar commissioned a series of *carte de visite* while visiting London, which he circulated upon his return to Zanzibar, whetting local demand for similar portraits. Several photography studios, primarily operated by Goan families, opened on the islands to meet the surging demand. In Bombay, commercial photography studios opened even earlier, in the 1850s.[65] Photographers operating in both places quickly developed modes of accommodating gendered modesty. Studios used veils to block the photographer's view and employed women assistants. These practices allowed women to commission portraits they could selectively circulate, presenting themselves visually to some while shielding themselves from others' gaze.[66]

Janbai's photograph and its migration into the PEM collections should be read in this broader context. Her portrait resembles at least two other contemporary photographs of Zanzibari women, suggesting that it was produced in conversation with evolving aesthetic fashions both local and global in their reach. Janbai's pose in the photograph, with her head resting on one arm, resembles a well-known photograph of the Sultan's daughter, Sayyida Salme, taken at a Hamburg studio in 1868 after she eloped with a German merchant (see Figure 2.3).[67] The photograph became famous as an accompanying illustration to Sayyida's memoir, published first in German in 1886. Still, the photograph likely circulated earlier in Zanzibar, where copies can be found in private collections.[68] Given Janbai's close relationship with the Sultan's family, she may have seen a copy of the photograph and assumed a similar pose in her portrait. Alternatively, the photographer who took her photograph may have known of Sayyida's portrait.

At least one other early photograph exists of another Indian-Zanzibari woman assuming a strikingly similar position, part of a large archive of

FIGURE 2.3. Portrait of Emily Ruete (née Sayyida Salme) in Omani dress, photographer H. F. Plate, Hamburg, circa 1868. Shelfmark Or. 27.135 D 1 (5). Leiden University Libraries.

east-African photographs amassed by the British collector Humphrey Winterton and now housed at Northwestern University (see Figure 2.4). The woman, whose name is unknown, was also photographed with books on a small table, suggesting a shared visual vocabulary.[69]

Viewing the three photographs in tandem suggests that Janbai positioned herself within circuits of mobile and influential women not via words but through poses and images. Janbai likely did not even share a common language

FIGURE 2.4. Portrait of a Zanzibari woman, circa 1893. The Humphrey Winterton Collection of East African Photographs: 1860–1960, Herskovits Library of African Studies, Northwestern University Libraries.

with Caroline. Instead, she forged a lasting connection with her through the gift of the bracelet and photograph—leaving an impression that persisted in the memory of Caroline's daughter and later in museum records.

Yet, I also do not want to overstate the power that Janbai and women like her possessed. Here, the story of what happened to the rest of her jewelry

FIGURE 2.5. Comparison of portraits photographs. Center photo courtesy of the Peabody Essex Museum.

provides a critical counterweight and a reminder of how patriarchy curtailed even the savviest women. In his will, Tharia specified that Janbai was "full owner and proprietress" of the jewelry that the couple had left in Zanzibar, including "three treasures (safes) in which are jewels" and "one box containing things (of gold)."[70] I have encountered similar clauses in which men bequeathed jewelry to women, including provisions that Thamboosamy Pillai made for both Alamaloo and Tipah. For Hindu women, jewelry often formed the most valuable component of their *stridhan* (literally women's property), which was traditionally given to them by their families at the time of their marriage. While such payments were often not considered traditionally Islamic, the giving of *jehaz* (dowry) was also customary among many Muslims. Families also gifted women jewelry to mark important events, such as the birth of a child. Men sometimes specified in their wills that this jewelry belonged to their wives. Jewelry was, in theory, a crucial store of women's wealth.[71]

The reality, however, was often quite different, as Janbai would find out. According to Mohamed Hussein's biography, after his father's death, his half-brother Jaffer broke into the safes where Tharia and Janbai had stored the family's jewelry before departing for Bombay. In exchange for a fourth of the stash, he enlisted the help of Tippu Tip, a famous Swahili-Arab trader who was also a close associate of the Topans. Allegedly, Jaffer, fearing that Janbai would "take criminal action," asked Tippu Tip to secret away the stash of diamonds, rubies, emeralds, and pearls to a remote location and bury it. Jaffer passed away soon after, and when Tippu Tip returned, the jewelry had disappeared—"such was the justice of God."[72]

For evidence of Janbai's exquisite taste, I have relied on the bracelet that found its way to Salem, MA, and family memories of the jewelry she acquired, preserved via her son's biography, rather than family heirlooms that were materially passed from generation to generation. I have found that the Topans' experience was not particularly unusual among diasporic families. Many families were forced to sell jewelry during economic hardship when it was treated less as women's wealth than a family resource over which men often exercised the final say. Even when families held onto their jewelry, some preferred to melt it down in each generation, using a mother's gold to make a new trousseau for her daughter.[73] Often, jewelry only existed as a treasured recollection—material property transformed into an immaterial, but no less profound, inheritance—a reminder of the fluid ties between material and immaterial afterlives, perhaps particularly for women.

## The Ethics of Working in Legal Limbo

In writing this book, triangulating between different types of archives and sources has been central to my thinking about the process of family history as akin to artistic collage. As Janbai's story suggests, this approach led to insights I would not have gained had I limited myself to traditional archives. Legal records and the family biography provide a remarkable picture of how Janbai navigated between different nexuses of patriarchal authority—familial, religious, political, and legal. The bracelet and portrait add something even more profound: tantalizing glimpses of her interactions with other women. This multi-dimensional collage reveals how Janbai moved across geographical, political, economic, and cultural boundaries despite the constraints of the patriarchal worlds in which she lived.

While deeply gendered, these mobilities echo larger diasporic patterns. Janbai was thus not so different than Thamboosamy. Both were adept at navigating across the highly layered and variegated landscapes that characterized the British Empire in the nineteenth century. Rather than a uniform swath of red splashed across the world map, the British Empire incorporated colonies and protectorates. It selectively empowered ethno-religious communities, outsourced development to diasporic capitalists, and relied on myriad forms of juridical and political administration. Surviving in these worlds required dexterity in shape-shifting and the ability to work across many different boundaries—spatial, cultural, linguistic, and religious. Here, too, there is a parallel between how Janbai pitted patriarchies against each other and how diasporic subjects navigated between different nexuses of imperial authority to carve their own pathways through empire. For many families, the resulting habits of mobility proved long-lasting, contributing to modes of being diasporic that defy bounded constructions of identity. In both these chapters, speaking to descendants and attending to material and visual sources has deepened my understanding of how family and gender relations were entangled with these overlapping webs of authority and mobility. Collage, with its emphasis on creating multi-layered mixtures of mediums, proves a fitting method for studying how these diasporic families moved through the variegated landscapes of empire.

Yet, working across state archives, family collections, and other repositories, from cemeteries to museums, raises ethical challenges. I began excavating these questions in the previous chapter, and they also haunted this chapter. While researching legal records in Zanzibar, I strayed from the nineteenth-century files that formed the core of my research into more recent records. Inheritance disputes were often passed from one generation to the next. For example, by the time the dispute over Tharia's estate reached the Privy Council, Moosa and Jaffer were already dead, so Moosa's sons stepped in as the plaintiffs. Many cases lasted even longer, with proceedings stretching across decades. A decision in the litigation over Thamboosamy's estate was not delivered until 1929, almost three decades after his death.

As I pursued these trails through the Zanzibar archives, I unexpectedly came across a will for one of Tharia and Janbai's descendants written in 1960. The will showed that the Topans were still using legal instruments long after Tharia's death to exert influence over their family members. But some of the parties named in the will were still alive. Some of its contents were also matters that I could imagine they might consider private, even though the author of the will had detailed them in a public document filed with a law court. Complicating matters further, the will was transferred from the courts to the archive in the aftermath of the revolution of 1964, which ousted the Omani Sultans, and after which Zanzibar merged with Tanganyika to become post-colonial Tanzania. During this period, many court records appear to have simply been stashed in the archive. Circumstances in the 1960s likely prevented careful consideration of whether some of the records should be kept closed until individuals mentioned in them could be presumed dead. As noted in the introduction, working across many archives with different access to resources, I found that such policies were frequently the product of expediency. With so many archives barely able to preserve their collections, let alone evaluate them on a granular level, researchers must take responsibility for considering the ethics of using particular materials.

Yet, as a historian, when I find something interesting in the archives, I feel a deep urge to write about it, a drive that unites most of the practitioners of my craft. We often feel an ethical commitment not just to protecting individual privacy but also to exposing sometimes uncomfortable truths. When I first drafted this chapter, I therefore included a more extended discussion of the contents of the will from 1960, which allowed me to trace the family's litigation forward by several decades. However, I felt compelled to rethink my approach after speaking with Farouk, who generously allowed me to use his father's unpublished biography. He was surprised that the will was in the archives in Zanzibar and had mixed feelings about me incorporating it into the chapter. As he explained, he did not have a problem with me using it but thought that some of his family might not want some of its contents disclosed. I sensed that he wanted to say yes as a fellow scholar but did not feel he could consent on behalf of his entire family. He threw the dilemma back at me by neither saying yes nor no. I wanted Farouk to affirm or withhold his consent—mirroring liberal legal logics in which the sovereign individual is the central agent for determining right and wrong. Farouk offered something else—a reminder of the complexities of navigating family legacies that cannot be partitioned into proprietary shares.

While working on this book, I confronted many such dilemmas. In the last chapter, I wrote about the possibility that Alamaloo might be Malay, despite my knowledge that some of her descendants felt uncomfortable with that claim. But in this case, I knew it was important to some of the family to share this version of their history. In this chapter, I have instead held back some information because the possible damage that might come from including it outweighed the additional information that could be garnered from its inclusion. The fact that living people were named in the will also informed my decision. Yet, the boundary between the living and the dead alone does not solve these ethical dilemmas. Indeed, for many families, this distinction is not especially relevant—information about an ancestor can, for some descendants, be akin to disclosure about themselves. In many other cases, I have also used information from archives without consulting with descendants because tracing their families was simply impossible. Relying on families to become the exclusive gatekeepers to archival records about their ancestors also raises a host of ethical and practical challenges. I return to these questions in the next chapter, which looks at archives of indenture, some of which require proof of descent or permission from descendants to consult and publish materials, while others have favored more open access.

I do not have an easy answer to these questions, but I am convinced solutions relying exclusively on legalistic methods are deeply problematic. All too often, scholarly ethics is reduced to signing forms, whose language is drafted by university lawyers rather than researchers or subjects. These protocols seem more designed to protect universities from litigation than to cultivate ethical relations between researchers and subjects. Conflating signing legal forms with ethics echoes larger legal fictions that offer up law as a means of resolving conflicts. In practice, they more often enrich lawyers and empower legal bureaucracies. Tharia himself was a victim of such fictions. He put great effort into crafting a will that would prevent his family from battling each other in court after his death. He even threatened to revoke their inheritance if they litigated. Yet, all the fees he paid to Bombay's top lawyers did not help him accomplish this goal. Law more often ripped families apart than tied them together.

Similarly, legalistic protocols, such as signing consent forms, certainly have a role in research protocols. But often, this was the beginning, rather than the end, of my effort to collaboratively engage families in crafting an ethical approach to writing their family's histories. Farouk Topan, for example, looked over multiple drafts of this chapter, and other family members have also read and made helpful suggestions on the book's text. Yet, while sharing my work with families and incorporating their feedback, I am sure that some will disagree with some aspects of the texts. I have had to weigh competing interests—of living family members, who sometimes disagreed; of the dead, whose desires I could never fully ascertain; of subjects who were not blood relations but embedded in the family, including concubines and enslaved people. I have also had to consider my professional commitments not to censure uncomfortable pasts and to meet scholarly standards. Balancing these required many ongoing conversations with families and colleagues. In the depths of the night, as these questions swirled in my mind, I also sensed the presence of the ghosts of the dead disturbing my rest. Through these conversations, I have not arrived at law-like rules but rather research habits. These include looking for descendants, asking about their understanding of the past, and sharing my findings with them. They also suggest that being haunted by ethical dilemmas, rather than being able to solve them through set protocols, pushes scholars to think deeply about who and how we are accountable beyond the boundaries of the academy. While imperfect solutions, I hope they will keep us all out of court!

# 3

# Jahaji Roots

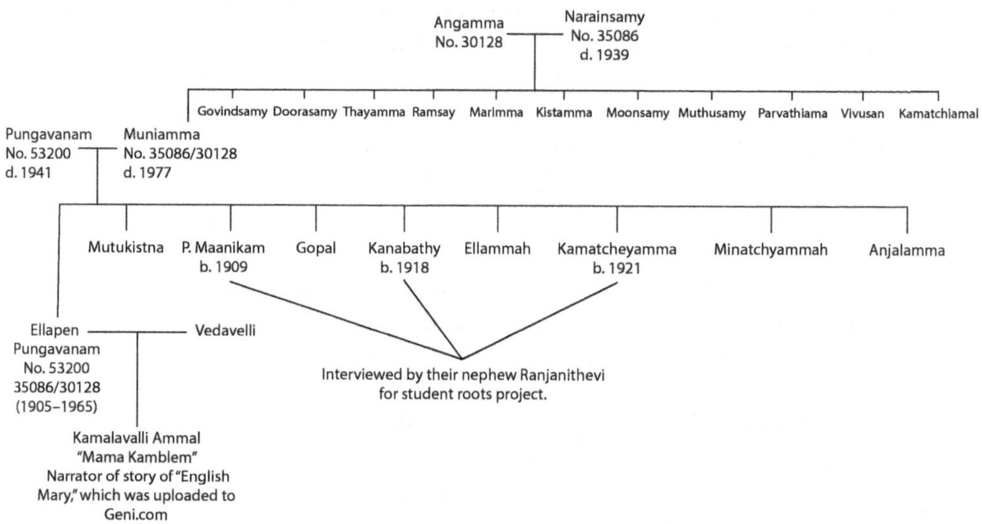


FIGURE 3.1. Partial Family Tree for Angamma's Descendants. Image drawn by author from information compiled from the death certificates of Narainsamy and Pungavanam, which can be downloaded from familysearch.org, and the family tree of Anneline Bernice Moodley, published on geni.com. The names of many of Angamma and Narainsamy's grandchildren and great grandchildren have not been included due to space constraints. Information from public and personal records reproduced with permission of Anneline Bernice Moodley.

AFTER THE deceased's funeral was finished and their assets divided, their afterlife stretched onwards across decades as kin and communities retold their stories. For diasporic families, these processes unfolded across generations and across shifting political boundaries. Many kept moving, and even those who stayed put lived through the cataclysmic shifts of war, anti-colonial nationalism, and post-colonial nation-building. In researching the families of

Thamboosamy and Alamaloo and Janbai and Tharia, I saw how narratives about family roots shifted from generation to generation and were told differently even within families. When my research turned to families who traced their roots through voyages of indenture, selective remembering and forgetting proved even more profound.[1]

My interest in the intersection of political change and family memory drew me to South Africa, which was a major destination for Indians, including over one hundred and fifty thousand migrants who travelled under contracts of indenture. It was also a fluid landscape, repeatedly reshaped by the currents of volatile politics.[2] Migrants and their descendants lived through the unification of South Africa as a self-governing British dominion in 1910, the formalization of racial Apartheid in 1948, and the transition to constitutional democracy in 1994.

For indentured migrants, the vicissitudes of these shifting political landscapes intensified the complexities of narrating family stories that were rooted in traumatic beginnings. Economic distress, coupled in some cases with outright coercion or deception, but also sometimes dreams of a better future, propelled these migrants. Their journeys began with terrifying sea journeys and back-breaking labor. They bore the scars of families divided—extended families reduced to a few mobile members, the young running away from elders, and women from patriarchal oppressions. But they were also stories of extraordinary agency, in which the most vulnerable migrants built legacies of survival and sometimes even significant wealth, often manifest in their fierce struggles to own land.

These stories, a sort of narrative heir*loom*, became keepsakes for their families. They were the looms on which their descendants interwove the stories of their own lives with those of their ancestors. But these stories were also sometimes hidden away or lost, much as Thamboosamy's trophies disappeared from the family armoire. Their descendants' own struggles against racial discrimination and property dispossession added to the pressure to selectively remember. More recently, the end of Apartheid and, for some, further migration inspired efforts to recover pasts that had been forgotten. These efforts have taken descendants into new geographies of archival research and digital genealogy where our paths crossed.

The story of Angamma, who left India when she was eight and traveled to Natal, where she joined other indentured Indians on a coffee plantation, is one such story of selective remembering, forgetting, and recovery. I first encountered her not as a name but as a barely legible number recorded on the birth certificate of her grandson, P. Manikam Moodley. A century after Angamma arrived in Natal, her great-grandson Ranjanithevi interviewed his uncle Manikam in 1984 and used information from his birth certificate to complete an undergraduate project. Today, his paper is preserved alongside dozens of similar roots projects in the archives of the Gandhi-Luthuli Documentation Centre at the University of KwaZulu-Natal's campus in Westville, Durban, which was formerly reserved for Indian students under Apartheid education policies.[3] These papers are a remarkable resource. Many students interviewed relatives who had been indentured or were the children of indentured migrants. They also captured the students' own experiences of a moment of rupture. The projects were shaped by a still segregated and censored institutional context but foreshadowed how the end of Apartheid would empower new engagements with the past.

Working in this context, Ranjanithevi offered a patriarchal recounting of his family's past. He researched the life story of his grandfather (Angamma's son-in-law), Pungavanam Moodley. Pungavanam, in 1893, at age twenty, traveled from North Arcot in Southern India to Natal, where he labored for five years on a tea estate. He rose from laborer to *sirdar*, or foreman, and worked in a general store run by the tea estate. After over twenty years on the estate, Pungavanam struck out on his own, first moving to Durban and then settling in Port Shepstone. There, he purchased nine acres of land and began growing tobacco. Like many former indentured laborers in Natal, the family also engaged in "market gardening," raising and hawking produce.[4] In 1920, he opened his own store, P. Moodley and Sons, and profited from savvy real-estate investments. According to family lore, his growing wealth allowed him to become the first Indian in town to purchase a car.[5] His economic ascent imparted to his descendants a lasting attachment to investing in land. This attachment to real estate persisted even after, under Apartheid policies of race-based dispossession, the family lost much of the physical property that Pungavanam amassed. The family rooted itself in land—but in ways that had to adapt to continually shifting tides, which eventually took some branches of the family to Australia and Qatar. This was the nature of family roots that originated not on land but on the *jahaj*, or boat, which transported indentured migrants from India. These roots were dug up, divided, and then replanted in new places where they grew anew, only to restart the process when forced to relocate again.

This process of re-rooting often entailed selective pruning, and memories of the women who bore branches of the family were sometimes trimmed away. In his biography of his grandfather, Ranjanithevi mentioned that Pungavanam was supported by his wife Muniamma, with whom he had twelve children. Her background, however, was barely mentioned beyond giving her father's name, Narainsamy Naidoo. Muniamma's mother was unnamed. I would only later come to know her as Angamma based on archival records. Her absence from Ranjanithevi's recounting of his family's history was not unusual. In the 1980s, when Indians in South Africa began to more systematically research and publicly celebrate their roots, families often remained hesitant to probe too deeply into their ancestors' experiences under indenture, and this was especially true for women. As I would learn was likely of Angamma, women who traveled under contracts of indenture frequently did so outside of conventional patriarchal units, sometimes as single women. Her story echoes the findings of a remarkable body of scholarship on gender and indenture. These studies show that women engaged strategically and creatively with systems of labor recruitment, plantation discipline, patriarchal domesticity, and colonial law to shape their own fortunes.[6] This chapter builds on this scholarship by considering how such remarkable acts of agency were suppressed in future generations, as the stories of indentured women were flattened into unwitting victims, restricted to the role of supporting companions, or excised entirely. Yet, the chapter also explores how these histories have been recovered, not just by historians, but also by roots researchers, and the deeper understandings of agency and memory that can emerge when the two work in tandem.

## Colonial Documentation Re-"Rooted" as Digital Genealogy

In previous chapters, family stories, photographs, and material objects proved the most essential sources for recovering suppressed histories of women. In this chapter, somewhat counterintuitively, state documentation proved particularly crucial to writing against the grain of patriarchal remembering. The number on Ranjanithevi's father's birth certificate, when used in conjunction with archival search engines and genealogy websites, revealed multiple trails leading back to Angamma—still incomplete but far richer than I had imagined possible. With their ability to rapidly process vast amounts of data, digital tools open new possibilities for triangulating between state records and family memories. Using conventional methods, most of the thirty million Indians who left India during the long nineteenth century are difficult to track through archives as individuals. Only an exceptional few, primarily wealthy, powerful men like Thamboosamy and Tharia, were mentioned repeatedly in official correspondence. A smaller minority of women, including Alamaloo and Janbai, appeared in legal records but in ways that foregrounded their relations to men. Many more Indian migrants surface only occasionally in colonial archives. However, the unusually extensive documentation that the British kept recording the lives of migrants who traveled under formal contracts of indenture means that some of their stories have been preserved in archives, laying trails for future historians and descendants to follow. The digitization of some of these collections, including many of the indenture records in South Africa, has made it considerably easier to pick up these trails.

The reason indenture produced more extensive archival trails is deeply entangled with how it emerged as an alternative form of labor recruitment after the abolition of slavery. In 1833, the British Parliament passed the Slavery Abolition Act, which gradually phased out legal enslavement in most parts of the empire, but excluded territories controlled by the East India Company. In India, the Slavery Act of 1843 outlawed financial transactions involving enslaved people, in theory shutting down the slave trade. However, it was notoriously piecemeal in its effects, particularly in relation to unfree household labor.[7] The formal abolition of plantation slavery in many parts of the British Empire created an acute need for alternative mechanisms of labor recruitment. Asian indenture was one such alternative, with Chinese and Indian migrants transported under contracts that bound them to work for specific employers for three to five years, with penal sanctions punishing those who did not serve out their contracts. Indentured laborers were theoretically provided housing, food, and modest wages, regulated by statute but prone to abuse in practice. In Natal, wages were set at ten shillings per month for men, with the rate increasing by one shilling for each year of employment. Women received half the rate of men, and children under ten received wages proportionate to their age. Bound to their assigned employer, laborers could not negotiate for better wages or working conditions. In South Africa, wages remained constant for over a half-century despite rising prices.[8]

Almost from its inception, indenture was haunted by criticism that it reproduced the very conditions that abolition was meant to abolish. As early as 1840, Lord John Russel while serving as secretary for the colonies asked whether indenture was none other than "a new system of slavery."[9] In some ways, the answer to Russel's question was yes: indentured Indians moved into barracks previously occupied by enslaved people and toiled under overseers armed with whips. But in other ways, the pressure to prove that indenture was *not* slavery demanded new methods of labor exploitation. Although encompassing only a fraction of Indian migration, indenture served as a testing ground for broader strategies for governing mobile labor. From international labor laws to ID photos, policies first applied to indentured Indians were later expanded to control global flows of labor, many facets of which remain in use today.[10]

The identifying number on the birth certificate Ranjanithevi used in his roots project, which allowed me to trace Angamma, was one such facet of this bureaucracy of documentation. The brutal work conditions and elevated mortality that characterized indenture led to periodic calls for investigation both in Britain and India. In response, officials collected data on recruitment, transportation, labor conditions, and health that were simultaneously supposed to help weed out the system's worst abuses while also proving that indenture, unlike slavery, was based on contractual consent.[11] Colonial officials also documented kinship ties and tried to encourage migrants to maintain links to their kin by providing free or subsidized postal service, remittance services, and, after death, by remitting their estates to kin in India.[12] Officials viewed this often elaborate bureaucratic process as crucial to labor recruitment. As an official from the Government of Bengal noted in correspondence, "Nothing would tend more to encourage emigration than the fact of sums of money left by relatives being sent by the colonies to their families in India. At present the relatives of an emigrant look upon him as cut off from them for ever [sic]. Any measure that tended to dissipate this feeling would help to popularise voluntary emigration."[13] Unlike slavery, indenture relied on embedding laborers in kinship networks and property relations, even though the harsh realities of plantation labor often curtailed these possibilities in practice.

The pressure for documentation generated population-level data about indentured migration, with officials regularly compiling statistics on relative mortality, rates of return, and remittances. Critically for family researchers, it also produced dossiers of individual biographical information. Both during the recruitment process in India and on arrival in Natal, Mauritius, British Guiana, Trinidad, and Fiji, among other places, migrants were queried about their backgrounds and this information was expanded on during and after their period of indenture. This information was cross-referenced with identifying numbers assigned to each migrant—a use of ID numbers that today is such a ubiquitous feature of modern bureaucracy that we largely take it for granted. In the nineteenth century, however, it was novel. Countries like Britain and the United States only began introducing numerical identification to facilitate mass conscription, rationing, and social-welfare programs during and after World War I.[14]

In Natal, each migrant was assigned a number, sequentially from 1 to 152,184, alongside which was recorded their name, father's name, age, sex, caste, place of origin, the date and ship on which they arrived, and their employer. The lists were compiled and stored at the office of the Protector of Indian Immigrants, which was tasked with the general governance of Indians both during and after their period of indenture. The Office of the Protector managed the assignment of Indians to employers, performed periodic inspections of conditions at plantations employing Indians, investigated complaints, and adjudicated civil suits. His office also served as a functional archive: in addition to compiling the Ships List, the Protector and his assistants recorded deaths, marriages, births, returnees, and probate, all of which were cross-referenced with the number that the migrant was initially assigned in the Ships List. From 1883 to 1903, the office in Natal was also continuously headed by Louis H. Mason, whose long tenure in the position probably facilitated the amassing of more systematic records.[15]

Ironically, while in their initial use these numbers worked to transform individuals into units of labor, in the late twentieth century they have proven a

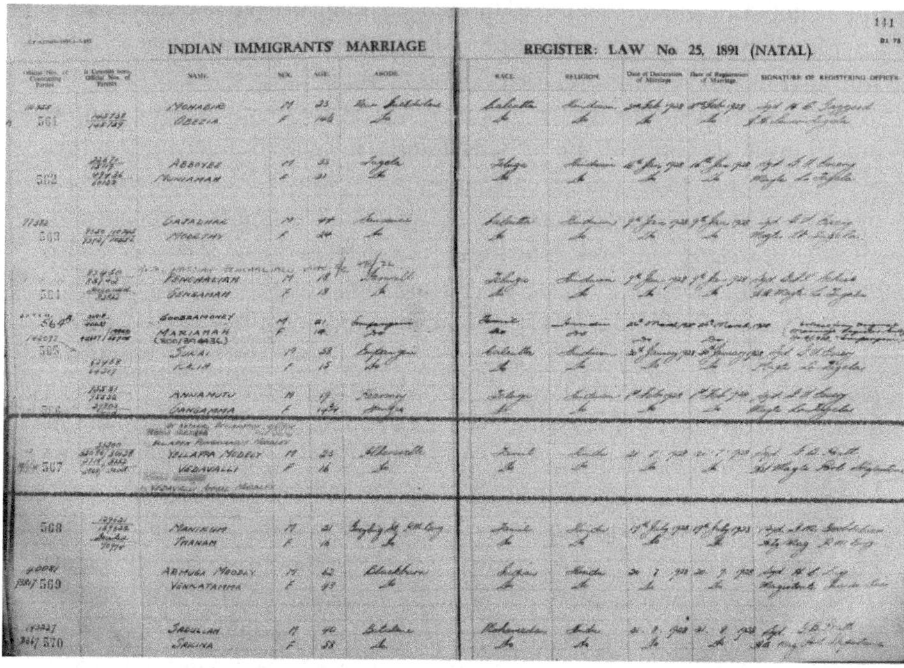


FIGURE 3.2. Marriage Registration of Ellapen Pungavanam Moodley to Vedavalli, July 21, 1928. Note the use of ancestral Ships List numbers to identify subsequent generations. Natal Marriage Registers, 1922–28, available digitally on familysearch.org.

great asset to families researching their roots. The power of these numbers as a genealogical tool is particularly pronounced in South Africa, as I quickly learned when I discovered that many of the people who occupied the desks beside me in the archives were there to research their roots. They came carrying birth, death, and marriage certificates for older relations, which had a series of numbers alongside their names. Rather than bearing unique individual ID numbers, the children and grandchildren of indentured laborers were identified with the numbers that their ancestors had been assigned on arrival. Thus, Ranjanithevi found the numbers for his grandfather, Pungavanam (53200), and his maternal great-grandparents, Narainsamy (35086) and Angamma (30128), on his uncle's birth certificate, while I found similar numbers on the marriage certificate of Manikam's elder brother, Ellapen when searching on the free database, familysearch.org (see Figure 3.2). This system was not abandoned until the early 1960s, so many families still have documents that include these numbers.

The transformation of these records into a genealogical treasure trove began in the late 1970s. Joy Brain, who was then a member of the history department at the University of Durban-Westville (UDW), became interested in the records while working on a book on the history of Indian Christians in Natal. She eventually acquired permission to consult and photograph the Ships List, a crucial step in preserving the rapidly deteriorating records. From 1981 to 1986, a period that overlapped with the student roots projects, a team of researchers at UDW transcribed the information from the Ships List into a specially built computer database. The process was immensely labor-intensive and unfolded against the backdrop of rapid shifts in who controlled various government repositories as the country transitioned from Apartheid to democratic government. In 2003, Brain finally completed the project, releasing a CD-ROM with all 152,184 biographical entries. Soon after, K. Chetty, then the director of the Gandhi-Luthuli Documentation Centre, which was housed on the campus of UDW, now the University of KwaZulu-Natal, published the Ships List as nine Excel spreadsheets that could be downloaded from the Centre's website.[16] They can be downloaded by anyone interested without the need to enter a physical archive, prove a family connection or academic credential, or pay a subscription to a genealogical website. They are thus among the most accessible collections I have worked with. I had some of my most interesting conversations while working on this book with families from Natal. The accessibility of these records played a huge role in facilitating these connections and demystifying the relationship between archival and roots research. I spent many hours exchanging screenshots of these spreadsheets with families, which we could both cross-check against other documents, including undigitized materials from archives and family papers.

Through one such triangulating search, I found not just Angamma and Ranjanithevi's roots project but eventually another branch of their family tree. Anneline Moodley, now living in Qatar, had constructed a family tree which included a profile of Angamma titled "English Mary," along with a vivid account of her life, albeit one that bore little resemblance to the stories I had reconstructed from the archives. As it turned out, Mary, aka Angamma, had not been pruned from the family's past but had been carefully cultivated in a different field of memory-making, one in which women were crucial both as subjects and as storytellers.

## Jahaji Number 30128

Before tracing the evolution of her memory in subsequent generations, let us first return to the journey that brought Angamma to Natal. When speaking about the experience of indenture, Indian migrants and their descendants often appealed to the bonds between *jahaji bhai*, or brothers of the boat, to convey the radical remaking of social relations they experienced. While the term itself is somewhat less common in South Africa than in the Caribbean, the phenomena it describes are equally powerful in both places. On the ships that brought them to Natal, migrants were thrown together in close and uncomfortable quarters. They rubbed shoulders with other migrants who spoke different languages, practiced different religions, and were from diverse caste backgrounds. Their shared suffering forged new bonds—the brotherhood of the boat. These ties have subsequently been celebrated through cultural hybrids such as Trinidadian musician Brother Marvin's calypso hit "Jahaji Bhai." But what of the *jahaji bahin*, or sisters?[17] While their stories have not been as widely publicly retold, their experiences of rupture and remaking were often even more profound.

According to the Ships List, eight-year-old Angamma traveled onboard the Castleton, which set sail from Madras in southeast India in August, arriving sixty-eight days later in Natal on October 10, 1883 (see Figure 3.3). During the 1880s, transportation between India and Natal shifted from sail to steam, significantly shortening the time of the journey. Angamma, however, was among those who still had to suffer through the slower journey by sail. When Angamma boarded the Castleton, which had been built in 1862, it was already an old ship, surely adding to the discomfort of its passengers.[18] Even by the standards of passages by sail, the Castleton's trip was unusually long, and the ship had to stop in Mauritius to re-provision, perhaps due to weather-related delays. The surgeon who traveled onboard recorded four deaths during the voyage and numerous cases of dysentery.[19]

During the journey, Angamma was accompanied by her younger sister, Poongavanam, who was five, and her elder sister, Muthamma, age twenty-eight. Given their age difference, it is also possible that Muthamma was the girls' mother, and the relationship was incorrectly recorded. The women do not appear to have been accompanied by any men who were their close relations. There were no other migrants on the ship who listed the same hometown, suggesting that they were probably not accompanied by any other immediate relations.

Muthamma gave their origin as Royapuram, a northern suburb of Madras. Unlike many of their fellow shipmates, they therefore had not traveled far to reach the dockside barracks where migrants were housed before being shipped out. Royapuram was best known for its railway station, the first to open in South India. Perhaps Muthamma had seen other migrants coming and going on the railway line and imagined a different life for herself far away from home. Did she decide to bring along her younger sisters for company, or did she fear what would become of her daughters if she left them behind? Was she running

| Indenture No | Names | Father | Yr | Mo | Sex | Caste | Zillah | Thanna | Village | Remarks | Arrival | Employer | Returned_Deceased |
|---|---|---|---|---|---|---|---|---|---|---|---|---|---|
| 30127 | MUTHAMMA | NARRAINAN | 28 | 0 | F | Vannia | MADRAS | MADRAS | RAYAPURAM | | Oct 1883 Castleton I Madras | Bisset, Walter Other | [Deceased : 1884 BURNS] |
| 30128 | ANGAMMA | NARRAINAN | 8 | 0 | G | Vannia | MADRAS | MADRAS | RAYAPURAM | | Oct 1883 Castleton I Madras | Bisset, Walter Other | |
| 30129 | POONGAVANAM | NARRAINAN | 5 | 0 | G | Vannia | MADRAS | MADRAS | RAYAPURAM | | Oct 1883 Castleton I Madras | Bisset, Walter Other | [Deceased : 1884 ACCIDENTAL BURNS] |

FIGURE 3.3. Entries for Muthamma, Angamma, and Poongavnam from the Excel spreadsheets compiled from the Ships Lists. Courtesy of the Gandhi-Luthuli Documentation Centre of the University of KwaZulu-Natal.

away from trouble at home? Was she recently widowed, trapped in an abusive marriage, raped, or accused of sexual scandal—circumstances that sometimes drove women to sign contracts of indenture?[20] If so, her personal struggles played out against the wider backdrop of agrarian distress, including the Great Famine of 1876–1878, which left millions dead and was particularly severe in south India.[21] Perhaps the family was struggling to feed its members, and a recruiting agent told her a tale of easy riches, giving her the impression that Natal was a short journey away. Or could she and the girls have been forcibly kidnapped by a recruiter desperate to meet his required quota for women laborers? Although the British played down such incidents of outright coercion, many such stories are preserved in family memories.[22]

Muthamma's decision may seem unusual in the context of nineteenth-century India, in which many women would not travel to a nearby village on their own, let alone to a different country. British officials, however, believed that the presence of women was crucial for the stability of indenture, promoting, in theory, more stable, family-oriented communities. They implemented quotas mandating that ships carry a minimum of forty women for every one hundred men.[23] This quota proved difficult to fill, and many ships sailed with fewer than the required number of women. The Castleton left the port of Madras with 162 men and just 47 women. Many families seemed to have preferred to send young men abroad on their own, so recruiting agents scoured the countryside for women who were desperate, deceived, or daring enough to defy convention.[24]

In fact, Muthamma was not the only woman onboard the Castleton who was traveling alone with children. Of the twelve families with children, three were headed by single women. One, Mangamma, age thirty-five, was traveling with her eight-year-old daughter, Chinnamma. In the space in which the registration clerks normally recorded an employer, Mangamma's registration listed instead the name and number of another Indian migrant: Rangasami, no. 27512. She was the only adult on the ship not assigned to an employer, suggesting that her tie to Rangasami was far from casual. Tracing his number reveals that Rangasami, age twenty, had arrived in Natal less than a year and a half earlier in July 1882. Had Rangasami written to Mangamma, encouraging her to come and indicating that he would support her? If so, it is unclear what tied the two so strongly together. They were from the same *thana*, or district, in North Arcot, but Rangasami was not listed as the father of Mangamma's daughter. Were they lovers, or more distant relations? Ponnamma, age twenty-six, was also from North Arcot, and traveling with an infant girl and boy. Like Muthamma, there were no other migrants onboard the Castleton who hailed from her home village.

Did the three single women support each other during the harrowing two-month journey from Madras to Natal? Did they weep together when an infant died onboard, along with two adult men and a woman?[25] Did Angamma and Chinnamma, both eight years old, play together and help watch Ponnamma's babies? Were they shunned by the other families onboard?

Whatever bond the three women and their children may have forged on the ship, they were not to find comfort in each other's company during the next stage of their journey. Ponnamma and her babies were indentured to an Irishman, Alex Lawrence, who owned Grantleigh Farm in Mooi River. Mangamma and her daughter presumably joined Rangasami at his employer, H. P. Harrison, who owned Rosehill Estates, a sugar plantation in Avoca. Muthamma, Angamma, and Poongavanam were indentured, along with twelve of their fellow passengers from the Castleton, to Walter Bisset, who owned a coffee plantation in Lower Umzimkulu.[26] Their group consisted of nine men, three women, and three children. In addition to the sisters, the other child in the group was a two-year old girl, whose name was recorded as Hussein Bee, traveling with her mother and father. If Angamma had wanted to visit her agemate from the ship, Chinnamma, she would have to travel 150 km, several days' journey by foot, probably an insurmountable distance given her circumstances.

In the coming year, Angamma could have used a friend. A year or so after their arrival, Muthamma and Poongavanam were killed in a fire that broke out in the "coolie lines," where indentured laborers were housed, on the Bisset plantation. It is almost unfathomable how devasting this loss must have been to a young girl like Angamma. She was alone in a strange country. But many around her were also grieving. Even against the backdrop of the generally elevated rates of mortality among indentured laborers, the Bisset plantation was an exceptionally dangerous place to work.[27] In 1885, another of Angamma's shipmates, a young man named Nachi, died of a gunshot wound, purportedly after he accidently shot himself. In 1886, Hussein Bee's mother, Ashabi, died of "natural causes," a label applied to those who died of disease, overwork, malnourishment, or in childbirth. Despite being labelled as natural deaths, colonial officials admitted that "the principal diseases of coolies in Natal are eminently preventable [*sic*]."[28] Of the fifteen who had arrived together on the plantation four were now dead. Did Angamma, remembering her own insufferable sadness, comfort Hussein Bee who had traveled with her on the Castleton?

Despite these suggestive hints, there is much that remains unknown about Angamma's experience onboard the Castleton and her early years in Natal. Analyzing the scant information in the Ships List left me wanting something more—to feel the haunting presence of this brave girl. Thinking of how jewelry, from the ring I inherited from my own grandmother to Janbai's bracelet, had allowed me to connect with other women's legacies, I wondered: was Angamma able to salvage some small keepsake of Muthamma's and Poongavanam's from the fire? I have not found any records that suggest as much, but

Angamma's circumstances remind me of another striking example. Twenty-year-old Mangathoyi died in a hospital in 1905, just short of four years after arriving in Natal. As she was ailing, she made a point of telling someone at the hospital that her last wish was that her jewelry, including a small collection of bangles, anklets, earrings, and nose pins, should be given to her ten-year-old sister, with whom she had traveled to Natal.[29] I found the record of this jewelry in a tabulation of Mangathoyi's meager estate, indexed with her Ships List number, 90536. Reading this document, whose columns asked officials to translate the deceased "effects" into "assets in cash," reveals the limits of historical methods grounded in textual analysis. But conjuring the jewelry as familial objects, through which the living connect with the dead, allows the historian to feel the presence of the ghosts that haunt these records. It allowed me to hope that Mangathoyi found some comfort in her final days by imagining that her younger sister would find solace as the inherited jewelry rubbed intimately against the young girl's skin. Perhaps Angamma was also able to keep a bangle or nose pin to remind her of her family? But I also worry, as I learned in Janbai's case, that for these girls, jewelry was a fleeting inheritance, both financially and emotionally, all too easily appropriated by men.

In addition to omitting much that we would like to know, the Ships List and other colonial documentation also raise questions about the reliability of the information that they do contain. British officials were candid about the problems with the information that they collected about migrants due to linguistic and cultural barriers. In 1883, the same year that Angamma traveled to Natal, George A. Grierson, who was tasked with evaluating the recruitment system, declared that "the present system of registration is just about as bad as it can be."[30] Migrants were also not always passive victims of a muddled bureaucracy.[31] Instead, some migrants deliberately rewrote their biographies as they embarked on new lives in Natal. Among Ranjanithevi's classmates at UDW, several heard stories from their older relatives that suggested such agency. For example, R. Singh related the story of his grandfather, as related to him by his mother. The child of a soldier, Durga Singh lost his father at the tender age of eleven, a tragedy followed by the death of his mother soon after. Durga was left to the care of his aunt, who overworked and abused him. One day, Durga was swimming with one of his cousins, who accidentally drowned. Terrified that his aunt would blame him for the death of her favorite son, Durga ran away to Calcutta, where he was spotted by recruiters. As recounted by his grandson: "Being a Singh by birth and fifteen years of age, he misinformed the recruiters that he was twenty years old and of the Pasi caste since he was told by someone that the Singh's and Maharaj's were not supposed to be recruited because they were a warrior caste and not trained to do agricultural work in India. He also re-named his father for fear of being caught out by the authorities."[32]

The stories I have been able to piece together from the Ships List about Angamma are, therefore, archival fragments rather than definitive facts. But even if some of the details are inaccurate, the overall narrative that emerges fits historians' larger understanding of indenture. The Ships List document disruptions to patriarchal norms and traditional family units, exacerbated by the brutal conditions that migrants faced onboard ships and on plantations. As the following section suggests, the Ships List and associated records, thus, provide insight into histories that were marginalized as migrants forged new lives for themselves after indenture. For many, this meant burying traumatic pasts.

## Burying and Unearthing Roots under Apartheid

In 1984, a century after Angamma arrived in Natal, her great-grandson Ranjanithevi set out to research his roots. Between them stretched decades of intense struggle over the future of Indians in South Africa. White South Africans initially supported Indian immigration as a source of cheap agricultural labor. By the 1890s, however, they were frightened by competition from a rising Indian middle class. This included merchants who paid for their own passage and former indentured Indians like Ranjanithevi's grandfather Pungavanam, who progressed from small-scale farming to real estate investment and retail. In 1895, Natal, where most current and former indentured laborers in South Africa were based, passed a law requiring Indians to leave at the end of their term of indenture, re-indenture, or pay a three-pound, per-head annual tax. For many families, this was a prohibitive sum. A typical Indian couple with two teenage children might earn fifteen pounds per year on their farm, of which they would be required to pay twelve in taxes.[33] In protest against the tax and other discriminatory laws, South African Indians organized a campaign of non-violent resistance, led by the expatriate lawyer Mohandas Karamchand Gandhi, who would later famously adapt the same strategies when he returned to India. The tax was repealed in 1914 under a compromise that Gandhi helped to negotiate, but other discriminatory laws remained in place, including restrictions on the right of Indians to travel to, from, and within South Africa. The mistreatment of Indians in South Africa fueled a larger campaign against indenture, leading the Government of India to suspend transports to Natal in 1911 and to abolish indenture completely in 1917.[34]

In the coming years, South Africa constructed an elaborate legal apparatus that worked to consolidate political and economic power in the hands of its White minority. Many tenets of the Apartheid regime, which officially began in 1948 with the electoral victory of the Nationalist Party, were anticipated in earlier laws. In 1910, the Union of South Africa consolidated the territories of the Cape, Natal, Transvaal, and Orange Rivers to become a self-governing dominion of the British Empire. In one of the first acts passed by the new union parliament, the Natives Land Act (1913) restricted Black ownership of land to a miserly 7 percent of the country, leading to mass dispossession and dislocation.[35]

The government simultaneously introduced a series of repatriation schemes which were meant to solve the "Indian penetration" problem by sending them back to India. Yet most Indian-South Africans chose to remain, and the government responded with escalating discrimination. On the eve of independence, Indian nationalists in India lobbied the newly formed United Nations to pass a resolution censoring South Africa for racial and cultural discrimination. To shield itself from further international scrutiny, the new Apartheid regime began to insist that the "Asiatic question" was a purely domestic affair. This position shifted focus away from repatriation and towards a highly segregated system of hierarchical incorporation.

After the formal advent of Apartheid in 1948, the government introduced the Population Registration Act and Group Areas Act in 1950, expanding systems of racial classification and segregation. Whites, Asians, Coloured, and Blacks were assigned highly unequal access to land, political rights, education, and employment. Many Indians were pushed out of residential areas newly classified as White, losing valuable land in the process, and forced to rent poorly constructed houses on the outskirts of town at exorbitant rates. Yet they were simultaneously elevated above Blacks, occupying along with Coloureds a middle stature as "quasi" citizens, between the full citizenship accorded to Whites and the effective non-citizenship status assigned to Blacks.[36] Those who resisted the new regime, including building alliances across racial lines to oppose these new policies of divide-and-rule, were met with brutal suppression. Indian activists like Ahmed Mohamed Kathrada and Ebrahim Ismail Ebrahim served long prison sentences alongside Nelson Mandela at the notorious Robben Island Prison.

To buttress the Apartheid regime, the government built a segregated system of higher education. In the 1960–1961 school year, the government opened what would become the University of Durban-Westville, which catered primarily to the Indian population. Forced to occupy the decrepit infrastructure of a former naval base on Sainsbury Island, Indian students replaced Hungarian refugees, who had previously been housed in the abandoned military buildings. The university shared the island with an explosives manufacturer. When large shipments of explosives were scheduled to ship out, classes were routinely canceled, and residential students were forced to vacate their hostels for offsite "picnics."[37]

Although an improvement in physical conditions, the shift to a new campus in Westville, a suburb of Durban, in 1972 did little to improve the intellectual climate. Through the 1960s and 1970s, an overwhelmingly White professoriate, some of whom had direct links to the Apartheid government, taught a White-washed curriculum to predominantly Indian students. On exams, students were asked to "Outline the main features of the Indian problem in South Africa from 1900 to 1914, and the attempts to find a solution."[38] Defined as a "problem," students experienced the university less as a place of learning than—in their words—a "prison camp" and "a mortuary."[39] Professor Uma Dhupelia-Mesthrie, who studied at UDW in the 1970s (and who as a graduate teaching assistant graded the roots project before becoming an eminent historian herself), described the students as "there under duress."[40]

The broader cultural climate was also distinctly hostile to critically examining histories of Indian migration to South Africa, particularly for those who came under contracts of indenture. (The first historical novel to explore the experience of indentured laborers in South Africa would not appear until 2003, with the publication of Praba Moodley's *The Heart Knows No Colour*.) The muffling of histories of indenture during the Apartheid period was in part due to draconian censorship laws. But it was also notably limited in comparison to a more substantial body of radical texts written by Black South Africans during the same period, suggesting factors beyond formal regimes of state censorship.[41]

Histories of indenture, with their deeply diasporic mobilities, proved hard to incorporate into emerging nationalist narratives both in South Africa and in India. For Indian nationalists, including Gandhi, the existence of indenture was a symbol of how Britain had subjected Indians to dehumanizing conditions. The position of women indentured laborers, who Indian abolitionists sometimes equated with women forced into prostitution, was considered even more degrading.[42] When colonial officials abolished indenture under pressure from nationalists, they heralded this victory as evidence of how independent India would protect its most vulnerable citizens. After independence, India limited emigration by non-elite groups on the grounds that the new nation must prevent its citizens from becoming "coolies."[43] Indian nationalist framings of indenture sometimes stigmatized the indentured themselves, who were, by implication, passive victims or even degraded by their subjection.

The difficulty of narrating histories of indenture in the South African context was amplified by the racial politics of Apartheid, which were structured by a Black/White binary that mapped onto an indigenous/settler divide. The history of indenture, in which Indians were simultaneously colonized subjects and migrant settlers, was ambivalent in ways that were disruptive to both Apartheid ideology and the struggle against it. As literary scholar Pallavi Rastogi notes, "The Indian presence complicates the binary of settler and indigene by introducing a third state of national being: that of postcolonial diasporic. Yet the antiapartheid movement could not encourage such subtleties for fear of diminishing the effectiveness of a unified onslaught against segregation."[44]

Against this backdrop, in the late 1970s and early 1980s, a small group of researchers in South Africa began to dig deeper into the history of indenture, even as barriers to engaging with this past remained high. Amongst them was Surendra Bhana, who designed the roots research project during his tenure at UDW. Bhana spent his childhood in Sisodra, a village in Gujarat, while his father worked as a tailor in Johannesburg. Bhana would later recall that although he had a happy childhood, he remembered taunts from upper-caste neighbors. Bhana later joined his father in South Africa, who insisted that his son spend his time learning English and catching up with his peers at the Pretoria Indian Boys' School rather than learning the tailoring business. Bhana eventually secured a coveted bursary to study for his BA at the University of Witwatersrand, then an overwhelmingly White institution. He later was admitted to the PhD program in History at the University of Kansas. Bhana returned to South Africa in 1972, taking up a position at UDW, where he would spend the next fifteen years before returning to join the faculty at the University of Kansas.[45]

Bhana arrived at UDW during a pivotal moment, both in South Africa and on campus. In 1976, university students boycotted lectures in solidarity with the children of Soweto gunned down by the police in the Black township. The following year, UDW students walked out again to protest the death of Steve Biko, an anti-Apartheid activist who was beaten to death by state security officials. During this period, politics and academics came together in the classroom. At a conference on techniques of teaching history held in 1984, Bhana noted that, "we are at a period in our development when there is a great deal more interest in history among blacks generally than I think is the case with whites."[46] Students also "voted with their feet"; between 1980 and 1984 enrollments in History courses at UDW increased from 1007 to 1818.[47] Black students, amongst whom Bhana strategically included Indians, were clearly interested in learning about the past. Yet, in the early 1980s, the risks to unearthing suppressed histories remained high.

In this context, the roots project was conceived in response to student feedback that the curriculum lacked "local history," a seemingly politically innocuous phrasing that nonetheless hinted at a hunger to know more about controversial topics.[48] Given the time he spent in the US, Bhana may have also been inspired by Alex Haley's *Roots* (1976) and its TV adaption, which excavated the legacies of Atlantic slavery through the story of Haley's own family, with a liberal mixture of fact and fiction. Despite being officially banned in South Africa, *Roots* was widely viewed in informal community screenings.[49] More broadly, the assignment reflected efforts, both in South Africa and more globally, to upset established historical hierarchies to write new histories "from below." Yet, initially, Bhana's assignment met with grumbles from some of his students. One dismissed the paper as "an exercise in futility presented by the History Department under the guise of being an innovative way of introducing students to Historical research." In frustration, he asked: "What does the history of my grandfather, who had absolutely no claim to greatness, have to do with the course of my study as a final-year student of History?"[50]

By the end of the term, students had changed their minds. The same student now extolled the assignment for showing "that History has been at my doorstep all this time."[51] One enthused: "This triggered off a change in my values and attitudes to life. Prior to this project, I never had the urge to think or question my origins."[52] The project was especially transformative for students who traced their roots back to indenture, which was often still considered a source of stigma in South Africa.[53] Through their projects students recast this history as something to be proud of—evidence that their ancestors, who had come with nothing, had secured a place in the middle class.

Yet in doing so, they sometimes fell back on colonial tropes that associated belonging with claims to have settled the land, a pattern that Nienke Boer traces to some of the earliest Indian-South African writings both before and after the advent of Apartheid.[54] From the nineteenth century, the legal regimes of property and immigration that governed the territories that would become South Africa framed White bodies as exclusively capable of permanent "settlement," with their capacity to improve a barren landscape justifying their unique rights to citizenship and ownership. In attempting to write their own narratives of South African belonging, the UDW students resisted these logics by asserting their own "settler" pasts. In the process, they sometimes adopted scripts that required minimizing critical aspects of their family stories, from the experience of indenture itself to the lives of their great-grandmothers to the displacement and dispossession of Black Africans.[55] Under titles such as "He Helped to Make History," "They Owe the Indians," and "An Indentured Labourer as Pioneer to Our South African Society," the students crafted narratives that at once resisted White supremacy while also adopting some of its settler and patriarchal tropes (see Figure 3.4).

Ranjanithevi's retelling of his grandfather, Pungavanam's story fits this pattern. Unlike many descendants with whom I worked, I was never able to speak directly with Ranjanithevi about his family history. I found an old entry for him in the Australia Business Register, and more distant relatives told me that they thought that he had passed away.[56] I thus rely on how he viewed his family history in the particular context of the early 1980s, when he was Bhana's student. In this pivotal moment, the narrative he offered, which was based on interviews he conducted with two of Pungavanam's sons and one of his daughters, emphasized the family's ascent into the middle class through the hard work and talents of its patriarch. Ranjanithevi did not present his grandfather as a typical rags-to-riches

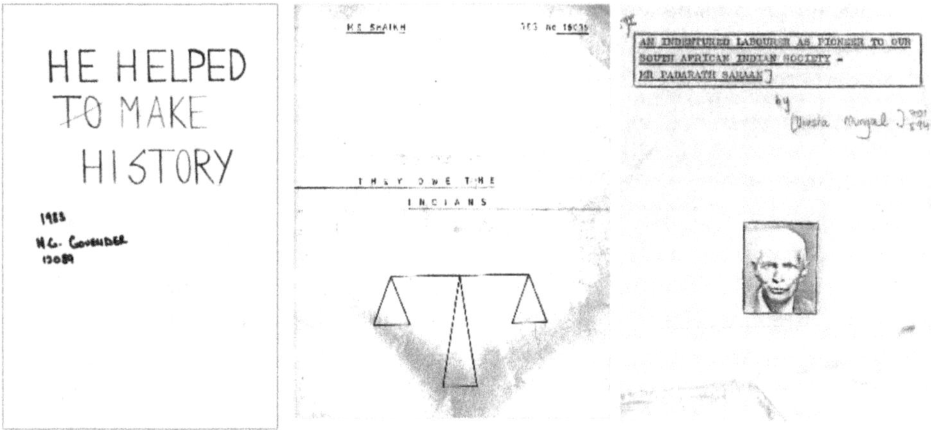


FIGURE 3.4. Cover images from student projects by N.G. Govender, “He Helped to Make History,” M.S. Shaikh, “They Owe the Indians,” and U. Mungal, “An Indentured Labourer as Pioneer to Our South African Indian Story.” Courtesy of the Gandhi-Luthuli Documentation Centre of the University of KwaZulu-Natal.

success. He noted that the family, who came from a village near Kanchipuram in North Arcot, had been well-off in India. Like many of the student biographies, Ranjanithevi included a discussion of his grandfather’s caste background, relying on cross-referencing information from the Ships List with scholarly compendium on caste. He used this information to conclude that the family was from a “clean non-Brahman” caste and noted that his great-grandparents were “land owners, cultivated crops and traded some of their produce at the market.” In India, they also wove silk saris, a trade for which Kanchipuram was (and is) famous. Ranjanithevi therefore concluded that his grandfather was “well placed socially, economically and religiously.”[57]

Given this information, Ranjanithevi struggled to make sense of why his grandfather emigrated as an indentured laborer. He noted that he left during a period of famine in south India. He also quoted from a secondary source on the history of indenture that indicated that many migrants had been told wild tales of “chilli trees [that] bore gold.” Yet, Ranjanithevi emphasized that his older family members did not talk about his grandfather as a victim of economic destitution or deception. They spoke of him as “an adventurous person with the desire to ‘see the world’ and ‘to do what he wanted.’” He also mentioned that one of his grandfather’s sisters had migrated to Singapore—suggesting that the family was connected to multiple circuits of mobility.[58]

While the precise reasons why Pungavanam left India remain obscure, the stories that Ranjanithevi heard are significant because they provided a foundation for a wider retelling of Pungavanam's life that emphasized his personal initiative (seeking out "adventure") and his progression from one economic success to the next. His time working as an indentured laborer on a tea plantation is quickly passed over while the astute financial deals he made to secure his family a place in the middle class are recounted in precise, quantitative detail. For example, Ranjanithevi noted that Pungavanam had "bought 100 acres in Umbango (North Shepstone) at £9 an acre and sold it shortly after that to Indian farmers at £30 an acre on terms for 9 years."[59] He also emphasized the critical role that Pungavanam played in opening schools for Indian children in the Port Shepstone area.[60]

In concluding his paper, Ranjanithevi summed up his grandfather's accomplishments:

> My grandfather emigrated to South Africa, decided to settle, and over a period of 48 years he helped to build it and regard it as his home and the home of his descendants who were South African born. The unfavorable laws based on prejudice did not deter him to achieve through self-help and to lay a solid foundation on which his descendants and the community have built. Today, 91 years, after his arrival, we can look with pride on the initiative, drive, determination and leadership qualities that my grandfather possessed. The reasonable position in life of his descendents is directly related to his brave decision to emigrate from India in 1893, at the age of 20 years.[61]

The paragraph encapsulated the contortions inherent to writing family histories rooted in indenture into scripts of White-settler colonialism. Ranjanithevi adopted many of the tropes of settlement and bourgeois improvement. These include the invocation of multi-generational ties to a homeland cast as barren before the settlers' arrival and the exaltation of "self-help" through which wealth is individually earned rather than colonially expropriated. Yet the haunting presence of the "unfavorable laws based on prejudice" suggests the yet unmentionable other pasts that undergirded much of the Indian experience in South Africa. Censoring these histories not only required silencing significant elements of the Indian experience; it also necessitated obscuring their connection to the experiences of other non-White South Africans. Ranjanithevi only mentioned Black South Africans to present Indians as a solution to South Africa's labor "problem," which he suggested was connected to the inadequacies of "Black local labour." As he summarized at the beginning of his project, the colony had "fertile land, skilled managers and capital" but lacked "reliable labour"—which Indians like his grandfather were able to provide.[62]

Ranjanithevi's retelling of Pungavanam's past was not unusual among the student projects. Repeatedly, the students framed the history of their ancestors in ways that linked them to White "pioneer" narratives while distancing them from overlapping Black experiences of coerced labor and land dispossession. A surprising number, like Ranjanithevi, found that their older relatives de-emphasized compulsion as an explanation for their ancestors' decisions to leave India. They instead presented their forebearers as adventurous young men who went "to seek fortune."[63] Like Ranjanithevi, many students also repeated the idea that South Africa was unproductive before the arrival of White and Indian settlers, and that Indians had "converted waste and unproductive land into well kept gardens."[64] For these families, like Ranjanithevi's, land ownership and cultivation—putting down roots in the most literal sense—was a potent symbol of implanting themselves in their adopted homeland. The projects, however, were largely silent about subsequent histories of land dispossession under Apartheid, during which many Indian families were forced to move from homes and farms their ancestors had acquired. I would hear of these memories when I connected with Ranjanithevi's extended relations decades later.

In pointing to how the roots projects replicated racist tropes of settler colonialism, my point is not to fault the student authors. It is to underline how, as Indian-South Africans began to excavate their roots in the early 1980s, the wider context of Apartheid limited what narratives could be explored. In fact, in many of the student projects, the pain of Apartheid discrimination and violence seeps through but is quickly cloaked in other less dangerous narratives. As one student wrote: "Through immense hardship, these pioneers made it possible for their children to achieve a firm foothold on the shores of Africa and share in her wealth and prosperity. Their deeds of courage and unflagging fight for justice, in the face of hostility and even aggression, on a strange shore, should be recorded for posterity and serve as a beacon for the struggle for future justice and freedom in South Africa." In adding the caveat "even" to aggression, the student author reminds us how difficult, and potentially dangerous, it was to challenge official narratives, or as the same student described it elsewhere, to "attack the veils of history."[65]

The relatively muted presence of women within many of the student projects, including the omission of Angamma from Ranjanithevi's paper, should also be understood in this context. The stories of many of their patriarchal ancestors could be edited to fit "pioneering" narratives, which downplayed forced migration and charted economic ascent into the middle class. The stories of women like Angamma, Muthamma, and Poongavanam were far more difficult to retell in these frames. We ultimately do not know why Muthamma, along with the two girls, left India. It is hard though to imagine that she would have chosen to travel alone with two young children other than out of desperation—whether because she had lost her husband, been cast out of the family, or faced economic hardship that made the previously unthinkable, thinkable. Her and Poongavanam's deaths, as recorded in the Protector's records, also point to the brutal conditions that indentured laborers faced. The deaths were officially recorded as "accidental," but at a minimum, poor-quality construction must have played a role. To tell such stories under Apartheid was both difficult and dangerous.

Of course, part of the reason that Ranjanithevi may have chosen to focus on his grandfather's migration was that he came to South Africa later, and thus the memory of his journey was better known to the family. But the absence of any mention of the women's migrations nonetheless marginalized their pasts. Historians Ashwin Desai and Goolam Vahed have argued that for indentured Indians, the "determination to build a family" was a form of resistance "to a system designed to brutalise them into units of labor."[66] This drive, in a cultural context that strongly favored patriarchal norms, provides vital context for why stories of indentured women had to be forgotten to create families anew. For indentured laborers, resisting the dehumanizing impacts of colonialism and capitalism required activating other forms of domination, in this case masculine, heteronormative norms. However, such processes do not mean that women's histories were lost forever. As I learned when I found the family online, instead, families crafted new narratives that allowed them to treasure their loved ones' memories in safer forms.

## Routes Revisited: Re-telling the Story of English Mary Post-Apartheid and in the Gulf

In the decades after the end of Apartheid, South Africans experienced what Devarakshanam Betty Govinden has termed "a time of memory," in which it became possible to revisit histories that were suppressed under Apartheid.[67] As I would learn when I pursued Angamma's trail out of the archives and across various digital searches, Angamma's story, which had been all but absent from Ranjanithevi's roots project, was retold in these new contexts. It migrated from a story preserved by her women descendants onto new online platforms. I picked up these digital trails on the ancestry website Geni.com, where I found profiles for Pungavanam and Muniama. They were included in a family tree constructed by the descendants of another of the couple's children (see family tree at the beginning of the chapter). The tree included a profile for Angamma but under the name "English Mary." Eventually, I connected with the creator of the family tree, Anneline Bernice Moodley, who was married to the great-great-great grandson of Angamma.[68] Through our exchanges, I gained new insight into how grappling with the legacies of Apartheid has also been instrumental in spurring deeper engagement with histories of indenture. Lifting the "veils" (to borrow from the UDW student) from more recent history also brought new insight into deeper pasts.

But it took many years to connect with Anneline. When I first reached out to her via messages on Geni.com in July 2018, they went unanswered. A year and a half later, in January 2020, I unexpectedly received a reply apologizing for the delay. Anneline explained that when I first wrote to her, she was moving to Doha after her husband, a pilot, took a job with Qatar Airways. While we tried to connect in 2020, the pandemic soon threw both of our lives awry, and we ultimately only spoke in January 2023. But the long wait due to the family's more recent diasporic perambulations proved well worth it. This elongated timeline echoed the alternative temporalities with which diasporic families often engage with the past. Diasporic memories do not unfold linearly in time or observe conventional geographical boundaries. Families may work on constructing these narratives—whether as oral stories or digital trees—quite intensely for a period. Then, they set them aside for long stretches before returning to them when circumstances arise that recall earlier experiences, including onward migrations, as was the case with Anneline.

When we finally spoke, Anneline provided some context for how the story of "English Mary" had been passed down in the family. She explained that she became interested in her roots when her daughter was assigned a school project to research her family's coat of arms. A distinctly Eurocentric and upper-class framing of family history, the assignment showed how colonialism and White supremacy continued to shape education even decades after the end of Apartheid. Yet while an assignment to locate one's family coat of arms was an odd entry to researching indentured roots, it set Anneline on a journey that eventually led her to vibrant new landscapes of family history. She created an account on Geni.com in 2013, finding there others who were also exploring connections to indenture. Projects like those sponsored by UDW and a new cultural center in Durban, the 1860 Heritage Center (named after the year in which the first indentured migrants arrived), were encouraging Indian South Africans to see links to indenture as a source of pride rather than stigma.[69] By the early 2000s, interest in indenture also overlapped with the growth of online genealogy. For many with South Asian roots, digital genealogy platforms are of limited utility, themes I explore in more depth in Chapter 5. But the comparatively extensive state archives for indenture in Natal and earlier efforts to digitize resources like the Ships List have made digital genealogy more accessible to Indian-South Africans. Yet, Anneline did not rely exclusively on such new mediums—she also drew on older tools, including organizing a family reunion. At the reunion, "Mama Kamblem," whose full name was Kamalavalli Ammal Moodley, and who was the great-granddaughter of Angamma, told the story of "English Mary." Anneline explained that Mama Kamblem was a teacher and "an awesome storyteller." She carried on a long tradition of powerful women in the family, who "were very forthright" and "took no prisoners."

Anneline would eventually post the story that Mama Kamblem told at the family reunion to her profile on Geni.com, where I found it. I have transcribed it as it appeared on her Geni.com tree:

> *The Story of English Mary*
>
> *In the 1860's Indian's were brought to South Africa. Two couples boarded the ship seeking a new life in South Africa. One couple had a daughter and the other had a son. Little did these two families know what a treacherous and arduous journey they were embarking on. These two couples did not survive the journey across the Indian Ocean. Finally when the ship docks at the Durban harbour, two young, starved, frightened and bewildered children disembark, not knowing what their future holds.*
>
> *After the Indians that disembarked had been selected by the farm owners, there stood these two children all alone. A white couple took pity when hearing their story and decided to take them to their farm. The girl, Mary, was trained as a parlour maid and Narainsamy was assigned to the kitchen. Mary was taught the English language and culture. She also learnt to ride a horse. She grew up into a beautiful young, tall, upstanding and a well-groomed lady. She was nicknamed by the Indian community as English Mary. When she walked on the road she was so well respected that the Indians would step away to the other side of the road as they would when the Whites walked on the road.*
>
> *Mary and Narainsamy became friends as both of them lost their parents and worked for the same family. They were well liked by the family they worked for. This White family decided to relocate to England and were concerned what would become of Mary and Narainsamy. So they decided to get them married.*
>
> *The Indians on the farm were all invited to attend the wedding ceremony and the celebration that followed. Their wedding gift from their employer was a piece of land and a house before they left the country. Mary and Narainsamy had lived a very happy married life. They had twelve children and one of their daughters was Papa's mother know to us as Vettu Patti. Patti was always immaculately dressed in a white sari. Sitting upright and very royal looking, she spoke softly and had beautiful manners. She was also known for her cleanliness. She married a young man named Pongavanum Moodley. Pongavanum came from Kanchipurum India.*[70]

Much about the story did not match what I had uncovered in the archives. My work with the Ships List suggested that Angamma lost her family not on the ship but on the plantation. Looking up her husband Narainsamy's number in the Ships List also yielded conflicting details. His Ships List number, which I confirmed through multiple documents, was 35086. His entry indicated that he traveled to Natal in January 1887 onboard the SS Laurel, which reported no deaths.[71] His age was also listed as eighteen, and there was no indication that he traveled with his parents. He was assigned to work at Sea Fields in Umzimkulu, the same area where Angamma had been indentured three years earlier, but not at the same plantation.

I found most striking, however, not the mismatch in some of the facts but the diverging ways in which violence and trauma were narrated in the archive and the family's story. Discrepancies in facts are almost always present when comparing oral and archival accounts, but the divergence here suggested more seismic ruptures. In the story of English Mary, the trauma of indenture was sequestered to the boat, where she is remembered as losing her parents and being "starved, frightened and bewildered." In contrast, she left India with her family intact in the story. The story also portrayed her time in South Africa as relatively benign, protected by the benevolence of her White employers, who are almost cast in the role of adoptive parents. (I found myself wondering, could this possibly be the same plantation where four of Angamma's fifteen shipmates died within the space of a few years?) One can imagine, however, that concentrating traumatic memories on the boats that carried migrants to Natal could play a protective role when Indian-South Africans felt pressure to romanticize their Indian past and self-censor critiques of White oppression. Submerging inherited traumas within the watery depths of remembered passages allowed families to endure the pain of burrowing roots into land saturated with tears. These roots, like those of a mangrove tree, drew sustenance from salty water before turning upwards to the sky to breathe in the present.

Yet displacing the trauma of death from land to water could also have subversive implications. As noted earlier, images of land pervaded Ranjanithevi's recounting of his grandfather's South African journey, reflecting how terrestrial attachment functioned as idioms for belonging under White-settler colonialism. The appearance of water as a traumatic force in the retelling of the story of "English Mary" is therefore noteworthy. It draws connections between the experience of the enslaved and indentured—defying the liberal construction of the "freely" entered contract as dividing them. These are what Caribbean theorist Édouard Glissant calls "submarine roots." Such oceanic, as opposed to terrestrial, roots opened possibilities for Indian attachment to Africa, not through settlement, but the shared pain of coerced migrations.[72] Oceanic roots moved outside ethno-nationalistic, bio-legal, and terrestrial constructions of ancestry. In the place of the conventional earth-bound family trees, which I also critique in the introduction, this imaginary of roots traces fluid intimacies across land and sea.[73]

This interplay between internalizing and subverting ideologies of White supremacy also provides context for the performance of Whiteness that permeated the story of "English Mary." In the narrative, Mary comes to associate herself so closely with her employers that she takes on multiple attributes of Whiteness—language, dress, and comportment. She is then implicated in racist hierarchies when other Indians feel obligated to step out of her way on the street. She also passed these qualities onto her daughter, Patti, aka Muniamma, who was "always immaculately dressed in a white sari" and "very royal looking." While not apparent in the story itself, the women's comportment may not have sat well with other Indians. The nickname "English Mary" might have carried an edge, since in South Africa "Indian Sammy" and "Coolie Mary" were derogative terms used to mock Indians.[74]

It is easy to dismiss the story of English Mary as evidence of false consciousness in which non-White South Africans imbibed ideologies of White supremacy. But there was also creative, subversive potential in the selective appropriation of markers of White privilege. The descriptions of Mary and Patti remind me of other accounts of Indian matriarchs in South Africa that similarly conveyed their authority through associations with Whiteness and royalty. In a Facebook post from 2021 celebrating the 106th birthday of Amartham Moodley, her daughter wrote that after her mother lost her parents, "she was raised by a strict but caring aunt who was like Queen Victoria in her dress and demeanour. 'North Street Ayah' as all the children called her, wore Harley Street shoes on her stocking clad feet and dressed in pale saris with a Queen Victoria pendant at her neck."[75] Donning the visage of Queen Victoria might be read as an internalization of imperial ideology, but the same story emphasized the brave way in which women in the family criticized racism. The post narrated how when Amartham was addressed as "Mary" by a White butcher's assistant, a name that conjured up the derogative term "Coolie Mary," "she replied with her head held high: 'Can I have a pound of lamb chops, please Jane?' To which the woman replied 'My name is not Jane,' and she retorted 'Well, my name is not Mary.'" I am thus inclined to read something other than false consciousness into the description of Amartham's "strict but caring aunt."

In the intimate act of wearing the image of Queen Victoria on her breast, Amartham's aunt channeled the Queen's authority into her own body. Just as tracing the migration of the bracelet from Janbai to Caroline Batchelder in the last chapter points to alternative networks of women's sociality, attending to how Amartham wore an image of Queen Victoria pushes us to consider the complexities of imperial identities as refracted through diasporic mobilities. Similarly, in *Through Space and Time* (2021), Renluka Maharaj, whose artistic practice has inspired my own, overlays the image of a South Asian woman

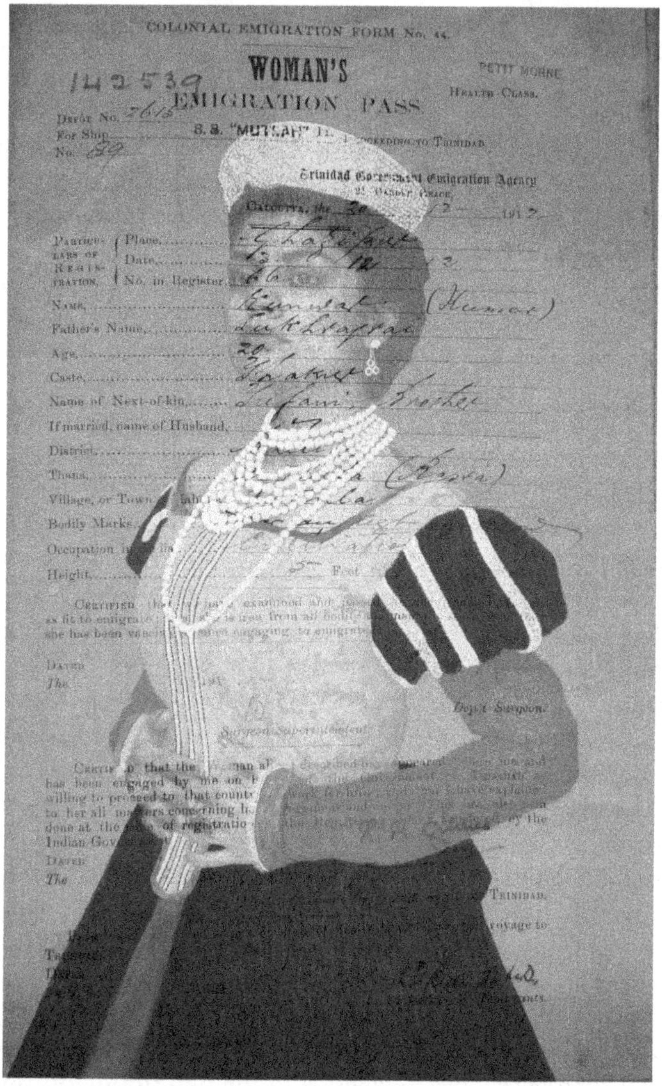


FIGURE 3.5. Renluka Maharaj, *Through Space and Time*, 2021, mixed media on pigmented ink print, 36 × 60 inches. Courtesy of artist.

wearing a Victorian dress, pearl necklace, and diamond crown on top of a record of an indentured woman's ship passage to Trinidad.[76]

The association of wearing White or pale colors with looking like a queen also transformed the meaning of clothing that, in an Indian context, might elicit images of widowhood. Upper-caste Hindu widows, particularly in north

India, were often forbidden from remarrying and forced to live austere lives of perpetual morning—a process symbolically embodied by removing a widow's jewelry and trading her colorful clothing for white. Social histories of indenture suggest that some women may have migrated to escape the stigma and deprivations of such practices. However, as these descriptions indicate, some Indian-South African women adopted white and pale-colored clothing as a marker of authority, associating it with royalty. This shift suggests the influence of Queen Victoria's decision to trade her crimson velvet robes of state for a white dress on her wedding day, popularizing it as a bridal color conveying purity.[77] For Indian women in South Africa, to don white saris thus simultaneously referenced inherited memories of widowhood and alternative visualizations of feminine respectability. Even when it may not have been possible to heroize their maternal ancestors, donning white saris was another way of claiming this past as their own. Such processes of embodying diasporic pasts were interwoven with empire, but in ways that deeply unsettled its dominant racial and gendered hierarchies.

As a historian, I read the story of "English Mary" against the grain to see how undercurrents of resistance create a mimicry of White supremacy that outwardly upholds its hierarchies while internally troubling its logic.[78] In her own quest to learn about her family's roots in the years after Apartheid, Anneline also revisited these stories with a new ability to critique how they were shaped by the family's experiences of losing property during Apartheid. She re-evaluated the evidence passed down through family oral histories in light of her experience living through the transition from Apartheid to constitutional democracy. She explained that she had doubts about the story that the couple had received a plot of land and a house from their adopted English family. According to her research, the family had been compelled to migrate towards Port Stepstone, and she wondered why they would have felt this need if they already had the financial security of owning their own home and farm in the Durban area. In thinking about how these stories of land and migration might have become muddled, Anneline noted:

> There was a lot of pain involved. E. P. Moodley [Pungavanam's son and Mama Kamblem's father] had built up quite a few assets and quite a bit of land in Port Stepstone. Then obviously [it was] South Africa and the Apartheid era, and they took that away from them. So with that pain was also the memories that were passed down because eventually they were left with only one house, and they would refer to the land they used to have . . . that is also how the stories were kept alive because of the great loss in terms of the land.

Anneline's ruminations suggest how, in the post-Apartheid moment, Indian-South Africans deconstructed White settler-colonial logics to assert different modes of claiming South African legacies. While emphasizing the family's economic ascent, or what Ranjanithevi described as Pungavanam's "achieve[ment] through self-help," she also reflected on their experiences of dispossession. As a result, she arrived at a very different understanding of their relationship to property. After speaking of the family's deep sense of loss, she explained that her husband "loves speculating on houses and land." In this habit, she saw evidence that "somewhere, something came down. We talk about DNA, it is so funny, it stays with you. That's for me the fascinating thing." Here, I interpret Anneline as asserting that while the family had lost the physical property they inherited from E. P. Moodley and Pungavanam, the Apartheid regime could not take away the habits of investment that had allowed them to amass it in the first place. Anneline called this "a mindset of wealth."

Anneline's description of her family's relationship to land was far more subversive than the sentimental attachments that Nienke Boer argued provided earlier Indian-South Africans with ambivalent grounds for resistance.[79] While also invoking sentiment through the family's feelings of loss, Anneline does not stake their claims to belong on their permanent settlement in South Africa. Instead, she made sense of their South African heritage by reflecting on the family's mobile habits of investing in real estate. Neither Apartheid nor further migration to the Gulf could squash such habits. While I take up genetic genealogy more explicitly in Chapter 5, here, I read her invocation of DNA (and of love) as underlining the embodied and emotive nature of this inheritance. In Anneline's retelling, the family's habits of real-estate investment became detached from a particular physical property, which could be seized, or which might be more profitably traded for an alternative location. They instead became familial habits, which could move with the family and be passed from generation to generation. The family, therefore, no longer stakes its claims to a South African inheritance by asserting their settled nature. Instead, they point to the experience of their ancestors, including indentured displacement and Apartheid dispossession, as inculcating habits that have *stayed* with them even as they have moved. The family's relationship to land is *unsettled*, replacing (White) settler-colonial logics with claims rooted in the family's mobility.

Anneline's narrative of her family's past resonated deeply with stories I heard from many others. For many diasporic families, migration entailed experiences of economic descent as well as ascent. Land, homes, and jewelry were often lost—whether through market collapse (as was the case with Thamboosamy's family during the Great Depression), in court cases (as with Tharia's estate), theft (as with Janbai's jewelry), or the seizure of the Moodleys' properties. But habits related to wealth—litigating, wearing gold, or buying real estate—persisted after objects and assets were lost. Often families clung even more closely to these habits because of the pain, but also determination, born of material losses. Heirlooms lost could become tools of a different sort as families recovered from past dispossession to reconstruct their lives in the present.

These afterlives have proved long-lasting in many diasporic families because they are adaptable to ongoing migrations rather than dependent on attachments to a particular place or stable ethnic/religious identity. While Anneline's initial forays into family history were shaped by the post-Apartheid landscapes of South Africa, she described to me how after moving to the Gulf, her appreciation for her family's past deepened. She explained that she could now personally relate to the stories she had heard about how her ancestors had left India. She cited the stories indentured laborers told of being deceived by descriptions of chili trees that bore gold but also the threat of their children starving if they remained in India. While her family's own circumstances were not nearly as dire as their indentured ancestors, they had left South Africa because her husband did not have a professional future there after its airline closed.

She also told me she appreciated how Indian-South Africans clung to their diasporic traditions, perhaps even more tenaciously than Indians who remained in India, because she was doing the same—"to the point where we are making our own biltong!" I found myself laughing to think that the first family tradition that came to mind for Anneline was biltong, a cured meat popular in southern Africa. Clearly habits of mobility and memory-making had been passed from generation to generation, but their contents also changed over time. Her stories reminded me of the plants in my garden that shifted colors when I transplanted them into a bed with more or less sunlight or different soil conditions. Existing frameworks for studying diaspora often fail to account for how repeated experiences of mobility create such diasporic habits. For families like Anneline's, being diasporic is about the ability to uproot as circumstances shift and to re-root in different cultural contexts. They are the perennials that flourish when you dig and divide them every few seasons, not the taproot that, once planted, is better left alone. Just as for some plants, this process of dividing and relocating is essential to their ongoing vitality, Anneline told me how her family's recent migrations kindled a renewed appreciation for their past.

As with many families, my conversation with Anneline was not a one-way exchange. She was also anxious to know about the archival trails I uncovered concerning the family. While Anneline had explored the story of "English Mary" through oral traditions, she had not previously connected it with archival records. Before we spoke, I sent her some documents I had found related to Angamma, including her Ships List number. I was concerned about how she might react to these rather different accounts of her ancestor. During our conversation, I tried to emphasize that the documents did not necessarily disprove the stories that had been passed down since government archives also contain inaccuracies and omissions. My concerns proved unnecessary; Anneline was excited to change the profile name for "English Mary" to Angamma and to add her Ships List number. She noted, "I would take a lot of that story [of English Mary] with a pinch of salt. I think it was romanticized." Having already been revisiting her family's past in light of her shifting circumstances, Anneline was open to further rethinking this history. We agreed that the supposed benevolence of a White adoptive family had to be confronted with her sense of the family's experience of dispossession under Apartheid and the evidence I had unearthed about the violent deaths of Angamma's sisters/mother.

Yet even as Anneline and I came to question its veracity as a matter of fact, the story of "English Mary" still says much about the past. Most critically, it shows how women's memories were not forgotten but preserved through different channels, even as they were edited to conform to prescriptive racial and patriarchal norms. Revisiting these stories with new critical lenses reveals these processes of editing, not necessarily to lead us back to an original truth, but to see the creative meaning-making at work in their retelling. The archival records leave me skeptical that Angamma and Narainsamy traveled and lost their parents onboard the same boat. But the knowledge I garnered from the archives, which present a different view of how Angamma lost her first family, deepens my appreciation of her struggle to forge a new family. Glimpses of this can be found in the archives and memories, but they emerge most powerfully when we collage them together.

## Whose Roots?

While certain aspects of these processes of forgetting and recovery are particular to Indian-South Africans, they have unfolded against the backdrop of a global effort to re-examine histories of indenture. This experience links them with descendants in Mauritius, Fiji, the Caribbean, and India itself. This process has opened new space for reflecting on gendered experiences of indenture, with previously suppressed histories of single women migrants being addressed and even celebrated. Several influential books have spurred this process, including Gaiutra Bahadur's *Coolie Woman*, which recounts the history of her great-grandmother who traveled from India to British Guiana alone and pregnant, and Amitav Ghosh's novel *Sea of Poppies*, in which the widow Deeti falls in love with a lower-caste man, with whom she runs away and becomes an indentured migrant to escape her in-laws' wrath.[80]

However, these books are only the most well-known of a wave of projects exploring indentured women's histories. Digital forums have encouraged a wider embrace of these pasts, inspiring descendants like Kaliani Lyle. Lyle grew up in South Africa but now lives in Scotland, where she served as the CEO of the Scottish Refugee Council, an experience that made her reflect anew on her ancestors' migrations. Along with her cousin and niece, Kaliani created a blog to tell the story of her grandmother, Rajwantia, who later became known as Janaki Chetty. Rajwantia traveled from Uttar Pradesh to Natal alone with her three-year-old son as an indentured laborer. She returned to India after her contract ended, only to return to South Africa as the wife of R. B. Chetty, an Indian Tamil merchant from Mauritius. As Kaliani explained to me: "My sense is that we are just at the start of exploring our history and that women's stories were until recently untold because they did not feature in our imaginings of indenture. But the context has changed. We are now celebrating the bravery and courage of people, both men and women, who travelled across the Indian Ocean to work as indentured labourers in SA." For Kaliani, revisiting her grandmother's past is about understanding her history and actively shaping her present as a migrant herself. It also inspires her work as an activist for highly vulnerable refugee populations, among whom she sees echoes of her grandmother's past. She explained, "Sure, I am interested in my background, but I think it's also about starting a conversation in Scotland about migration."[81] Such creative acts of retelling are deeply characteristic of *jahaji* roots.

My experience tracing Angamma through archival records and family roots projects reinforces my conviction that historians have a role to play in these creative retellings. But historians enter complex fields of memory in which families and communities also struggle to engage the past in ways that respect their forebearers and meet their own need to excavate buried traumas. The UDW students vividly captured just how wrenching these struggles can become. One student recounted how his grandfather, after repeated inquiries about his past, shouted at the family to "shut up." The family believed that the grandfather's silence was rooted in shame because he had left behind his widowed mother and sister in India without a man to provide for them.[82] To probe such stories can feel deeply troubling, but silencing the past also perpetuates shaming and robs future generations of the opportunity to reframe the past in light of shifting perspectives. While an older relative might be ashamed that he was unable to live up to patriarchal norms, his children and grandchildren might see this shame differently—as the product of oppressive economic systems that fractured households. In the ensuing conversation, the older relative might also re-evaluate a personal story—a process that could promote healing.

Such negotiations are also not just between the living. Tracing names and numbers through the archives, I sometimes felt like I was chasing after ghosts. I came to associate this feeling with encountering a glimmer of a past that had subsequently been suppressed. As noted in the introduction, Avery Gordon in her book *Ghostly Matters* evocatively describes such presences as "that which makes its mark by being there and not there at the same time."[83] I was not alone in feeling haunted by these absent-presences amongst the records of indenture. For example, one of the UDW student in her paper thanked her relations "who had managed to persuade the family ghosts to produce documents that were of direct relevance to my grandfather."[84] In attending to such ghosts, we acknowledge that they too have a stake in whether history remains buried or unearthed.

Attending to such varied claims on the past, both from the living and dead, reveals the shortcomings of approaching history through an ethics oriented towards ownership and individual rights. As I have encountered again and again, families' understanding of their history is deeply intertwined with the intergenerational transfer and loss of property. Yet treating history itself as a form of property governed by individualistic ownership is deeply problematic. As inheritance cases show, even partitioning control over material assets can be extremely difficult. Deciding who owns memories is even more difficult.

This is one reason why, early in my work on the book, I decided that I needed to look beyond inheritances of property as my central focus, branching out to look at heirlooms and stories as alternative afterlives. Looking beyond disputes over property, often involving land, (while by no means abandoning them) also helped me to think about roots in ways that resisted the imaginary of the nation-state, with its bounded territories and regimes of individual ownership. Studying indenture underlines the fluidity of roots—of families ripped apart, transported across oceans, and sewn back together in new soil, only to be unearthed and re-rooted again. Thinking about mobile roots that move through but are not bound to the land, whether perennial roots that must be divided or mangrove roots that reach from salt water into the air, opened other possibilities for thinking about how we might care for the past without claiming ownership over it. Parents' pasts are also their children's and grandchildren's inheritance; nor can ownership over family pasts be limited to blood relations or to a particular nation. The process of narrating these histories must also embrace a fluid approach to who might make use of this past, an openness which invites creative retellings across generations.

At their best, archives are custodians of widening personal pasts into public resources and thus have a role to play in preserving diasporic histories in ways that allow these fluid processes of retelling. Doing so, however, requires surrendering control over how documents might be used in the future to construct alternative pasts. Albie Sachs, a freedom fighter and former judge who served on the first Constitutional Court of South Africa, movingly described this process in a lecture recounting how he discovered records of his torture by the security police:

> the hidden archivists, maybe not even seen by anybody, getting these materials together, organizing them and making sure that they are not going to be destroyed by nature, copying them, conserving them, is doing something very beautiful in terms of our history, something very precious. It's linking up the generations. It's doing something intensely humane. The connections between our ancestors, and we speak a lot about our ancestors in South Africa in different ways: we become the ancestors of others through these material traces and remains . . . they are doing it, not as we used to think, to guard certainty; they are doing it to protect uncertainty because who knows how the future might use those documents.[85]

Working in this spirit, the scholars and archivists who contributed to the Gandhi-Luthuli Documentation Centre have made the records of indenture as widely accessible as possible. However, as I was in the process of completing the book, I noticed certain materials being removed from its website. The openness of collections in South Africa was essential to my ability to navigate back-and-forth between archival documents and memories preserved within families, and it saddens me to think that future scholars and families might not have the same access.

In contrast in Mauritius, which received the largest number of Indian indentured laborers, use of the Ships List and other indentured records is more tightly controlled. In general, the records are not open to "members of the public" due to concerns about "the physical fragility of these documents and the sensitive and confidential/personal information contained therein." Unofficially, researchers who have worked in the archive report that the restrictions were put in place due to fears that people might use the records to "expose" the caste background of the descendants of indentured laborers.[86] Under the policies, descendants can request information upon providing "proof of lineage," through documents such as birth and death certificates and notary deeds. Researchers apply for access by submitting evidence of their academic credentials and research topics. If they wish to include biodata for an individual immigrant, however, including their name or immigrant number (the equivalent of the Ships List numbers in South Africa), they must show that they have authorization from at least one descendant.[87]

While I respect the concerns that motivate these policies, I am uncomfortable with how they elevate consent and legal lineage as core principles for governing archival access. I have found that many families were already intimidated by archives and assumed that, as non-academics, they would struggle to access them. Entry requirements that mandate extensive paperwork, including the very documents that families may hope to find in archives, can further discourage roots researchers from using archives. These requirements also elevate forms of kinship that are recognized by the state, while marginalizing alternative understandings of family. Thinking back to Angamma's story, I wonder about who comforted her during the lonely years after she lost her sisters (or mother and sister) in the plantation fire. Family lore spoke of a White couple taking pity on the orphaned child, educating her, and arranging her marriage. Like so much of the story of "English Mary," I imagine that this memory was produced through repeated erasures and edits. Yet, it nonetheless suggests that for the indentured, kinship cultivated beyond relations of blood and law was often crucial to their survival. To govern access to the history of indenture according to a narrow construction of kinship does a disservice to the very pasts that these archives are entrusted with preserving.

I also believe that there are more effective ways to empower groups, including the descendants of indentured laborers, to shape how the past is narrated that move beyond the reductive logics of ownership and consent. This is crucial because these logics were so critical to producing indenture itself. British architects of Asian indenture used contractual consent as the core ideological defense against critics who accused them of perpetuating slavery in a new guise. Historians have argued over whether migrants understood the documents they were signing, but even when they did so knowingly, the mere act of signing, or applying their thumbprint, did little to give them greater agency. The procedure of signing a contract did not enable migrants to negotiate for shorter terms of indenture, better wages, or more humane conditions. Similarly, simply asking researchers to provide documentation of permission to publish a name does little to promote an ongoing conversation between researchers and descendants about how the past should be interpreted. I would prefer to see archives encourage researchers to broadly engage with relevant communities in ways that empower groups that have historically been denied access to research resources and platforms for disseminating their interpretation of the past. As part of applying for access, researchers might be asked to provide information about how they plan to engage with relevant communities, such as conducting oral histories, providing volunteer genealogical searches, giving public talks to non-academic audiences, or contributing to free digital archives. Asking researchers to regularly reflect on public engagement as part of the process of gaining archival access would open new conversations about the responsibilities that come with accessing archival records.

By de-emphasizing the need to trace descendants, this approach would also avoid incentivizing researchers to fall back on anonymization to avoid the bureaucratic hurdle of proving consent to use actual names. While historians pursuing particular case studies may be able to trace descendants, it is often extremely labor-intensive and practically impossible to do in large numbers. I eventually located Angamma's descendants, but I could have never completed this project if I also needed to locate descendants for all of her shipmates. I could have anonymized these other subjects, but I worry that anonymization denies the individuality and agency of the indentured. It was the glimmers of the stories of particular individuals that made me feel the presence of ghosts in the archives. As Black feminist scholars have long insisted, and Black Lives Matter protesters seared in our conscience, to "say her name" is often the first step to recognizing a person's humanity. Descendants of indentured laborers also often complain about histories that leave their ancestors "nameless and faceless."[88] I thus question a conception of "ethical" research that requires anonymizing the very migrants who were most violently dehumanized by empire.[89] Yet, I also recognize that the names I encounter in colonial records, and reproduce in the book, were often mangled Anglicizations of the names by which migrants knew themselves. However, it was often these very colonial inventions that became standardized as family names passed from generation to generation, bequeathing to many whose roots passed through indenture their unique surnames, another inheritance of empire which they have remade.

My attachment to using names, even in the absence of consent from descendants, also stems from my experience researching the next chapter. It involves a seaman, or possibly seamen, whose family I have not been able to connect with. In the absence of conversations with the family, I trace this history through photographs that have circulated through archives and public exhibits in Britain and the United States. While I try to imagine what it might mean to reassemble these photographs into a family album, I hold onto the hope that one day I might learn how the family itself has preserved this past. By publishing my version of their ancestor's story, alongside the names accompanying it in archives, I hope the family might one day happen upon my work while Googling their family history. I am sure this would be the beginning of a very interesting conversation.

# 4

# Seamen's Album

FIGURE 4.1. Album compilation of images by author. Top left image courtesy of The National Archives (UK). Top right image courtesy of University Archives, Rare Book & Manuscript Library, Columbia University Libraries. Bottom left image courtesy of the Redpath Chautauqua Collection, University of Iowa. Bottom right image courtesy of the New York U.S. District and Circuit Court Naturalization Records.

IN THE previous chapter, I considered how families remember, forget, and recover diasporic pasts and how working alongside historians might enrich how we both engage with the past. With the further passage of time, the stories of some migrants became unraveled from their family's histories and woven instead into public retellings of diasporic pasts. Here, they encountered new pressures—to provide historical roots to defend a precarious pluralism in the present, as I saw in Thamboosamy's case, or to document histories of racial discrimination and struggles for justice that could inspire more just futures. While drawing on diasporic narratives, these stories were often narrated in national frames—for example, of migrants from India who defended their status as British subjects and later citizens.

This is where I first encountered Jan Mohamed's photograph (see Figure 4.2). His image was part of the promotional materials for an audio play, which the National Archives in the United Kingdom (TNA) produced in the spring of 2021 in collaboration with playwright Hassan Abdulrazzak and Tamasha, a British-South-Asian theatrical company. The play was part of a heritage project, "Once British Always British." The phrase was from a petition written on behalf of a seaman who was facing deportation from Britain, and the project used its theme to engage the public around histories of discrimination against Indian and Yemeni seamen during the interwar years. Jan Mohamed's photograph served as the visual backdrop to the fictional oral narratives voiced by actors from Tamasha and inspired a graphic novel workshop for young author-illustrators. In the picture, Jan Mohamed sports a suitcoat decorated with war medals he earned during World War I while serving in the British Merchant Navy, the title King George V gave to Britain's civilian ships and crews, formerly known as the Mercantile Service, in recognition of their wartime service. The line between fact and fiction blurred as I viewed Jan's photograph and listened to the audio play. When the play's narrator described her grandmother pulling a photo of her father, a former seaman, out of an old biscuit tin, I imagined it as Jan's photograph, a handsome young man, dapperly dressed.[1]

In real life, the photograph of Jan Mahomed was preserved not in a biscuit tin but in a TNA file, part of a collection related to the elaborate surveillance measures implemented under the Coloured Alien Seamen's Order of 1925. Under the order, Asian, African, Caribbean, and Arab seamen, many of whom were British colonial subjects, had to prove their nationality to remain and work in Britain—an arduous process at a time when birth certificates and passports were still rare. The order was introduced against the backdrop of rising hostility in Britain towards non-White seamen, who had provided vital service and suffered high casualty rates during the war but who were scapegoated for rising unemployment among White working-class Britons during the interwar period.[2] The order also reflected anxieties about seamen, who circulated across continents, as possible agents for the spread of global radicalism. Such fears were not wholly ill-founded; seamen's unions were increasingly active in organizing non-White sailors in campaigns that combined leftist, anti-racist, and anti-colonial politics.[3] In an attempt to regulate their mobility,

FIGURE 4.2. Photograph of Jan Mohamed as incorporated into the project "Once British Always British." https://blog.nationalarchives.gov.uk/once-british-always-british-stories-of-indian-and-yemeni-sailors-in-britain-in-the-1920s, accessed December 4, 2024. Original in TNA, HO 45/13750. Courtesy of The National Archives (UK).

the 1925 order mandated that colonial seamen carry documentation with identifying photographs. In its use of photographic identification to limit and surveil Asian migrants, the order was a relatively late addition to a bevy of similar procedures adopted by the United States, Canada, Australia, and South Africa starting in the late nineteenth century. As noted in the introduction, one of the earliest uses of ID photography was to document indentured laborers in Mauritius beginning in the 1860s, a chronology that closely dovetailed with the contemporary development of forensic photography. But even as I knew the repressive context in which Jan's photograph was produced, I could also easily imagine it as an intimate keepsake, pasted into a family album or stashed away in a biscuit tin. Caroline Adams, who led a well-known oral-history project documenting the lives of British-Asian seamen, recounted that she frequently encountered such photographs in the early 1980s while traveling in rural Sylhet, a region of northeastern Bangladesh known for its seafarers. She would meet "old men, sitting with their hookahs, draped in shawls against the winter chill," who "from tin trunks . . . would produce creased and dog-eared 'continuous discharge certificates' identifying them (by a thumbprint or the faded photograph of a bright-eyed boy) and detailing their journeys around the world."[4] In transforming images of surveillance into mementos of their mobile pasts, the former seamen present another example of the creative acts of collage that I observed repeatedly when working with migrant families.

What circuits had Jan Mahomed's photograph traveled before being incorporated into the heritage project "Once British Always British"? Unlike the previous four chapters, I could not connect with Jan Mahomed's descendants, although I would eventually discover a trail of photographs he left in multiple archives. I did locate a tree on Ancestry.com that suggested a possible link, but my attempts to connect with this family have not been successful. This chapter, therefore, delves more deeply into what it might mean to engage in "family" history as a method without necessarily working alongside families themselves. It asks how centering visual and material analysis shifts our understanding of the traces that migrants left through their engagements with state authorities and how historians can assemble alternative albums out of archives originally designed to surveil mobile lives.

In Jan Mahomed's case, the alternative album I assemble across the following pages tells a story that is even more remarkable than the one captured in the fictional audio play. It suggests not only that he snuck into Britain as a stowaway but also that he may have had a prior life as a lecturer and businessman in middle America, where he went by the name John.[5] As Jan/John traveled between India, the United States, and Britain, he presented himself before the camera in different guises: dressed up in exaggerated Eastern garb in advertisements for his lectures on the "Wit and Wisdom of the Far East"; on the steps of a Detroit courthouse defending his US citizenship while refusing to remove his turban; and wearing a suitcoat and war medals in the ID photographs that he submitted while claiming British nationality.

A newspaper clipping was the first clue that set me along this transatlantic trail of photographs. British immigration officers seized the clipping from Jan when he tried to enter Britain from Antwerp in April 1925. The newspaper story described a US District Court case in which the citizenship of John Ali Mohamed was canceled because he was deemed not White and, therefore, ineligible for naturalization. On questioning by the officers about the story, Jan "admitted" that he was the same man. The possibility that Jan also went by John and had an American past led me to an article in the South Asian American Digital Archives (SAADA). In the US, John built a life for himself, converting to Christianity, marrying a White woman, and buying a house in a leafy suburb outside Detroit. He made a middle-class living, lecturing rural American audiences about the "East" while also building a career in marketing and import-export. In 1925, this all came crashing down when the US government brought a denaturalization case against him, eventually revoking his US citizenship on the grounds that he had falsely presented himself as White. In a landmark but ultimately unsuccessful case, John attempted to defend his citizenship by arguing that his ancestral links to the Prophet meant that he should qualify as White. A few months after losing his legal battle in Detroit, Jan appeared in the archives in Britain, now fighting to be recognized as a British subject based on his Indian origin and hoping to find employment on British ships.

I could not help but note the irony that the same man celebrated in a British heritage exhibit titled "Once British Always British" was also claimed as part of a project to archive the South-Asian-American experience. As a patriotic seaman, Jan was a powerful illustration of the struggle for British Indian belonging. As an entrepreneur fighting to retain his US citizenship, he embodied the promise and perils of the American dream. But how do we make sense of Jan/John, who converted to Christianity but claimed genealogical links to the Prophet and who alternatively presented himself as White, Hindustani, Arab, and British? Looking again at the photographs of Jan/John, he seemed to shift identities as easily as he traded an embroidered Punjabi vest for a suitcoat, or a turban for a trio of war medals.

As the previous chapters suggest, I have repeatedly encountered such mobile habits and fluid approaches to national, religious, and ethnic identities while working with diasporic families. Fitting lives and legacies marked by repeated movement into models of diaspora that treat them like de-territorialized nations entails selective cropping. Looking outside such frames reveals that many families have moved multiple times, confusing ties to a singular homeland and host land. Their relationship with identarian communities was also often more fluid, as evidenced by Jan/John's shifting racial and religious affiliations. They, therefore, complicate an approach that associates being diasporic with a bounded community, even in this case, a de-territorialized one organized around an ethno-religious identity.

The cropped versions of Jan/John's story that TNA and SAADA offer suggest that methodological nationalism shapes both scholarship on diaspora and heritage programs that engage the broader public. For these projects, many of which seek to exhibit a more inclusive version of national pasts, hyphenated identities like "British-Indian" or "South Asian-American" can offer a logical frame to link past struggles to present inclusivity. In this context, more mobile identities and the possibility that people assumed and cast aside categories like British and American can seem to undermine narratives of inclusive belonging. In this vein, the project "Once British Always British" did not mention Jan's potential connections to the US denaturalization case, nor was this aspect of his file noted when his photograph was incorporated into an TNA exhibit on life in Britain during the 1920s.[6] I found this exclusion significant given that it struck me as one of the most exciting aspects of his story—precisely the sort of plot twist that lent itself toward dramatization in an audio play.

To imagine a different way of visualizing Jan/John's mobile past, I have looked to family albums, literally printing out physical copies of the photographs I found in the archives and moving them around my desk and bulletin board as I wrote. Since the introduction of photography in the nineteenth century, families have gravitated towards photographs to maintain ties across geographical distances and generations. Migrants sent photographs home, and many families I worked with had preserved old pictures, even when they were forced to part with other material inheritances during harried migrations. I locate the essence of "albuming" as viewing photographs in combination rather than as singular framed images, and as assemblages, defined not just by their visuality but also their materiality. Albums are thus not just compilations of visual sources—they are collages of images, words, and material objects, that tell stories with photographs but also paper, glue, and thread. In contrast to the single images of John and Jan that were published as part of the TNA and SAADA's projects, I argue that we can learn more about diasporic lives and legacies through observing, and making, such multi-media visual and tactile albums. This includes viewing multiple photographs of John/Jan taken throughout their lives and photos of people in their orbit, including fellow seamen and family members. It also means attending to how these photos were assembled into official dossiers through cropping, pasting, piercing, and threading—as with the blue thread that ran through the image of Jan Mahomed that I first saw in the TNA's "Once British, Always British." Attending to these threads helps us to see how we might untangle them to weave new heirlooms.

Attending to the material manipulation of images empowers us to reassemble them into alternative albums that tell different narratives about mobile lives than those preserved in state documents. We learn about whom individuals identify with rather than just who they identify as. While inspired by my observations of the creative work that families do when they recover photographs from archives, this emphasis on attending to the materiality, movement, and assemblage of photographs is of broader relevance to historians working with images, including those who do not think of their research as related directly to families. In this chapter, by stepping away from family history as practiced by descendants, I reflect on how families' engagements with the past might inspire historians more broadly.

## "Love . . . Cannot be Measured by a Hat": The American Lives and Afterlives of John Mohammad Ali

According to the petition he submitted to naturalize as a US citizen, John arrived in New York on June 2, 1900, on board the St. Paul, which had departed from Southampton, England, a week earlier.[7] John listed his last foreign residence as Lahore and his date of birth as January 10, 1875.[8] To audiences at his lectures on the cultures of the East, he also told of his childhood in the princely state of Kapurthala, where his father was the personal physician to the Maharaja. Some were familiar with the Maharaja of Kapurthala because he had attracted much attention as a visitor to the World's Fair in Chicago in 1893. Most Americans would have been less familiar with the other credentials John cited. These included studying at the prestigious Muhammadan Anglo-Oriental College at Aligarh, the alma mater of many of India's leading Muslim political figures, and the Forman Christian College in Lahore.[9] John disappeared from the official gaze for the next several years, but he resurfaced on January 10, 1906, when he married Emily F. Lambourne in Detroit.[10] Emily was also a migrant, having traveled from Putney, England, with her parents in 1895 at age fourteen. Her father, Thomas, had worked as a postman but listed his profession as "bootmaker" when arriving in New York.[11] The family traveled onward to Michigan, where John and Emily met.

At the time of their marriage, John listed his profession as a tea merchant. Four years later, when the census was taken in 1910, the couple was renting a single-family house at 318 Holbrook Avenue in Detroit. They had two young children, one-year-old John Jr. and three-year-old Ayesha. Emily's widowed mother and one of her cousins were also living with the family, suggesting that John had a close relationship with his in-laws. The home was in a solidly working-class neighborhood. The men supported their families through skilled, blue-collar jobs: machinist, carpenter, printer, iron worker, chauffeur. The women, including Emily, were mostly housewives. Most had been born in Michigan, but there was a smattering of immigrants from Canada, England, Austria, and Germany. Most (including John) gave their race as White, although a Black family lived a few blocks down the road.[12] In describing himself as White, John reflected prevailing ambiguity concerning how Indians fit into

American conceptions of race, which fluctuated between biological, phenotypical, cultural, and geographical constructions of difference. Some typologies of racial origin treated Indians as Caucasian, drawing on theories that ancient Aryans migrated into the Indian Subcontinent. Yet, as more Indians migrated to America, conceptions of Whiteness progressively shifted to exclude them.

In 1910, John was still making his living selling tea, but perhaps with two young children to support, he felt added financial pressure and saw an opportunity in the Redpath Chautauqua. Redpath Chautauqua staged phenomenally successful traveling tent shows across rural America, which brought together music, educational lectures, and Christian preaching. Theodore Roosevelt purportedly described Chautauqua tent shows like the one in which John featured as "the most American thing in America."[13] They were meant to be both entertaining and enlightening, and John excelled at this balance. As the promotional pamphlet for his lectures touted: "No Anglo-Saxon ever saw India as Mr. Ali has seen it, and few natives of India have had the command of English and the understanding of American audiences which enable Mr. Ali to present the results of his observations in such instructive and delightful form." During the summers of 1910 and 1911 (and possibly more), John traveled with the tent show across Michigan, Wisconsin, Minnesota, and Missouri, lecturing on topics such as "Wit and Wisdom of the Far East" and "India's Millions." His audiences were captivated by his scholarly presence, noting that "his English would have done credit to an American or English professor."[14] They were also moved by his account of giving up "his wealth[,] his worldly honors and native land in order to become a follower of Christ."[15]

The promotional materials for John's lectures feature portraits in profile and full body (see Figure 4.3). In both, he is wearing a white turban, but his dress otherwise captures alternatives modes of asserting his authority. In the first, he wears a three-piece suit and cravat while staring dreamily off into the distance. His picture is framed on either side by images of a minaret and domed building, which appear to have been taken from postcard images of the Taj Mahal. In a second photograph in the pamphlet, John is pictured in whole body, but this time clothed in a tunic, silk jacket, vest with heavy embroidery, and upturned slippers, described as "the native costume of Punjab." Facing the camera, he wore a thin pair of wire spectacles, evoking the professorial qualities praised in the text. The overall style is a mélange of photorealism with fantastical visualizations of Orientalism. The photos also have a vaguely art-deco aesthetic, lending them a sense of placelessness—an imagined "East" that could as easily be conjured under a tent in rural Wisconsin as in Lahore. Within the pages of the same pamphlet, we see John shape-shifting, presenting a kaleidoscope of familiarity and difference to the American audiences he hoped to attract.

FIGURE 4.3. Photographs of John Ali (here as Mohammad Ali) published in a pamphlet advertising the Redpath Chautauqua, circa 1910–1911. Identifier MSC0150, Redpath Chautauqua Collection, University of Iowa. Also available via the South Asian American Digital Archives, https://www.saada.org/item/20111208-527, accessed December 4, 2024.

By 1918, the Ali family, perhaps with funds John earned on the lecture circuit, had purchased a new home at 201 Ravine Road in Birmingham, a leafy suburb north of Detroit. The family's new neighbors were solidly middle-class managers and salesmen. Some had servants living in their homes. There was a large park just a few blocks away.[16] John also initiated the paperwork to naturalize as a US citizen. He made a sworn statement "to renounce forever all allegiance and fidelity to any foreign prince, potentate, state, or sovereignty, and particularly to George V, King of Great Britain and Ireland of whom I am now a subject."[17] The same year, he registered for the US draft. Perhaps for the first time, he confronted a new category of racial identification, checking a box labeled "Oriental," whereas he had previously described himself as White.[18] John, using the name Jan, would later tell British officials that he served on a British merchant vessel that was torpedoed in 1918.[19] Is it possible that John renounced King and country, only to feel called back to them later the same year? It is one of several mysteries emerging from reading the American and British archival trails together. If so, by 1921, John had settled back in the suburbs of Detroit and officially became a US citizen that summer.[20] He must have felt he had truly made a life in America. Yet, with anti-Asian xenophobia on the rise in the United States, perhaps he also feared for his family's future.

If John was worried, it was with good reason. In the late 1910s and early 1920s, Indians were subject to increasing surveillance and racism. From the late 1800s, several thousand Indians, overwhelmingly men, began to put down roots in the United States.[21] Some of the earliest were seamen, often Muslim Bengalis, who jumped ship in US ports and made new lives amongst the racially diverse populations of cities like New York and Detroit, sometimes marrying African American and Latin American women. Many supported themselves as peddlers, selling tea, silk, and spices.[22] John would have likely known men from these communities through his commercial activities. Given the little information we have about how he arrived in the United States and his possible subsequent maritime career, perhaps he traveled similar routes. At the same time, Indian laborers, mostly Sikhs from the Punjab, were arriving to work on railways, lumber mills, mines, and farms along the west coast of Canada and the United States. The number of Indians, however, remained quite limited. Consequently, during the early years of migration, they did not face the same systematic racism and legal bars as Chinese migrants targeted under the Chinese Exclusion Act of 1882.

In the 1910s, however, anti-Indian racism intensified against the backdrop of global anxieties about transnational networks of anti-colonial, communist, and anarchist revolutionaries. In 1907, anti-Asian riots in West Coast cities from Vancouver to San Francisco terrorized the Indian community. During the next decade, opposition to Indian migration mounted, spurred in part by British complaints that Indian students and activists in the US and Canada were organizing global, anti-colonial networks. Expatriate Indians in the United States and Canada founded the Ghadar Party in 1913, which sought to overthrow British rule. The party quickly spawned branches amongst diasporic Indian communities in Panama, Manila, and Shanghai, among other places.[23] M. N. Roy, who founded the Indian Communist Party in 1925, immersed himself in Marx's works in the reading room of the New York Public Library.[24] Fearing that the United States was providing a safe harbor for anti-colonial and communist organizers, Britain pressured the US government to ramp up surveillance and limit the mobility of Indians. Responding to rising fears about Asian migration, the US Congress passed the Immigration Act of 1917. The act created an "Asiatic barred zone" stretching from the Middle East to Southeast Asia. Individuals from these regions were forbidden from entering the US, with some exceptions for religious figures, professionals, merchants, students, and tourists. Even more worrisome for John, the Supreme Court ruled in the case *United States* v. *Bhagat Singh Thind* (1923) that Indians were not White and, therefore, ineligible for citizenship.

In 1790, Congress had set out in the Naturalization Act that citizens must be "free white [men] . . . of good character," setting in place a racial bar that was not removed until 1952. In the wake of the Civil War, Congress extended eligibility for citizenship in 1870 to "persons of African descent." However, the Chinese Exclusion Act of 1882 made clear that persons of Chinese origin were still excluded from citizenship. The status of other groups remained ambiguous, and during the first two decades of the twentieth century, federal courts litigated the meaning of "Whiteness" in relationship to naturalization cases involving Japanese, Indians, Afghans, Arabs, Armenians, Turks, Syrians, and Iranians. In several cases involving Indians, the courts identified them as Caucasian and, therefore, eligible for citizenship. In 1922, the Supreme Court ruled in *Takao Ozawa* v. *United States* that Japanese people were ineligible for citizenship. The decision argued that while having visibly white skin, the Japanese were not of the Caucasian race. According to this logic, Indians might have been eligible for citizenship as Caucasians. Ultimately, however, the courts would prove that White privilege relied on mixed and contradictory logics, vacillating between categories of color and race in service of excluding anyone whom the White majority perceived as alien.

Thus, just one year after *Takao Ozawa* v. *US*, when the Supreme Court considered the citizenship application of the Indian American Bhagat Singh Thind, they deployed a different logic of exclusion. Thind was a US veteran and, like John, a lecturer on Indian spirituality. In contrast to its earlier decision in the *Ozawa* case, the court set aside contemporary "scientific" categories of racial origin, like Caucasian. Instead, it appealed to what it described as a "common" understanding of Whiteness rooted in supposedly outwardly apparent differences. In an originalist approach, the court insisted that appeals to Caucasian origin according to certain contemporary "scientific authorities" were irrelevant given that these ideas were unknown at the time of drafting the Naturalization Act in 1790. "Free white persons" were, therefore, to be defined according to "the understanding of the common man." According to the decision, Hindus were not White because:

> It is a matter of familiar observation and knowledge that the physical group characteristics of the Hindus render them readily distinguishable from the various groups of persons in this country commonly recognized as white. The children of English, French, German, Italian, Scandinavian, and other European parentage quickly merge into the mass of our population and lose

> the distinctive hallmarks of their European origin. On the other hand, it cannot be doubted that the children born in this country of Hindu parents would retain indefinitely the clear evidence of their ancestry. It is very far from our thought to suggest the slightest question of racial superiority or inferiority. What we suggest is merely racial difference, and it is of such character and extent that the great body of our people instinctively recognize it and reject the thought of assimilation.[25]

As several scholars have pointed out, the language of the decision, including terms such as "familiar observation," "clear evidence," and "assimilation," encouraged an understanding of race that was premised on the ability to present as White to an Anglo-American audience visually. In this context, people threatened with exclusion from citizenship turned to photography to prove that they were recognizably White, for example, submitting images of their families set against bourgeois domestic backdrops and dressed in American military and police uniforms. Inverting the pattern I have observed elsewhere of family transforming official photos into family heirlooms, images from family albums were repurposed into state documents, subject to legal logics.[26] Even as they contested their exclusion, in adopting this strategy, Indian Americans reinforced visual regimes that equated respectability and Whiteness as qualities that could be outwardly performed. As we will see, John also attempted to use photographs to advance his citizenship.

In the wake of the decision, the Department of Justice pursued an unprecedented mass "denaturalization" campaign against Indian American citizens. The Department instructed district attorneys across the country to initiate cancellation proceedings against Indians who had become US citizens. They argued that Indian Americans had misrepresented their racial identity in their initial applications, retroactively applying the logic of the decision. Up to that point, denaturalization cases were virtually unheard of—the only precedents involved a man convicted of pimping prostitutes in Montana, and six German Americans denaturalized for disloyalty during World War I.[27] In contrast, no such campaign was initiated against US citizens of Japanese origin, despite the ruling in the *Ozawa* case just a year before *Thind*. The startling decision to pursue cases against Indian Americans was likely due to the influence of British diplomats. The British feared that Indians would use the US as a base to build transnational anti-colonial networks while using their status as US citizens to shield themselves from extradition and trial in British India.[28] In fact, one of the first denaturalization cases involved Taraknath Das, who served two years in Leavenworth Penitentiary in Kansas on charges of conspiring with the Germans to foment an uprising against the British.[29] While technically denaturalization did not lead to expulsion, some Indian Americans who lost their citizenship also lost their property under state laws that excluded "aliens" from owning land. In a particularly tragic case, Vaishno Das Bagai committed suicide after being forced to surrender the prosperous retail business he had built in San Francisco. Unable to return to India because he was deemed a political radical for his participation in the Ghadar Party, Bagai left behind a suicide note in which he lamented: "Is life worth living in a gilded cage?"[30]

John soon found himself caught in this cage, with the government initiating proceedings for the cancellation of his citizenship in late June 1923.[31] In October, Emily was at home when the deputy US marshal visited the Ali home to inform them of the case against John.[32] It must have been a terrifying experience, but at least the Alis were informed about the proceedings and could prepare a defense. In some cases, the government canceled Indian Americans' citizenship without the subjects even knowing about the proceedings.[33] John was better positioned to fight back. He hired a Detroit-based lawyer, Humphreys Springstun, and enlisted as an expert witness Professor H. H. Bartlett, a prominent botanist and anthropologist based at the University of Michigan. In organizing his defense, he possibly drew on connections to other Indians facing similar proceedings. John may have known Sakharam Ganesh Pandit, who had represented Thind before the Supreme Court, and would subsequently battle and ultimately win legal challenges to his own citizenship status. Like John, Pandit also lectured for the Redpath Chautauqua, and the two men might have met.[34] Interestingly, Pandit also enlisted the assistance of prominent academics in his case, suggesting parallels in their legal strategies.

In other ways, however, John took a different approach than Pandit, whose defense emphasized his elite class status as a lawyer and property owner. In contrast, John appealed to his Arabian and Muslim genealogy as evidence of his Whiteness, given that the legal status of people from western Asia remained unsettled. Like Indians, courts had naturalized some Syrians and Armenians on the grounds that they were Caucasian. The *Thind* decision did not directly address their status, leading John and his lawyers to see a possible opening. In federal court, he explained that his family could trace their genealogy thirty-one generations back to the Prophet Muhammad, and thus, the decision in the *Thind* case, which referred to the racial status of high-caste Hindus, did not apply to him. John further explained that his family migrated to the Punjab about three hundred years earlier, but "the stock was kept pure" through exclusive marriages to cousins. He claimed that his marriage to Emily was the first one to occur outside the family line.[35] He explained that he had only described himself as Hindu in his citizenship application to conform to the colloquial use of the term in the United States, where it was often loosely used to refer to all Indians. As John put it: "I am Hindoostanee," not a "Hindoo." As he further elaborated, had Columbus not confused the Americas with India, "we would be called Indians, our rightful title." Professor Bartlett further contextualized John's claims for the American court, noting "the excessive care with which these people preserve records of their genealogy."[36] At the same time, he anticipated that the court might not place much value on John's own account of his origins and racial status and therefore turned to "scientific" methods. In court, he measured John's head and reported that it "possessed the elongated characteristics of the Arabian sheik," which he explained meant "elder or chief." Bartlett informed the court that John was, therefore, a "white man." The government's lawyers immediately protested, asking if he was using the term "in a scientific sense or in the popular sense," a question Bartlett left unanswered. Perhaps feeling that his defense was faltering, John emphasized he was battling for citizenship "for patriotic reasons" and to aid his two American-born children, Ayesha and John Jr.[37]

In John's legal performance, which shifted between claiming identities based on ties to Arabia, Hindustan, and White America, we see in rapid motion the fluidity of diasporic identities constructed under constraint. But, even as he navigated from one identity to another, John returned again and again to family to create throughlines. Thus, despite converting to Christianity, he appealed to genealogy to maintain ongoing ties to a Muslim past rooted both in the land of Arabia and the person of the Prophet, even as he noted how his new family rooted him in the American landscape. The importance John gave to family in performing varied identities suggests how logics of kinship, which are based on building bonds between insiders and outsiders, can take on particular importance in diasporic settings, which require adapting to continually shifting surroundings.

John focused on optics to make this case to broader publics within and beyond the courtroom. At the time of his trial, John listed his employer as Mathew Advertising Agency, suggesting he had some professional experience with marketing. He certainly seems to have approached the trial as an opportunity to sway public opinion in his favor. The trial itself, as reported in the press, took on a semi-theatrical quality through the public performance of pseudo-scientific racism and references to Orientalist tropes. The *Los Angeles Times*, which likely reported on the story due to the large number of Indian Americans in California, described the sight of "a University of Michigan professor measuring a swarty [*sic*] turbaned head" as a "spectacle." It also made note of the "story of the petitioner's love for his British wife," tapping into contemporary fascination with border-crossing romances.[38] At the time, references to John's status as a "sheik" would immediately elicit associations with E. M. Hull's *The Sheik* (1919). The novel revolved around the abduction and repeated rape of the White protagonist by an Arab *sheik*, with whom she subsequently falls in love. Widely popular on both sides of the Atlantic, when an

American edition of the novel was released in 1921, it went into fifty printings in that year alone. Its cinematic adaptation the same year was a blockbuster hit that propelled Rudolph Valentino to international stardom.[39] In claiming an ancestral tie to the Prophet Muhammad, John would have more accurately described himself as a *sayyid*, but he likely understood the term *sheik* would be more evocative for an American audience.

John may have imagined that he could gain sympathy with American audiences by both emphasizing his romantic status as "A Sheik in Distress," as the *Detroit Free Press* described him, and a patriotic American. In imagining this balance, he may have drawn on his successful stint as a lecturer for the Redpath Chautauqua. In this setting, his ability to "self-Orientalize" had been crucial to his popularity as a speaker, even as he also forged emotive bonds with his audience by relating his experiences as a Christian convert. John sought a similar balance when he explained in court that although he wore a turban, "His love for the country of his adoption . . . can't be measured by a hat."[40] He also reiterated this performance outside the courthouse, posing for cameras in a suit and turban while boasting to the crowd: "I wish I had an American flag in my hand, and I wish somebody would try to take it away from me."[41] While his audience does not seem to have obliged, or the scene was not captured on camera, the following photograph was published in *The Detroit Free Press* (see Figure 4.4).

Yet, while John's performance may have been successful at garnering public attention and perhaps even sympathy, it had little impact on the court. Six months after hearing the case, on August 3, 1925, Judge Arthur J. Tuttle, who had ironically also signed John's original citizenship papers, filed a terse written opinion rejecting John's defense. He declared: "I am unable to follow the argument thus sought to be made. No reason has been suggested, and I can discover none, why the mere fact that the early ancestors of the defendant came to India from Arabia, where they had been called Arabians, renders the defendant a white person. His skin is certainly not white, but unmistakably dark, like that of the other members of his race."[42] While John constructed a multilayered visual performance of his ties to India, Islam, and the United States, the judge flattened his image into a static, monochronic image of a person of dark complexion.

It is unclear what happened next to John. His citizenship was canceled in September 1925. He then disappeared from the US archives until June 1927, when his lawyer filed a motion of appeal. The paperwork, however, unlike that filed in the original case, was signed only by John's lawyer, not himself, suggesting that he may not have been present in Detroit. The motion to appeal pointed to the recent decision of the US Circuit Court of Appeals for the Ninth District in California, which ruled in favor of Sakharam Ganesh Pandit's

FIGURE 4.4. Photograph of John Mohammed Ali, printed during his denaturalization appeal in *The Detroit Free Press*, February 3, 1925, available via subscription at newspaper.com, accessed October 20, 2022.

appeal against denaturalization in November 1926. Both the trial judge and the appellate judge in Pandit's case deemed that his citizenship could not be reversed *ex post facto* based on subsequent case law. Did John hear about the positive outcome in Pandit's case via their mutual connection to the Redpath Chautauqua? Unfortunately for John, Judge Tuttle disagreed with the opinion of the Ninth Circuit, which was not binding on the courts in Michigan.[43]

Where was John, as his case was being reconsidered? Losing his case did not necessarily mean that he had to leave the US, although, after *Thind*, many Indians did.[44] Some of the most prominent targets of the US government denaturalization campaign, however, remained in the United States and battled to make lives for themselves and their children and secure citizenship rights. They did so in the face of significant obstacles. Without US passports, many found themselves stranded in the United States, fearing they would be refused re-entry if they left. Many felt effectively stateless since it was unclear whether the British would grant them British Indian passports after renouncing their loyalty to the King and Empire when applying for US citizenship.[45] The American wives of men who were denaturalized also risked losing their citizenship due to laws that mandated that a woman lost her US citizenship on marriage to a foreigner. These laws had been amended in cases of women marrying Europeans in 1922 but still applied to American women who married men who were "ineligible for citizenship."[46] The material, as well as emotional, costs to these Indian American families were substantial; many were forced to sell or give up their homes, farms, and shops in states where "aliens ineligible for citizenship" were prohibited from owning or leasing land.[47] Michigan did not have such a law, but John may have feared it would adopt one. By the 1930 census, John, Emily, and their son had left their home in the Detroit suburbs and were living in an apartment on Sanford Avenue in Brooklyn, New York.[48] As the following section discusses, John may have traveled even further as he sought to reassemble his life.

## "Jan or John (or Ali John) Mohamed": The British Lives and Afterlives of Jan Mohamed

In the spring, following his trial before the US District Court, but before a final decision in his case, John, or a man claiming to be John, disembarked at the British port of Harwich on April 1, 1925. He was carrying a "Continuous Certificate of Discharge" (CCD) with the name Jan Mohamed and the number 976527. A CCD served as a sailor's record of employment, listing the various ships on which he had worked, and it served in lieu of a passport for international travel.[49] Jan's paperwork indicated that he had traveled to Britain from Antwerp, where he had earlier arrived as a sailor aboard a Finnish ship. His CCD also listed his service on British ships during World War I. While awaiting a final decision regarding his citizenship, did John try his luck in Britain? Had John perhaps purchased papers from a British Indian seaman in Detroit named Jan?[50] Even with his CCD, he was refused permission to enter Britain on the grounds that he had no proof of British nationality.

Having left behind one regime of xenophobic legal persecution in the United States, Jan/John found himself ensnarled in another on the other side of the Atlantic. In the aftermath of World War I, Britain became an increasingly hostile place for seamen of Asian, African, Arab, and Caribbean origin. These men powered the ships that knit together the British Empire—delivering the mail, transporting troops and bureaucrats, moving raw materials to factories, and transferring manufactured goods to consumers. In 1914, on the eve of World War I, one in five men working on British ships were *lascars*, a term associated with sailors from British India, although sometimes used more broadly to describe all Asian maritime labor. By 1937, the proportion had risen to one in three.[51] Most of these men were employed under "Asiatic articles," a legally codified system of racially differentiated wages and working conditions. They received one-third to one-fifth the wages of "British" seamen.[52] They also performed the most grueling work on board. Many shoveled coals into the fires that produced the steady supply of steam needed to keep the ships moving, working in temperatures reaching 60 degrees Celsius or 140 degrees Fahrenheit.[53]

During World War I, these seamen, even those serving on non-military vessels, were effectively conscripted into combat positions, drowned at sea after their ships were torpedoed, and captured as POWs. Yet, in the postwar period, those who tried to remain in Britain faced unprecedented hostility. Small numbers of Asian, African, and Arab seamen had "jumped ship" and settled in Britain from at least the eighteenth century, if not earlier. Their numbers began to grow during the early decades of the twentieth century. Many who put down roots married White, working-class women. Their interracial families became embedded in close-knit, racially diverse communities concentrated in dockside neighborhoods in London, Liverpool, Cardiff, and South Shields. Some of the men were able to shift from working under Asiatic to British contracts, gaining better wages and working conditions. Increasingly, British authorities viewed these men with suspicion, as a mobile population with links to anti-colonial and labor activism. Shipping companies also resented paying more to employ them as British seamen. As demobilization and a postwar economic slump led to a shrinking labor market, elite politicians and business owners encouraged White working-class men to blame "coloured" seamen for taking "their" jobs, deflecting broader criticism of the postwar order.[54] These forces combusted in a series of riots in 1919, during which White crowds attacked African, Caribbean, Asian, and Arab seamen and their families in British port cities.[55] The mobs were galvanized by racist propaganda blending fear of colonial men as economic competitors with sexual panic about them "stealing" the wives of White men.[56] A small number of American GIs were also among the rioters, testifying to the global circulation of anti-Black and anti-Asian racism during the interwar period.[57]

The 1919 riots gave the government and shipping companies the justification they needed to introduce draconian limits on colonial seamen's ability to live and work in Britain, refusing them entry into the country and deporting those already in residence. Technically, the target of these policies were "alien" seamen, not men who held British nationality as subjects of British colonies like India. However, officials increasingly demanded that colonial subjects prove their nationality by providing birth certificates or passports, documents that few seamen carried. These policies were consolidated in the Coloured Alien Seamen's Order of 1925, under which non-White seamen had to establish their British nationality or register as aliens. The registration process required being fingerprinted and photographed. Seamen were then required to carry their alien registration booklets or face detention. The act encouraged local police to view all non-White subjects as aliens, subject to intensified surveillance and vulnerable to intimidation and abuse. In 1932, the government further codified this system of racially differentiated documentation by implementing a "Certificate of Nationality and Identity" exclusively for coloured seamen, who would no longer be granted British passports, even if they possessed proof of their nationality. The authorities were also instructed to seize the passports of coloured seamen, if they had them, and to provide them instead with the new certificates. Henceforth, only colonial subjects who were literate and of "established position" would be eligible for passports.[58]

Seamen and their families fought these new requirements. Many resisted carrying papers that marked them as racial others. One Indian sailor, when asked to surrender his passport to authorities at the Barry docks in exchange for a certificate, responded that "he did not require the certificate if the issue of it signified that he would be registered and that he preferred to retain the passport."[59] Other men accepted the certificates but used them to facilitate wider mobilities than those intended by British officials. The Chief Commissioner of Aden complained that a group of Somali men, who were no longer working as seamen, arrived in Aden with certificates of nationality that they intended to use to travel to Colombo.[60] Some were even more creative in repurposing the documentary regime to their own ends. When a district official in the Northwest Frontier Provinces in India visited the mother and brother of Gul Hassan Shah to verify his photograph and place of birth as part of an investigation into his nationality, his relatives conveyed their own message asking him to return. Perhaps seeing his photograph elicited a renewed longing for his presence, while the questions from colonial authorities made them fear for his well-being in Britain. The police reported that they passed along the message from his family to Gul Hassan when he picked up his certificate of nationality. It is unclear whether he heeded their bidding to return home.[61] In these examples, seamen linked the official circuits they traveled as maritime laborers with alternative routes. These included building side businesses selling foreign goods, sometimes derisively labeled as peddling. Others used official circuits to cultivate their own affective networks, as was the case of Shah's family, who turned an official photographic inquiry into a sort of family reunion.

When Jan arrived in Harwich, he entered this documentary tussle.[62] The immigration authorities at the port would not accept his CCD booklet as proof of British nationality, although it detailed his prior employment on British ships during World War I and listed his birthplace as India. Instead, they interrogated him about his past. In response, Jan told them that after serving on British ships during the war, he was sent back to India as a passenger but was able to gain employment on another ship in Bombay in late 1919. He disembarked in New York and traveled onward to Detroit. He indicated that he had worked as a laborer there before traveling back to India in 1923. These were the years that John and his family were moving into a new home in the suburbs of Detroit. In 1923, when Jan indicated he traveled back to India, the US government instigated denaturalization proceedings against John. Fearful that these legal proceedings might leave him stateless and landlocked in middle America, could John have acquired a second identity as Jan as he contemplated his escape from what his fellow target called "a gilded cage"? We know that many other seamen were creatively altering paperwork to resist efforts to curtail their mobility in the context of global restrictions on their migration and employment.

Immigration officials also searched Jan's belongings and found a newspaper clipping about John's US denaturalization case. On further questioning, Jan admitted that he was the article's subject. However, other information he provided to British authorities, including his date of birth, listed as 1897, did not match John's US paperwork, in which his birthdate was 1875. But Jan/John must have been scared, and he had many reasons to obscure the details of his life story. Perhaps John needed to claim to be younger to secure maritime employment. Or could Jan, whom immigration officials described as speaking in broken English, have misunderstood officials when they asked him about the newspaper article? John's English was immaculate. But perhaps, scared by his legal ordeal in the United States and seeking a new identity as a British Indian seaman, he felt the need to disguise his background.

Beyond such factual discrepancies, much about Jan's case was the subject of dispute between the officials who reviewed his papers. The first immigration officer who wrote up his case stated that since Jan/John had naturalized as a US citizen, he "would thus have lost his British nationality," effectively becoming stateless after his US citizenship was canceled. Another official reading over the file later disagreed. He noted in the margin: "No . . . his holding an American cert. wd. not operate in these circ. to deprive him of his British nationality." This official was nonetheless no more sympathetic to Jan's case, noting instead: "The main point here is that he has no proof of his birth in Punjab." On returning to Antwerp, Jan found at least one British official who found this requirement absurd. The British consul there wrote to the Foreign Office that "there is generally no reasonable doubt" that he was a native of India and, therefore, a British national. The Foreign Office, however, was unsympathetic, noting that Jan had last worked on British ships in 1919, and thus "had little claim to return to this country"—introducing an entirely novel definition of nationality based on recent employment. Yet, while bearing little basis in law, it was an accurate statement of fact. When Asian, African, and Arab men were needed by Britain to man its ships during the war, they were welcomed as British subjects. When their labor was no longer needed, their claims to be British were cast in doubt.

But Jan firmly believed he had a claim to British nationality, a right he would stake on foot. After traveling back to Britain on board a ship that landed in Leith, near Edinburgh, he walked the country's length over the next few months and applied for a passport in London in June 1925. As part of his application, he submitted the striking portrait photograph that, nearly a century later, would grace the promotional materials for the project "Once British Always British." His suitcoat was perhaps a little large, and the scarf in his pocket a bit rumpled, but he looked polished with his war medals prominently displayed along with a lapel pin bearing the insignia of the Merchant Navy. Jan, like John, believed in the importance of optics, and thus the power of photography, in claiming belonging.

The back of the photograph, however, told a different story (see Figure 4.5). It was endorsed by the superintendent of the Strangers' Home for Asiatics, which provided free or inexpensive housing to destitute seamen. Jan tried to look his best for the camera but was in a precarious position. The need for an endorsement, which read "To certify that Jan Mahomed is the original of the Photo," reflected official anxiety about their ability to identify Asian subjects visually. British officials routinely complained that they could not distinguish one Asian from another. Some seamen turned this confusion to their own purposes by trading out photographs in their paperwork. The tension between the two sides of the photograph—the front in which Jan performed imperial patriotism and the back in which he was bureaucratically marked as a subject of suspicion—suggests both the potential and constraints of ID photography as a mode of subaltern self-fashioning.

Jan received a diminished document in return a month after submitting his application. Instead of a passport, he was granted only a "Document of Identity Issued to an Applicant Who Cannot Obtain a National Passport" (see Figure 4.6). In the box that should have specified his nationality, the words "is registered as" are struck out, and instead, the words "claims to be a native of Punjab, India" are written in a hand that almost screams out its suspicion. The document could only be used for a single journey, and authorities granted it to Jan on the understanding that he would travel to America to collect his belongings and $250 deposited in a US bank account. The photograph attached to the certificate was also cropped to remove his war medals, even as

FIGURE 4.5. Photograph of Jan Mohamed from file TNA, HO 45/13750, as provided by their imaging services. The back reads, "To certify that Jan Mahomed is the original of this photo" and is signed and stamped by the superintendent of the Strangers' Home for Asiatics. Courtesy of The National Archives (UK).

the official form provided ample space to include them. For the official preparing the document, the visual evidence provided by Jan's medals seems to have been too starkly at odds with the suspicion that the certificate registered concerning his claims to British belonging. Here again, we see how the photograph operated as a site of struggle between subaltern and official regimes of presentation, not just at its moment of capture but repeatedly as it circulated across different paperwork regimes. Seeing the photograph cropped and pasted onto the "Document of Identity" also made me think about an album in which photographs are trimmed and glued into place. While purporting to offer scientific modes of accurately identifying subjects, bureaucratic files are also albums, selectively manipulating images to narrate certain stories while suppressing others.

These dynamics of self-fashioning and selective editing illustrate how photography played a crucial role as a site of contestation within racialized regimes of documentation in interwar Britain. Thousands of similar photographs from the 1920s and 1930s are preserved in archival records. In addition to the dozens preserved in files related to "alien" registration, I have located a much more

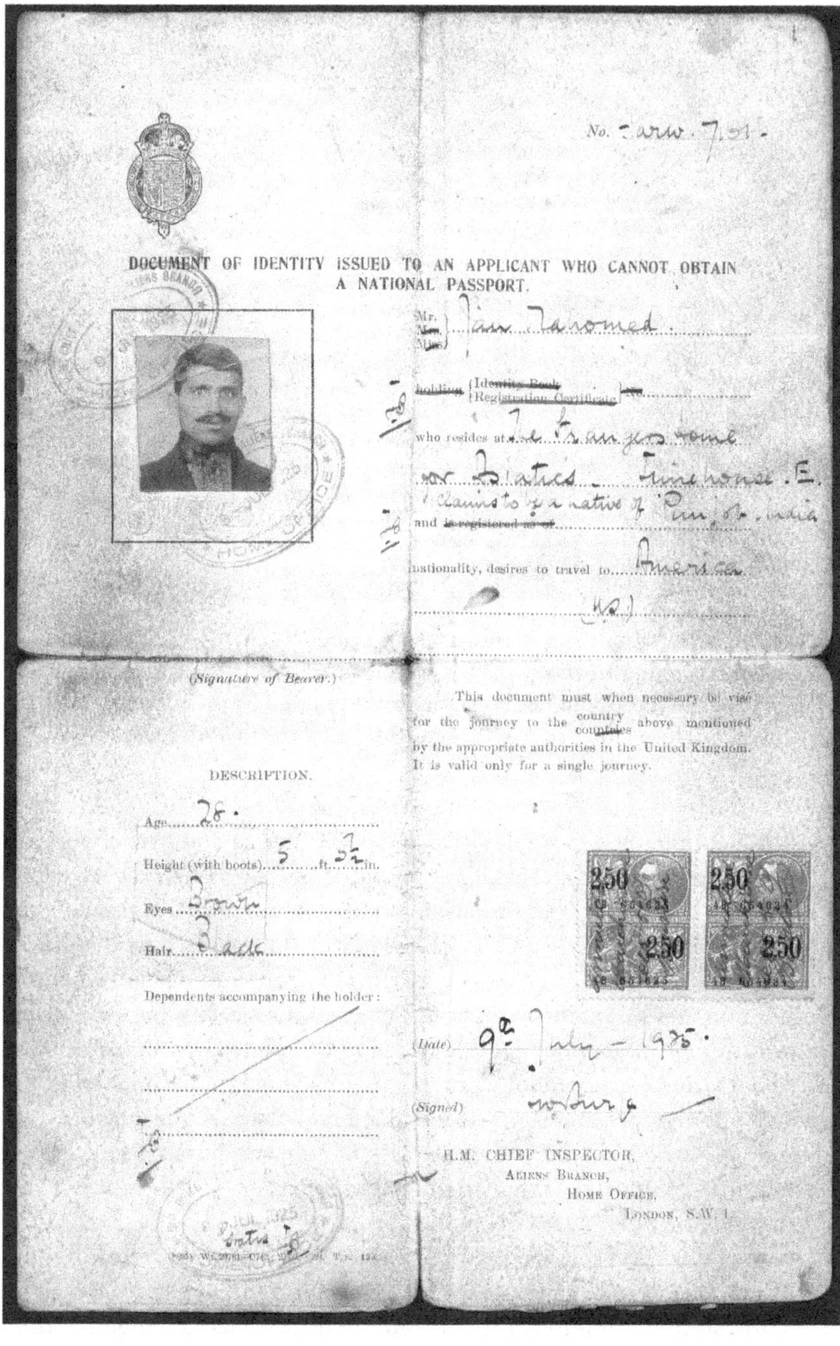

No.

DOCUMENT OF IDENTITY ISSUED TO AN APPLICANT WHO CANNOT OBTAIN A NATIONAL PASSPORT.

Mr. Jan Mahomed.

holding ~~Identity Book~~ ~~Registration Certificate~~ No. ........

who resides at ........

and ~~is registered as of~~ ........

nationality, desires to travel to ........ America

(Signature of Bearer.)

This document must when necessary be visé for the journey to the country ~~countries~~ above mentioned by the appropriate authorities in the United Kingdom. It is valid only for a single journey.

DESCRIPTION.

Age ........ 28.

Height (with boots) ........ 5 ft. 5½ in.

Eyes ........ Brown

Hair ........ Black

Dependents accompanying the holder:

(Date) 9th July – 1925.

(Signed)

H.M. CHIEF INSPECTOR,
ALIENS BRANCH,
HOME OFFICE,
LONDON, S.W. 1.

FIGURE 4.6. Jan Mohamed's "Document of Identity Issued to an Applicant Who Cannot Obtain a National Passport," July 9, 1925, TNA, HO 45/13750. Courtesy of The National Archives (UK).

extensive collection known as the "Seamen's Pouches," which includes identity documents for over a half million men who served in the British Merchant Navy. The Merchant Navy consisted of the civilian crews that manned commercial vessels but which the government closely regulated and could commandeer during wartime for military needs.[63] Run through the joint efforts of the government and British shipping companies, the Central Registry of Seamen compiled biographical files on men serving in the Merchant Navy, stored in so-called "pouches" between 1913 and 1972. These records were subsequently transferred to the British National Archives, where they remain today. Each pouch, which is, in fact, a brown paper envelope, contains employment records for a particular seaman, including the paperwork he filed for a Continuous Certificate of Discharge, listing the various ships on which he served and, in some cases, details about next of kin, medical discharges, etc. Many of the pouches also contain multiple ID photographs of the same man during his maritime career. Unlike records related to the 1925 order, the collection includes pouches for seamen of all backgrounds. From 1918 to 1921, all British merchant seamen were required to carry identity documents with passport-style photographs to comply with the heightened security measures implemented at many international ports during the war to prevent the entry of migrants from enemy territories. This requirement, however, was discarded after the war. It was reintroduced during World War II when all British seamen were required to carry British Seamen's Identity Cards (BSIC), which included both photographs and fingerprints, to again comply with wartime security measures.[64] In contrast, photographs in the pouches from the 1920s and 1930s are almost entirely of so-called "coloured" seamen, testifying to how war-time surveillance was repurposed during peacetime to monitor populations that were cast as internal invaders.

The presence of photographs from the interwar period in a seaman's pouch marked him as a racial other. As visual artifacts, however, they convey a different story. The photographs from this period are stylistically distinctive from those taken when they became a universal requirement for all seamen, regardless of race, during and after World War II. The earlier photographs of "coloured" seamen from the 1920s and 1930s are studio portraits taken by professional photographers. A few even include the name of a local photography studio stamped on the reverse side. In visiting portrait studios, seamen entered spaces of bourgeois consumption, in which photographers made their living by producing images that were meant to flatter their customers. Studios had specialized lighting and backdrops and often kept stores of clothing and props so subjects could borrow aspirational accessories. The portraits of seamen bear the hallmarks of the genre, including professional lighting and, in some cases, signs that the negatives were touched up, including to lighten skin tone and

FIGURE 4.7. Mohamed Ali's elegant portrait photograph from 1935 alongside other photographs in his "seamen's pouch." As he aged, the style also shifted from studio portraiture to a more forensic style. File TNA, BT/372/50/13, R124667. Courtesy of The National Archives (UK).

remove blemishes, a common practice among studio photographers. In comparison, the photographs from the 1940s onwards are often poorly lit, and the men show little extra care in their appearance. Many also hold placards with their CCD numbers. Ironically, the transition of ID photographs from tools of racialized surveillance to a universal requirement corresponded with their aesthetic degradation. Seamen, including those identified as White, complained that the inclusion of registration numbers in later photographs made them look like a "convicted criminal."[65] From the 1940s onwards, photographs were also likely taken within the physical space of the Mercantile Marine Offices in ports like Liverpool and South Shields, as the government encouraged local offices to make arrangements with a photographer to take photographs onsite.[66]

For seamen marked as "coloured," the contrast in the style of the photographs across different time periods is stark enough that the same men can appear dramatically different, accentuating the visual impact of physical aging. For example, Mohamed Ali, another seaman, appears elegantly posed in the portrait photograph he submitted in 1935, his face set off against a light scarf wrapped around his throat (see Figure 4.7). One can imagine him sending a copy of the photograph home to his family in Sylhet or giving a copy to Esther, the woman he would later marry.[67] The later photographs in his pouch appear crude and invasive in comparison to the elegance of the 1935 image. In the photograph attached to his BSIC from 1943, his face is poorly lit, and he looks uncomfortable, even slightly stunned. The inclusion of the registration number made it unlikely that he would repurpose the photograph, which was fit only to appear alongside other invasive biometrics. These include fingerprints

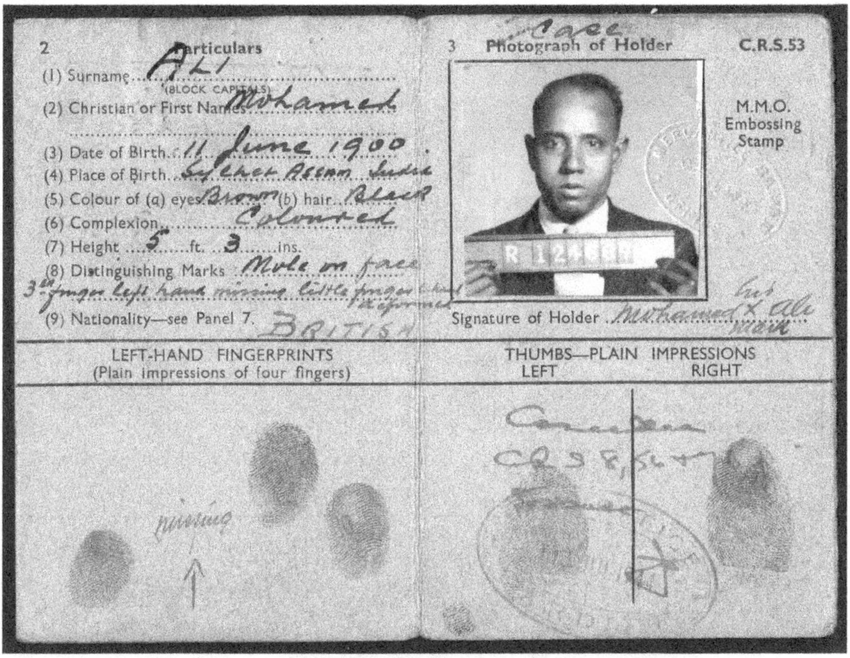
2 Particulars
(1) Surname ALI (BLOCK CAPITALS)
(2) Christian or First Name Mohamed
(3) Date of Birth 11 June 1900
(4) Place of Birth Sylhet Assam India
(5) Colour of (a) eyes Brown (b) hair Black
(6) Complexion Coloured
(7) Height 5 ft. 3 ins.
(8) Distinguishing Marks Mole on face
(9) Nationality—see Panel 7. BRITISH
3 Photograph of Holder C.R.S.53
M.M.O. Embossing Stamp
Signature of Holder Mohamed X Ali
LEFT-HAND FINGERPRINTS (Plain impressions of four fingers)
THUMBS—PLAIN IMPRESSIONS LEFT RIGHT
missing

FIGURE 4.8. British Seamen's Identity Card of Mohamed Ali, 1943. TNA, BT/372/50/13, R124667. Courtesy of The National Archives (UK).

revealing a missing finger, also visible in the hand gripping the placard with his registration number (see Figure 4.8).[68]

While the men in the earlier and later photographs mostly wore suits, they appeared dressed up for the camera in the former: many sported lapel pins, pocket handkerchiefs, ties, and scarves. Maung Aung Sein, who listed his birthplace as Burma, wore a delicate butterfly pin in a photograph attached to the forms he submitted in 1938. He was fond of bodily adornments; his identity card also mentioned elaborate "vernacular" tattoos on his back (see Figure 4.9).[69] Suna Meah, from Sylhet, wore a flower pin (see Figure 4.10).[70] In these sartorial choices, one can sense an element of playful resistance even as the men subjected themselves to a racist system of documentation.

Most men in the photographs appear bareheaded, likely having been instructed to remove their hats or turbans, a common requirement in identity photographs. But in October 1939, after working together on the ship "City of Rangoon," Mohamed Mottassim and Surcoom Ali submitted pictures to the Merchant Marine Office wearing similar, or perhaps the same, fez (see Figure 4.11).[71] Did Mohamed admire Surcoom, who was ten years his elder and literate enough to sign his name and ask to borrow his headgear for his

FIGURE 4. 9. ID Photographs of Maung Aung Sein. TNA, BT 372/127/51, R 166967. Courtesy of The National Archives (UK).

FIGURE 4.10. ID Photographs of Suna Meah. TNA, BT 372/148/100, R175479. Courtesy of The National Archives (UK).

FIGURE 4.11. ID Photographs of Mohamed Mottassim and Surcoom Ali. TNA, BT 372/200/144, R195170 and BT 372/200/145, R195171. Courtesy of The National Archives (UK).

photograph? Did they associate the fez with sentiments of Muslim cosmopolitanism and anti-colonial nationalism, aware of its links to Pan-Islamist movements? John would have found common ground with their use of headgear to assert their own claims to belonging.

Perhaps my personal favorite of the photographs is an image taken of Pakianadar Swaminathan, a seaman from Colombo (see Figure 4.12). His date of birth is listed as 1903, but in the picture he submitted in 1938, he looked more like a teenager than a man in his mid-thirties. His wide-collared shirt, whose fabric has a slight sheen, falls exaggeratedly atop his suit coat. A patterned scarf, perhaps a batik design, peaks out beneath. His outfit at once anticipates a disco vibe from decades later while also suggesting the flamboyant sailors of Herman Melville's novels. Nestled in his pouch, alongside two additional photographs from decades later, one cannot help but feel the vicissitudes of time whiz past.[72]

The poignancy of the men's dress in these photographs becomes even more apparent compared to other contemporary images of lascars. Among the most widely circulated images of Asian seamen in the late nineteenth and early twentieth century, which continue to be reproduced in historical exhibits today, are the brochures and postcards sold by British cruise lines.[73] In many of these photographs, Asian seamen wore uniforms explicitly designed to appeal to Orientalist stereotypes. For example, in a photograph taken on the

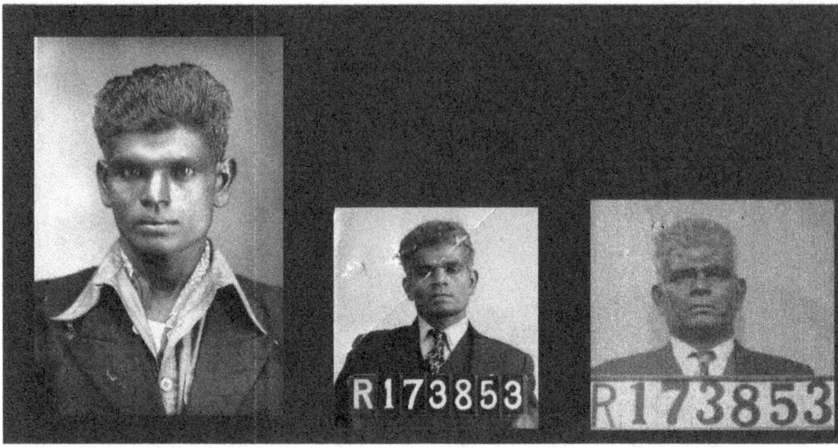


FIGURE 4.12. ID Photographs of Pakianadar Swaminathan. TNA, BT 372/144/121, R173853. Courtesy of The National Archives (UK).

Peninsular & Oriental (hereafter P&O) cruise liner, the Viceroy of India, three seamen appeared in generically Asian-style tunics decorated with embroidery (see Figure 4.13). The men also sported turbans and appeared without shoes. Their white pants, while distinctly impractical for performing heavy labor beneath the decks of a coal-fueled steamship, set off the bright hues of other aspects of the uniform. Such clothing was crucial to packaging the onboard experience for European passengers as a taste of the Orient. As a souvenir sketchbook produced for the P&O company explained: "Life on board a P&O steamer is one continual round of pictures kaleidoscopic in its quick change and variety of color." Of particular importance to the creation of this visual tableaux was "the Lascar crew, who appear in pure white, with red turbans bound around their curious straw hats, and with sashes around their waists. Backed by the deep blue of the Mediterranean Sea, they present a picture not easily forgotten." The colorful clothing made the sailors appear "striking and picturesque objects"—offered up for European consumption.[74]

Seamen's choice to don suitcoats and ties for their portrait photographs when registering under the 1925 order must, therefore, be read as an act of resistance against their being visually Orientalized in other contexts. By wearing suits marked as European, they asserted their Britishness. In an interesting inversion of the Indian office worker who traded his suit for the comfort of a *kurta pajama* (a tunic and loose pants) at home, seamen who cast aside racialized uniforms to don the cosmopolitan garb of the urban dandy claimed leisured selves outside regimes of maritime discipline.

FIGURE 4.13. Three lascars standing behind the wheel on board one of the motor tenders of the Peninsular & Oriental Steam Navigation Company cruise ship Viceroy of India (1929). Image ID P85233. Courtesy © National Maritime Museum, Greenwich, London.

The men's stylistic choices should also be understood in the larger context of their experience shifting clothing, at times by choice and at other times due to compulsion, as they moved between different spaces. In their writings and oral histories, seamen repeatedly noted the importance of changing clothing as a marker of critical life transitions. Nawab Ali, a leading member of the British-Bangladeshi community in East London, who helped to found one of

Britain's first halal butchers, repeatedly commented on clothing in an interview he contributed to a local history project in the 1980s.[75] Orphaned as a young boy, Nawab Ali ran away from home to join a riverboat crew. He reminded the older men of their sons and grandsons at home, and they affectionately dressed him up in "white short pants." During World War II, Nawab Ali secured employment on a steamship sailing from India to Britain, jumped ship in Cardiff, and eventually secured work at a seamen's coffee shop in London run by an Egyptian. Nawab Ali described how when the police visited the coffee shop and began checking the customers' paperwork, they let him go because "I always used to look too smart, suit and tie and all."[76] Nawab Ali's pride in looking "too smart" captured the seamen's distinctive swagger. Did Jan/John also engage in such strategic costume changes—trading the Orientalized garb he wore while lecturing on the Chautauqua circuit for an exaggerated display of loyalty by pinning his war medals to his suit coat? Did he remove the turban he wore to court in the US by choice or because he was required to do so by the photographer?

There is a hint of the dandy to the swagger with which coloured seamen dressed up for their ID photos, and as suggested earlier, some of the seamen recall sailors from Melville's novels. In *Billy Budd*, for example, the African "Handsome Sailor" appears with "a gay silk handkerchief thrown loose about the neck danced upon the displayed ebony of his chest; in his ears were big hoops of gold, and a Scotch Highland bonnet with a tartan band set off his shapely head."[77] Yet, unlike Melville's characters, actual Asian seamen in interwar Britain were more constrained in mixing Western attire with elements of South Asian or Muslim clothing. In most of the ID photographs in the Seamen's pouches, there is no sign of non-Western attire. When such articles appear, they were circumspect—a hint, for example, of a silk batik scarf peaking from beneath a Western collar. While donning suits may have been an act of resistance to the Orientalist trope of the *lascar*, seamen marked as coloured adopted these outfits under tremendous pressure to prove their status as British nationals. For many, this context precluded more creative mixing of clothing genres although a few like Mohamed Mottassim and Surcoom Ali did assert more hybrid visual aesthetics. Yet despite these constraints, the seamen still exhibited elements of the dandy's spirit of "opposition and revolt," as Baudelaire famously celebrated the aesthetic.[78] By adopting an exaggerated emphasis on dress, more associated with women and the outmoded fashions of the aristocracy, dandies underlined the artifice of prescriptive identities of gender and class. In their careful curation of Western attire, Asian seamen did the same work for nationality and race—flaunting their ability to shapeshift from the prescribed role of Asian lascars at sea to British seamen ashore. The very concept of identity, or the idea that we might understand some more

FIGURE 4.14. Comparison of photographs of John taken in Detroit in 1925 and the passport photograph that Jan submitted in London the same year. Right image courtesy of The National Archives (UK).

profound truth about these men through labeling them Indian, Asian, or British, unravels in the face of what instead appear to be continually shifting performances. Hyphenated labels may accurately capture the experience of diasporic communities that migrated once, for example, from India to Britain, and cultivated deeper attachments to a singular home and host land. However, they are ill-suited to describing the intensely mobile lives of seamen. They were the most diasporic of subjects, at least according to my framing of diaspora, defined by their mobility and facility with adapting to different contexts rather than their attachment to any particular place.

Was Jan/John such a mobile shapeshifter? If we line up the photograph from the Detroit newspaper in February 1925 and the one he submitted with his passport application in London in June 1925, they appear to be of a different man (see Figure 4.14). At the very least, John in Detroit appears much older than Jan in London. But could Jan have submitted a photograph of himself taken years earlier with his passport application? John largely disappears from the US archives after his citizenship was canceled. He briefly reappeared in the 1930 census, living with Emily in Queens and importing Indian products. Still, it is not clear whether he was physically present when the census taker dropped by or whether Emily provided that information. Could John/Jan have used employment on British ships to travel between the US and India while running an import/export business from New York?

On the other side of the Atlantic, Jan was certainly on the move. His CCD showed that he signed onto a ship in London in September 1925 and headed to New York. Did Jan/John find paid employment on a ship as a means of securing free passage to visit Emily? Only a few months later, however, Jan was again working on ships, disembarking in Hong Kong in January 1926. Jan then disappeared from the British archives for nearly four years, showing up again in September 1929 in Harwich, where he was refused leave to land, just as he had been in 1925. Again, Jan found a way back to Britain, this time landing at Poole in the south. From there, he made his way back to London, where he again applied for a British passport. This time, he told officials that he wanted to either travel to Belgium to sell silks or to India to visit his family, including providing the name of a wife in India. Did John/Jan have a family both in the US and India? If so, he was hardly unusual among seamen, many of whom had multiple partners.

Back in London in December 1929, Jan applied for a new CCD, and in January 1930, he received a new "Document of Identity," permitting him to travel to India (see Figure 4.15). Both documents included additional portrait photographs, although neither was as striking as the first that he submitted in 1925. Perhaps he was losing faith in the power of optics. A notation in his records from the Merchant Navy suggests that he then signed onto a ship in September 1931.[79] In December of 1931, *The Nottingham Evening Post* reported that one Jan Mahomed had been the victim of a theft by a homeless man who snatched his suitcase containing a number of scarves.[80] Instead of traveling to Belgium, was Jan working as a peddler in Britain? Could John, the importer of Indian products listed as residing in Queens in the US census in 1930, have also been Jan peddling silks in Britain in 1931? In asking such questions and contemplating the possibility that Jan was John, we trace alternative biographies from those recorded in official documentation, like the seamen's pouches, which reduce seamen to their maritime employment. Instead, we see glimmers of men who mixed work onboard ships with other pursuits, including transnational business ventures, and who strategically turned maritime employment into multiple circuits of mobility.

Jan/John's collective archival biography peters out in the 1940s but lacks a definitive ending. Jan's seamen's records, which include an additional undated photograph (see Figure 4.16), include a notation that he was "presumed killed" in October 1940 after his ship was torpedoed. However, someone named Jan Mahomed reappeared in the British archives in 1942, this time as a suspected

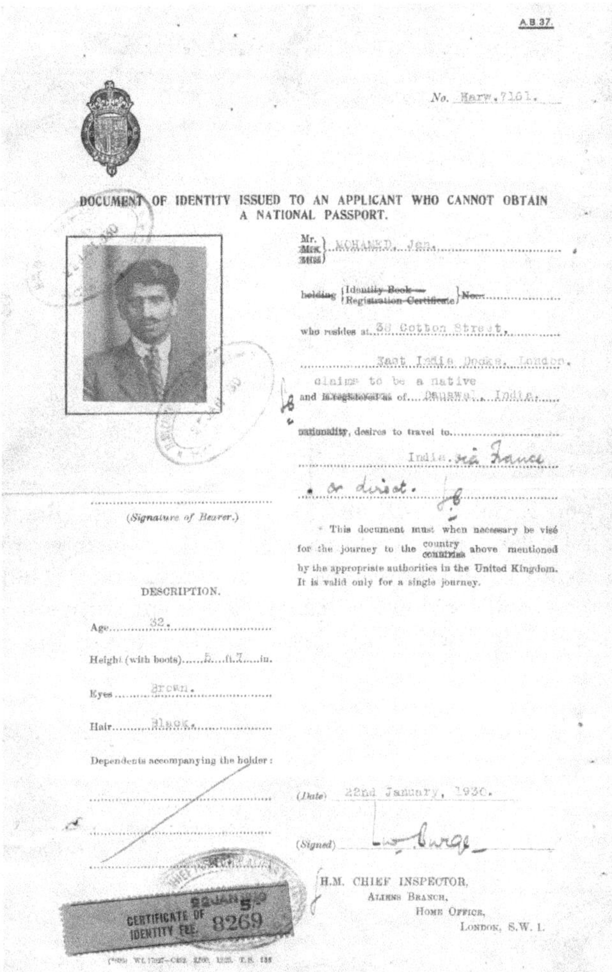
A.B.37.

No. Harw. 7161.

DOCUMENT OF IDENTITY ISSUED TO AN APPLICANT WHO CANNOT OBTAIN A NATIONAL PASSPORT.

Mr. MOHAMED, Jan.

holding Identity Book — Registration Certificate No.

who resides at 38 Cotton Street, East India Docks, London.

claims to be a native and is registered as of Dausawal, India.

nationality, desires to travel to India. via France or direct.

(Signature of Bearer.)

This document must when necessary be visé for the journey to the country above mentioned by the appropriate authorities in the United Kingdom. It is valid only for a single journey.

DESCRIPTION.

Age 32.

Height (with boots) 5 ft. 7 in.

Eyes Brown.

Hair Black.

Dependents accompanying the holder:

(Date) 22nd January, 1930.

(Signed)

H.M. CHIEF INSPECTOR, ALIENS BRANCH, HOME OFFICE, LONDON, S.W. 1.

CERTIFICATE OF IDENTITY FEE. 5/- 8269

FIGURE 4.15. Document of Identity issued to Jan in January 1930. TNA, HO 45/13750. Courtesy of The National Archives (UK).

political radical, making speeches in Hindustani and "broken English" at anticolonial rallies in Britain.[81] Could Jan have survived the torpedo attack, or was this a different man entirely?

Across the Atlantic, Emily submitted a form declaring her intention to naturalize in 1942, including a photograph, and received her US citizenship in 1944, still using the surname Ali (see Figure 4.17). In 1946, a local newspaper in Lewiston, Maine reported that John attracted considerable attention when he passed

FIGURE 4.16. Photograph of Jan from his seamen's CR2 record (Register of Seamen, Central Index, Numerical Series, 1921–1941), originally microfilmed by the National Archives (UK). Now available (with subscription) at https://search.findmypast.com/search-world-records/britain-merchant-seamen-1918-1941, searching with his discharge number 976527. Courtesy of The National Archives (UK).

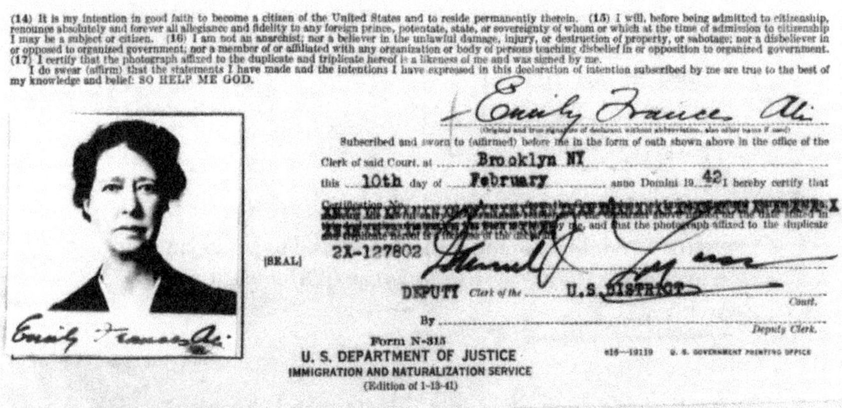

(14) It is my intention in good faith to become a citizen of the United States and to reside permanently therein. (15) I will, before being admitted to citizenship, renounce absolutely and forever all allegiance and fidelity to any foreign prince, potentate, state, or sovereignty of whom or which at the time of admission to citizenship I may be a subject or citizen. (16) I am not an anarchist; nor a believer in the unlawful damage, injury, or destruction of property, or sabotage; nor a disbeliever in or opposed to organized government; nor a member of or affiliated with any organization or body of persons teaching disbelief in or opposition to organized government. (17) I certify that the photograph affixed to the duplicate and triplicate hereof is a likeness of me and was signed by me.

I do swear (affirm) that the statements I have made and the intentions I have expressed in this declaration of intention subscribed by me are true to the best of my knowledge and belief: SO HELP ME GOD.

Emily Frances Ali
(Original and true signature of declarant, without abbreviation, also other name if used)

Subscribed and sworn to (affirmed) before me in the form of oath shown above in the office of the Clerk of said Court, at Brooklyn NY this 10th day of February anno Domini 1942 I hereby certify that ... and that the photograph affixed to the duplicate ...

[SEAL] 2X-127802

DEPUTY Clerk of the U.S. DISTRICT Court.

By ... Deputy Clerk.

Form N-315
U. S. DEPARTMENT OF JUSTICE
IMMIGRATION AND NATURALIZATION SERVICE
(Edition of 1-13-41)

16—10119 U. S. GOVERNMENT PRINTING OFFICE

FIGURE 4.17. Photograph of Emily Frances Ali from her Declaration of Intention to Naturalize, February 10, 1942. Original in the records of the New York, U.S. District and Circuit Court Naturalization Records, 1824–1991, now available at familysearch.org.

THE UNITED STATES OF AMERICA

DUPLICATE
TO BE FORWARDED TO
IMMIGRATION AND NATURALIZATION SERVICE

No. 6714270

CERTIFICATE OF NATURALIZATION

Petition No. 449795

Personal description of holder as of date of naturalization Age 72 years sex Male
complexion Dark color of eyes Black color of hair Grey height 5 feet 11 inches
weight 150 pounds visible distinctive marks Pock markson face
Marital status Married former nationality British
I certify that the description above given is true, and that the photograph affixed hereto is a likeness of me.

John Mohammad Ali Allison
(Complete and true signature of holder)

UNITED STATES OF AMERICA } SS:
EASTERN DISTRICT OF NEW YORK }
Be it known, that at a term of the District Court of The United States held pursuant to law at Brooklyn on August 5th 1947 the Court having found that JOHN MOHAMMAD ALI ALLISON then residing at 136-05 Sanford Avenue, Flushing, New York intends to reside permanently in the United States (when so required by the Naturalization Laws of the United States), had in all other respects complied with the applicable provisions of such naturalization laws, and was entitled to be admitted to citizenship, thereupon ordered that such person be and (s)he was admitted as a citizen of the United States of America.
In testimony whereof the seal of the court is hereunto affixed this 5th day of August in the year of our Lord nineteen hundred and forty-seven and of our Independence the one hundred and seventy-second

John M. Ali Allison

Seal

It is a violation of the U.S. Code (and punishable as such) to copy, print, photograph, or otherwise illegally use this certificate.

Perry T. B. Gilkes
Clerk of the U.S. District Court.
By Thomas MacPherson Deputy Clerk.

DEPARTMENT OF JUSTICE

FIGURE 4.18. Certificate of Naturalization for John Mohammad Ali Allison, August 5, 1947. From record search provided by US Citizenship and Immigration Services, Genealogy Program.

through town working as a jewelry dealer and driving a specially equipped automobile, with "an Indian plate bearing the crown seal and the inscription 'Kapurthala 4,'" and "an electric air cooling system."[82] John resurfaced in official records in August 1947, anglicizing his last name to Allison. Finally, he regained US citizenship after Congress passed new legislation in 1946 permitting Indians to be naturalized, receiving his Certificate of Naturalization on August 5, 1947. In the attached photograph, signed John M. Ali Allison, he appears notably aged but with the same handsome mustache (see Figure 4.18).[83]

John Jr. and Ayesha were also forging accomplished paths of their own. John Jr. was a handsome young man and sported a handlebar mustache like his father in the photograph that appeared of him in 1930 in Columbia University's yearbook (see Figure 4.19). After earning his BA from Columbia, John Jr. earned an MA at the University of Michigan and pursued further graduate study in physics at the University of Colorado. Tragically, in 1954, when he was just forty-five, John Jr. fell ill in Zurich, while traveling home from Pakistan, where he had

FIGURE 4.19. John L. Ali (1908–1954), Columbia University Yearbook, 1930, photograph by Robert Kopp and the White Studio. Courtesy of University Archives, Rare Book & Manuscript Library, Columbia University Libraries.

been working temporarily as a radio engineer for the International Telephone and Telegraphic Company. In John Jr's obituary, John was mentioned as surviving his son. Still, he was not included as a next-of-kin on the official paperwork processed by the Department of State when Americans died abroad, which only gave contact information for John's wife, his sister Ayesha, and Emily.[84] John would have been proud of his son if he outlived him. John Jr.'s obituary noted that he "was said to have descended from one of Pakistan's oldest families and his ancestry was said to date back to the first Caliph of Mohammed"—hinting that John's narrative of his lineage, although rejected by the US courts, nonetheless remained vivid in the memories of his children.[85] He also clearly passed on his wanderlust to his son. In contexts where migrants were often unable to choose which national and religious labels were assigned to them, as was the case when the courts denaturalized John, these alternative diasporic legacies of family stories and habits of mobility took on particular salience.

Tracking John's daughter, Ayesha, has been more challenging. In public records, her past is primarily subsumed under her husband, Norman Maier, an esteemed psychology professor at the University of Michigan. While her brother traveled the world, Ayesha raised her three sons, Carl, John, and Richard, in Ann Arbor. As is often the case with women, her photograph has been preserved not in public records, but in family collections. Today, it appears alongside that of her mother, Emily, in a digital family tree on Ancestry.com, raising more questions than answers. In addition to Ayesha and John Jr., the tree lists two other children of John and Emily Ali, whom I had never seen listed as their children in public records. One, Jack L. Ali, is listed as born in India in 1911, and the other, Solomon Ali, is listed as born in Michigan around 1922. On his World War II draft card, Solomon checked the box not for "Indian" but for "Negro." Could John and Emily have unofficially adopted Solomon, and did John have a son, Jack, in India? Was Solomon Emily's son from a relationship with another man, perhaps conceived while John was away? Or did Solomon check "Negro" as a different expression of racial solidarity, rejecting his father's (or stepfathers') politics of assuming a White identity? The tree reminds us how official records only record a limited range of kinship, while family albums incorporate a much broader range of ties. However, it is also striking that John's photograph is not included in the tree, suggesting how families also lose track of certain facets of their past, sometimes intentionally and sometimes not. I have tried contacting the family through Ancestry, but I have not received a reply, only further adding to the mysteries surrounding John's life and legacies.[86]

## The Rogue's Thread: Unravelling the Archive

As it should be clear by now, the more I looked at John's and Jan's archival trails together, the less certain I became that they were the same person. Yet, I have tried to resist the urge to answer this question of identity one way or the other. To do so risks falling back into the logic of surveillance, identification, and control that defined the state's drive to photograph men like John and Jan. Instead, I have tried to work with their images through the logic of the album, seeking not to identify individual subjects but to chart a network of relations. When families look at photographs, they deploy different ways of seeing than states, sometimes in ways that blur the boundaries between individuals. When I look at photographs of my mother and mother-in-law as toddlers, I see my daughter staring back at me. Nor does such logic have to be biological. In this respect, "albuming," despite some dubious historical associations with eugenics, can be a more open means of documenting family than genealogical trees, which privilege blood and legal relations.[87] Most family albums include different types of kin—friends, neighbors, classmates, perhaps even total strangers caught in the background but drawn into a visual relation of being present together in a particular place and time.

My archival method in this chapter was deeply enriched by a conversation with a colleague, Michele Bambling, who has spent many years studying and exhibiting family photo albums, primarily in the United Arab Emirates. When I showed Michele some of the photographs I had gathered of Jan/John, she immediately noticed something I had taken for granted: the blue thread that ran through the picture of Jan exhibited as part of the "Once British Always British" project. Michele told me she was struck by the color and texture the thread brought to a black-and-white and two-dimensional collection of images. As she explained, the thread reminded her of an album in which flat photos are transformed into a three-dimensional and tactile assemblage. I admitted that I had not previously thought much about the blue thread, even as I had been trying to think about how images were cropped and pasted into the file, much as they would be into an album. Such colored threads are ubiquitous in archives, which often use them instead of staples to collate records. However, once Michele noted it, I remembered that the blue thread visible in the image of the photograph used for the heritage project was no longer there when I consulted the file in the archive. It had been removed, and a plastic case was added to protect the photograph, with a new reddish-orange yarn threaded through the plastic so as not to damage the picture further (Figure 4.5).[88] This altered arrangement was evidence of routine archival preservation, although also a testament to the new importance of the photograph after being included in a heritage exhibit celebrating multi-ethnic Britain. Yet, after speaking with Michele, I pondered the deeper significance of this alteration because the metaphor of threads has been crucial to recent discussions about methods of researching global histories.

In recent years, many historians interested in writing global histories have navigated its potentially overwhelming scale by turning to micro-history.[89] Micro-histories look at broader social patterns by focusing on an individual (or family), object, or event, often showing how zooming in on a smaller scale of analysis reveals historical dynamics overlooked in studies that aim at broader generalizations. This book is deeply influenced by this method. Researching micro-histories often involves tracing individuals across multiple archives, and two of its earliest practitioners, Carlo Ginzburg and Carlo Poni, described an individual's name as akin to the red thread of Greek mythology, which Ariadne gives to her lover Theseus to allow him to navigate the labyrinth and slay the Minotaur.[90] More recently, historians Emma Rothschild and Francesca Trivellato have returned to the metaphor of following Ariadne's thread to describe the experience of researching micro-histories in the digital age, in which search engines have turbocharged the ability to trace a name through a labyrinth of archives. These new tools allow historians to quickly identify documents related to their query in archives scattered across the globe, sometimes downloading digitized copies without leaving their desks.[91] The power of these digital tools can seem almost mythological. But they have also thrown into sharp relief how archives are structured to ease the writing of certain histories and to suppress others. In Anglo-American archives, non-English names are often mangled in transliteration, appearing in so many different forms that it can be nearly impossible to know whether they refer to the same or different people. Perhaps to pre-empt such confusion, many seamen adopted a simplified "ship's" name. Many used the same simple names, such as Ali and Miah. Such aliases were common among a range of mobile subalterns, paralleling the naming practices that Durba Ghosh has written about concerning the Indian wives of British officials.[92] In such cases, names can appear more as a red herring than a red thread.

In a more recent and less widely cited essay, Carlo Ginzburg returned to the image of the red thread in a meandering meditation on identity, family resembles, family trees, and a series of photographic experiments conducted by the eugenicist Francis Galton. Early in the essay, Ginzburg points to a passage from the writings of philosopher Ludwig Wittgenstein. Wittgenstein alludes to a reference from Goethe's novel *Elective Affinities,* originally published in German in 1809. The passage describes how the British Navy commissioned its rope with a red thread running throughout to mark it as crown property. (The British Navy did incorporate an identifying thread to prevent the theft of its rope, sometimes referred to as the "rogue's yarn," although different colors were used depending on where the rope was manufactured.[93]) The metaphor of the red thread in Goethe's novel originally referred to the idea of a single continuous idea that unites a text. Ginzburg notes, however, that Wittgenstein subverted this original meaning, writing instead that "the strength of the thread does not reside in the fact that some one fibre runs through its whole length, but in the overlapping of many fibres."[94]

There is much to think with here for practitioners of global micro-history. For many, the historical connection to the imperial British Navy will feel more immediate than to Greek mythology, a tie that is especially strong for John/Jan's story. The idea of a single thread that, on closer inspection, reveals itself to be composed of many fibers also raises questions of identity that have been central to this chapter. The fuzziness of identification, or what Ginzburg describes as the "blurred edges, mistakes, and anomalies," have long preoccupied micro-historians.[95] Many have found that following an individual across multiple archives troubles disciplinary norms of empiricism. Micro-historians offer informed speculation based on historical context to fill the gaps in what can be known from archival sources, particularly for non-elite subjects. They hover between the biography of an individual, in all its particularities, and the cultural and social history of broader populations.

This balancing act has led some to question the nature of identity itself. Natalie Zemon Davis, who, along with Ginzburg, was one of the most influential pioneers of micro-history, was preoccupied with the nature of identity in her celebrated book *The Return of Martin Guerre* (1983). Davis writes about how a rural community in sixteenth-century France sought to determine whether a man was their former neighbor or an imposter when experiencing new opportunities for self-fashioning. Just as her historical characters ask how could you tell "who a man was," Davis also grapples with the slipperiness of identity.[96] In the various ways that John and Jan presented themselves before the camera, we see how such opportunities for creative re-invention further proliferated in the nineteenth and twentieth centuries, raising the question of whether we are all playing the role of the imposter. If there is an element of the imposter in all of us, so too is a hint of the novelist in all historians. We do not merely pick up a red thread in the archives and follow its pre-ordained path. We carefully spin it together by selectively incorporating some fibers while abandoning others.

Whether John and Jan were the same person recedes in importance when we focus on the fact that all threads are made up of many fibers. Instead, we see the richness of viewing their archival traces in tandem. Noting how only a few months separated John's battle to defend his citizenship in the US, and Jan's efforts to claim subjecthood in Britain, shows how regimes of racial exclusion and surveillance developed across global geographies. The possibility that Jan *identified with* John and his struggles, perhaps so intensely that he felt them to be a single person, also points to bottom-up resistance to these top-down regimes. If the British and US governments collaborated to curtail the mobility of men like John and Jan, they built their own alternative global solidarities. Flipping through thousands of ID photographs of Asian, Arab, and African seamen, I was struck by how these solidarities could be expressed as much physically and aesthetically as through words. Using a common visual vocabulary—a carefully knotted tie, pressed suitcoat, fez, and touch of personal flair—was itself an act of collective resistance to regimes that sought to reduce non-White seamen to a pool of disposable foreign labor. We see these patterns best when we look deeply at particular photos, in all their captivating individuality, and *en masse*—a visual protest which relied on each individual fiber and the thread they collectively wove through the archive.

These archival threads are not pure metaphors. Archival files are themselves collages—assemblages of paperwork (and sometime images and objects) physically bound together, sometimes with staples but more often with thread. Paying closer attention to actual threads in the archive can aid our ability to think creatively about historical method. As noted in the introduction, historical scholarship often assumes that archives are stable repositories of knowledge about the past, which historians enter and exit without leaving a trace. We know that archivists routinely alter records to preserve and organize them, just as the thread in Jan's file was changed from a blue to an orange one. Many of the archives I have used were disassembled and reassembled in the context of decolonization and partition, which created new national archives out of the refuse of colonial bureaucracies, even as the British also took many records home. Yet historians rarely view themselves as part of these processes. To remove a record from the archives is anathema, and we are trained to meticulously ensure that the papers in a file remain in the same order in which we found them. These practices serve an essential purpose. I am not advocating archival theft or vandalism, although I admit to identifying with the character of the rogue stealing ropes from the British Navy. Yet historians' professional training can exaggerate the distance between past and present and obscure the fact that historians, too, exert their disruptive presence in archives. As noted in the introduction, I was vividly reminded of this fact when an archivist slit open a sealed will at my request, releasing the haunting photograph of Sher Dilkhan onto the desk before me. Seeing historians as themselves altering and creating archives in their wake empowers us to reassemble materials into assemblages that resist the top-down logic of the states that oversaw the creation of the original paperwork. By mentally unraveling the threads that bind together archival files, we open the possibility of twisting them into new narratives.

Re-thinking the red thread as a series of fibers that can be unraveled and twisted into new formations also has implications for roots researchers, whose work shares much in common with micro-historians. For the former, however, the red thread often appears as the black lines that link the boxes in their family tree, which likewise have become more accessible to trace across time and space through the turbocharged powers of digital searching. The process of building family trees using platforms like Ancestry, Geni, MyHeritage, and FamilySearch, which are built around digitized collections of state records of births, marriages, deaths, etc., offers an almost addictively empirical approach to answering the question "Where do I come from?" They suggest that the more branches we add to our family tree, reinforced with links to census data, immigration records, etc., the closer we will get to a definitive answer to that question. While rendered in black, these lines are tinged with red, as family trees often privilege blood and legal relations, pushing users towards a particular way of approaching identity. However, as the family tree I found for John Ali's descendants suggests, some users are making trees that resist these logics. As I explore in the following chapter, for diasporic families with ties to South Asia, the seductive appeal of these sites is often quickly tempered by the discovery of dramatic inequalities in their geographical coverage. The fact, however, that the platforms were not designed with South Asian families in mind has meant that some diasporic families have rejigged digital genealogy in creative ways, opening up possibilities for tracing more mobile kinship. They approach the process of mapping their family roots in ways that are more akin to weaving a tapestry of threads—in which the pattern is not predetermined by blood or law but instead a creative act of unraveling and remaking.

# 5
# Digital Genealogy

FIGURE 5.1. Priyanka Sacheti in her childhood home in Muscat, as posted on the Instagram account *Gulf ⇄ South Asia*. Courtesy of Priyanka Sacheti.

HAVING DRAWN on techniques of micro-history in the last four chapters, this chapter steps away from this approach to delve more deeply into contemporary mediascapes where diasporic families are engaging with the past. It pulls together insights from the previous four chapters, all of which were critically shaped by digital as well as in-person research. The chapter also reflects on how my research shifted in the spring of 2020 with the onset of the COVID-19 pandemic and how these shifts affected broader landscapes for researching family history. During this period, most archives closed their doors, and in some cases, they remained closed for several years. I was stuck at home with my daughter, not even a year old, and would spend much of the next two years struggling to take care of her during repeated interruptions to our childcare while also learning to teach online. Meanwhile, my mother-in-law was in Chennai caring for her ailing mother amidst India's almost complete lockdown during the early months of the pandemic. My daughter uttered some of her first words in a mash-up of English, Tamil, and Malayalam while speaking daily on Facetime with her grandmother and great-grandmother. Despite the stress of those early pandemic months, we are all now a bit nostalgic for these calls, which dwindled in frequency as we cobbled together a new normal.

I shoved the book in mental cold storage. But late at night, when I relaxed by scrolling online, I noticed a proliferation of family photos on media linked to the South Asian diaspora. While some of these projects predated the pandemic, during the months in which many individuals found themselves homebound and glued to their screens, digital spaces opened new terrains for mapping diasporic pasts. The legions of the dead also grew more rapidly as many older relations succumbed to COVID—losses that perhaps kindled a greater desire to connect with older relatives as the pandemic threatened to snatch them away. The projects I discovered, like *Brown History* and *Gulf ⇄ South Asia*, echoed themes I had begun encountering while using various online tools to research this book, from genealogy websites to Facebook. Before the pandemic, my engagement with these tools was pragmatic and a bit clandestine. I worried that colleagues would think along the lines of one librarian, who, when I asked about obtaining an institutional subscription to Ancestry.com, informed me that university libraries did not consider it a serious research resource. He recommended that I try a local public library, some of which subscribe to these resources. During the pandemic, I realized I needed to return to these digital spaces with the same critical perspective that historians have long brought to physical archives. I needed to read them both along and against the grain—understanding how their structures encouraged certain normative approaches to studying family history, but also how individual users subverted these logics.[1]

The seismic impacts of the Black Lives Matter movement were also reverberating through digital diasporic spaces, fostering new efforts to decolonize the past. Despite all their problems, platforms like Instagram allowed individuals outside of academia and museums to bypass institutional gatekeepers to explore their family histories on their own terms. In recent years, we have been inundated with stories about the myriad evils of social media. It can be easy to forget that social media can be used in creative ways that resist its profit-seeking algorithms. In speaking about how social media opened new vistas for exploring histories of indenture, Esha Pillay, whom I also discuss in the introduction, explained: "It's just a whole new different world on social media when it comes to Cooley histories, indentured descendants and history."[2] Many of these efforts foregrounded family histories recognizing both their relatability and radical potential. New ways of thinking about the past, and family as a means of connecting with it, were evolving before my eyes.

I knew I needed to write about these developments, but it was only in mid-2022, when I took up a visiting research fellowship at New York University in Abu Dhabi, that I had the time and mental space to do so. I returned to the book project after two years away and from the vantage point of myself being a short-term migrant to the Gulf—the epicenter of twenty-first-century South Asian migration. However, when I began asking people whom I should talk to about local migrant histories, many pointed me back to digital spaces, particularly Instagram. In the United Arab Emirates, South Asians are outwardly excluded from the many government-funded "heritage" exhibits that feature Emirati culture. (Often, though, they are a silent presence—for example, as the expert craftsmen who build models of historic *dhows* for museums across the Gulf.[3]) More well-known heritage projects center migrations between South Asia and the Global North, such as those I encountered at the British National Archives and the South Asian American Digital Archives while working on the last chapter. South-South migrations, including those within Asia and between Asia, the Middle East, and Africa, are often underrepresented despite their historical importance. The importance of South-South migrations remains true today, with the Gulf states top destinations for South Asian migrants, including the UAE, which in recent years has hosted the largest number of Indian migrants.[4] These migration pathways have their own temporalities and subjectivities from the experiences of migrants who relocate to the United States and Europe. Like much of the migration explored in earlier chapters, circuits between South Asia and the Gulf are multi-sited and circular. Gaining citizenship in countries like the UAE is virtually impossible for South Asians. Gulf governments structurally encourage migrants to maintain links to their homelands, often pushing them out once their labor is no longer needed, during economic downturns, or as they age. Yet, many South Asian families have been linked to the Gulf for generations—defying official constructions of them as temporary guest workers. The experiences of those who travel these routes often do not conform to models of diaspora that are oriented towards one-way relocations from a singular home to host land, but nonetheless involve long-lasting diasporic legacies. In recent years, online spaces have emerged as crucial zones for exploring these alternative mobilities.

This chapter brings together my experiences navigating across these spheres of digital genealogy. It pays particular attention to digital projects involving ties between South Asia and the Gulf while meandering across different geographies. In this respect, I followed the multi-stepped migrations of the individuals I encountered, many of whom had moved multiple times, sometimes to different destinations, sometimes also along circular pathways that brought them back to South Asia. Similarly, I define digital genealogy broadly because my subjects frequently triangulated between purpose-built genealogy websites; DNA tests, which are integrated with websites like Ancestry.com; and other platforms, particularly Instagram, which is not designed for family history, but which has emerged as an essential space for exhibiting family photos and recording oral histories.

Despite the popularity of digital genealogy, which attracts millions of users and billions of dollars of revenue, it has attracted surprisingly little attention from historians. The research that exists has been top-down, focusing on the corporate evolution and ideologies of companies like Ancestry.com rather than what users make of these sites.[5] Like social media, there is ample reason to be wary about these platforms, with their explicit aim to monetize others' pasts, often profiting from privatizing public documents, and their focus on resources catering to Anglo-American families. These dynamics are even more pronounced when their services are integrated with genetic testing. As research on groups from African Americans to Pacific Islanders has shown, genetic science, while denouncing eugenics and colonial racism, has produced its own troubling regimes of knowledge. While claiming to offer "the master key to inheritance and heredity," DNA research has often diminished other modes of genealogical knowledge while exploiting Black and Brown bodies to advance its own reductive "population"-based conceptions of human difference.[6] Yet, despite these critical limitations, I have been interested in how users of diverse backgrounds work against the platform's own logics, for example by incorporating family photos and stories rather than relying on state documents and DNA results to build their trees. This chapter, therefore, takes a more bottom-up, ethnographic approach to studying digital genealogy, arguing for the creativity with which users who trace their roots through Indian Ocean and Global South itineraries are retrofitting these platforms.

My sampling method drew on families I had already met while researching the previous chapters and whom I asked to refer me to others who were active roots researchers. This "snowball" sampling method was particularly helpful in studying the digital networks through which my research subjects were themselves often connected.[7] In 2022 and 2023, I also sent hundreds of blind emails to individuals whose trees I found interesting or whose family photographs on Instagram caught my eye. Most of these emails went unanswered, but several dozen yielded willing interview subjects. They are not a representative sample; my interview subjects were delightfully quirky. In some cases, our initial conversation evolved into months-long exchanges of texts and calls as they updated me on their research and looped me into chains of WhatsApp messages forwarded among family members and fellow history buffs.

As a professional historian, I was primed to view these subjects as amateurs and potential pawns to the billion-dollar companies profiting from their hobby. Historians, alongside other scholars, have written with considerable skepticism about digital genealogy and DNA testing, seeing these tools as prone to reinforcing ideas about family and race that are elitist, heteronormative, and prone to biological determinism.[8] I certainly encountered elements of these attitudes. Still, I also connected with many sophisticated fellow researchers, who taught me much—from the distinction between autosomal, Y, and mitochondrial DNA tests—to the differences between Instagram and TikTok algorithms. Some were interested in tracing kinship through blood but not necessarily to corroborate normative family narratives. DNA testing was critical for many in their efforts to locate people who had been excluded from family stories—including women and illegitimate children. Others spoke of how social media allowed them to cultivate alternative diasporic kin—people who could relate to their migration experiences in contrast to some of their extended family who remained in India and found their habits alien. Most recognized that many available genealogical tools were biased towards White users but jerry-rigged them to their purposes. They offered provocative templates for interdisciplinary research—publicly engaged, and inclusionary of marginalized pasts—models from which historians have much to learn.

## Digital Family Trees

Historians' skepticism about genealogy is in part rooted in its history. Historically, elites have often practiced genealogy, from British royals to Muslims claiming descent from the Prophet. Tracing one's roots has thus frequently been a means to "claim power over others," to borrow a phrase from Maya Jasanoff, a fellow historian of empire interested in family history.[9] Yet, from at least the 1970s, family history has also become a critical way of engaging with histories of previously marginalized historical subjects—Alex Haley's *Roots* (1976), a book and later television serial that traced the author's roots to his enslaved ancestors, being one of the most prominent examples. While now accessible to many more, roots research, to a certain extent, remains a hobby of privilege, particularly via genealogy websites. Ancestry is the largest of these websites, with over a billion dollars of annual revenue and 50 million visits per month in 2023. In the US, it ranks as the eighty-fifth most popular website.[10] Its services, however, come at a premium: $39.99 a month for a worldwide subscription, with access to additional newspaper and military records costing up to $59.99 a month.[11] In frequently cited statistics gathered in 2012, the average Ancestry.com user was a fifty-five-year-old, White, American woman.[12] This data may now be somewhat dated: more recent surveys of internet traffic to the site, for example, suggest a reasonably even age distribution, with approximately 20% drawn from users aged 55 to 64, closely followed by 17% of users aged 25 to 34. The gender distribution of users was roughly equal, with 52% women compared to 48% men for the US-based site, while being somewhat more skewed for the UK, with the website attracting 46% women to 54% men.[13] It is more challenging to get data about how users identify their race. Still, Ancestry has been aggressively marketing itself as a tool for diverse users to research their pasts.[14] On its YouTube channel, it features a segment with actor Kal Penn discussing his family roots in Gujarat with African American professor Henry Louis Gates Jr. on his show "Finding Your Roots," also sponsored by Ancestry. When Gates asks Kal Penn whether the research results make him feel "more Indian," he replies: "I actually think it makes me feel a lot more global"—a claim to worldliness that has echoed through my conversations with other diasporic families.[15]

However, geographical information about the user base of Ancestry.com suggests a significant gap between this image of global diversity and the services it provides. In addition to its main US-based site, it maintains websites in the UK, Canada, Australia, Germany, Italy, France, Sweden, and Mexico.[16] Users in South Asia can access the US-based site, and India is the fifth most common location for visitors to Ancestry.com. This traffic, nonetheless, accounts for less than 1 percent of its user base.[17] Although in no way statistically representative, my own informal survey of Ancestry family trees with South Asian connections yielded only one conversation with a user based in India. The rest of my interview subjects recruited through the platform were mostly in the US, Canada, and the UK. This result is unsurprising. The birth, death, census, and property records that can be accessed via Ancestry skew heavily towards collections drawn from North American and European archives, or in the case of India, relate primarily to British families in India or Indian Christians.[18]

Other sites involved similar challenges for researchers of South Asian roots. Familysearch.org, the largest free genealogy website run by the Church of Jesus Christ of the Latter-Day Saints, lists a substantial collection of Hindu pilgrimage records, a vital resource for tracing Hindu ancestors. The collection, however, is only accessible to members of the Church or on physical microfilms housed in Salt Lake City, Utah.[19] To connect with families in Malaysia and the Gulf, I found other platforms, including Facebook and Instagram, far more helpful. It was via the Facebook group "Malaysia History and Heritage" that I first connected with some members of Thamboosamy's family. Another digital genealogy website, Geni.com, proved invaluable for my work with families with links to South Africa, many of whom preferred its services due to the availability of a free basic plan and less expensive enhanced options, which at $120 a year are significantly cheaper than Ancestry.

Individuals with South Asian roots were simultaneously aware of the disadvantages they faced in using platforms like Ancestry while working creatively to repurpose the site to meet their needs. For example, Karanveer Sahota, a flight attendant working for Air Canada who is in his twenties, has built a tree on Ancestry with over four thousand relations and counting (see Figure 5.2).[20] Tracing his roots to Punjabi Sikhs who began migrating from India during the nineteenth century, Karanveer explained that he had wanted

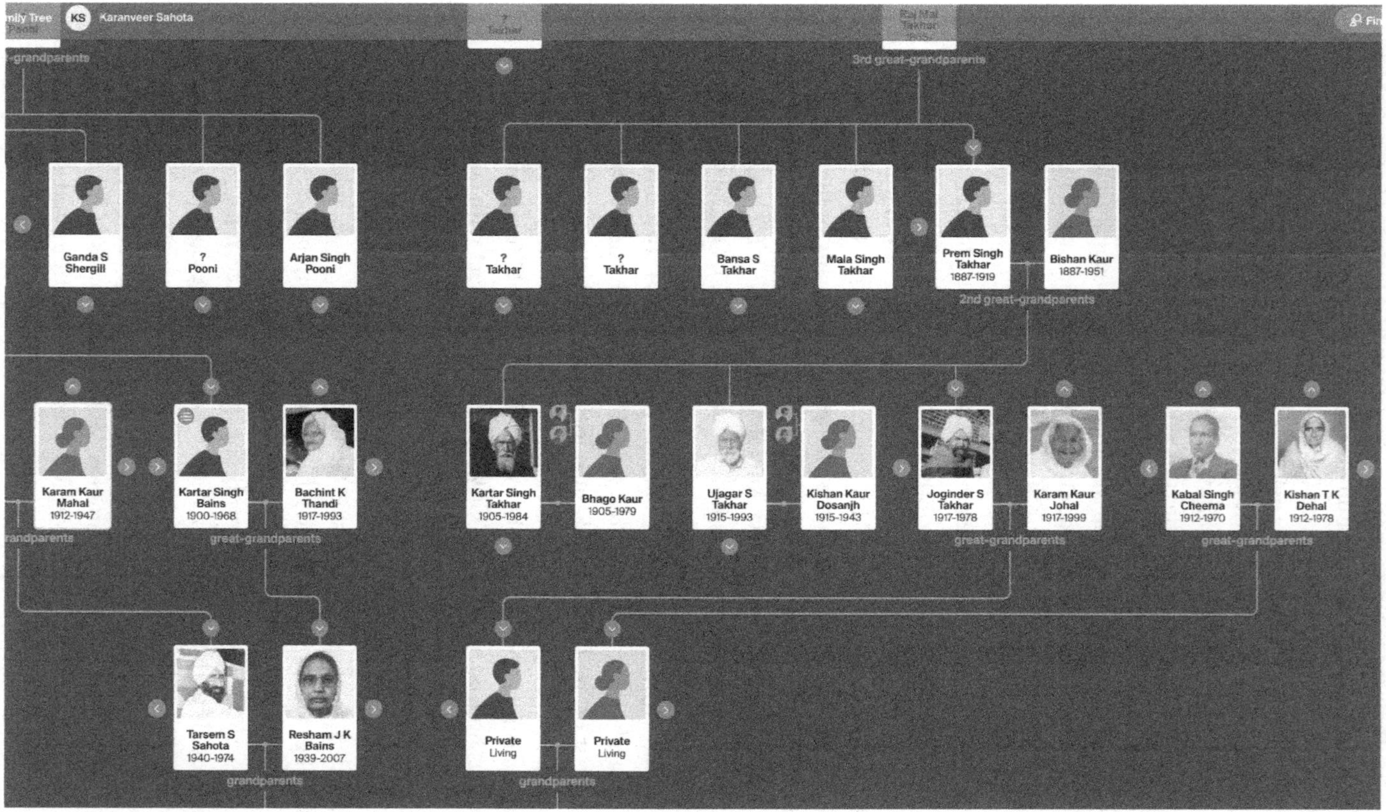


FIGURE 5.2. Online Family Tree of Karanveer Sahota. Posted on Ancestry.com, accessed November 16, 2023. Courtesy of Karanveer Sahota.

to explore his family history from a very young age. As a small boy, he used to share a bed with his grandmother, and he remembered asking her about her childhood while they lay together at night. Karanveer began pursuing this interest more seriously after his history teacher assigned a family roots project in seventh grade. He quickly discovered that his experience researching his family differed from some of his peers. He explained: "It is so easy for American, European, Canadian people. You can [use the census to] find the address where your ancestor was living, siblings, age, occupation, if their house was on a mortgage . . . Punjabi history is all oral." Using platforms like Ancestry can, therefore, be frustrating for people of South Asian origin. As Karanveer put it: "You see the ad, these people building their trees—yeah, those are people of European descent!" As a result, he noted that "people give up." Karanveer, however, did not give up and instead became a self-taught oral historian. As a teenager, he begged his relatives to tell him stories, and he used the Voice Memo app on his iPhone to make recordings. He also learned more about India's unique archival landscapes, including the land records kept by *patwaris* or village registers/accountants. He asked relatives to visit these offices to collect information during visits to India.

He was also surprised to learn that they had amassed a particularly rich collection of family photos because his family had a long migration history, spanning Malaysia, Fiji, Australia, England, Scotland, Canada, and the US. Long before cameras were common in Punjab, his relatives made a special effort to have photographs taken during special occasions, especially weddings, so they could send copies to relatives who could not attend in person. Karanveer incorporated many of these photographs into his Ancestry tree, generally adding photographs after a relative died. He explained that part of his motivation for adding the photographs to the tree was his acute sense of their fragility as physical heirlooms. His family had lost many photographs when forced to flee their homes during Partition and during the mundane vicissitudes of life. He recounted one photograph older relations had described to him, in which his great-grandfather was pictured wearing a flower garland after being released from jail during the struggle for Indian independence. In the 1960s, however, the photograph was destroyed when rain flooded the family home. Kareen explained, "I would have been so happy to see a picture of my great-grandfather, this freedom fighter, coming out of jail. And not coming out of jail being disrespected, but being celebrated." His efforts to collect, scan, and upload photographs to Ancestry ensure that other family photographs do not meet the same fate. At the same time, even the photograph of his great-grandfather has not been entirely lost but instead shifted to the immaterial archive of family memories.

Karanveer also related to me that although his family had lost many other treasured keepsakes during their multiple moves, they had managed to keep a few of his grandmother's old steel vessels engraved with her name. Running his fingers along the engraving, Karanveer explained to me that these labels allowed the dishes to be gathered for large communal functions like weddings and then returned to their proper owners, women's work that is rarely recorded in archives but here etched into a family's everyday archive of material heirlooms. Such creative reflections about the dynamic relationship between material and immaterial inheritances have helped deepen my understanding of family history as a distinctive method, including its significance in bringing out gendered pasts.

Karanveer's attention to the importance of such objects arose from his efforts to work against the grain of patriarchal norms in Punjabi society, which meant that "women weren't documented." But as he told me, "We came from mothers!" To compile a more inclusive family past, Karanveer also turned to DNA testing, particularly kits that provide information about mitochondrial DNA, which is inherited through the maternal line. He used this information to locate the villages where some of his women ancestors grew up, which he then visited to collect more information to fill in maternal lines in his family tree. Karanveer's openness to unconventional sources allowed him to unearth women's pasts that might have otherwise remained hidden if he had relied exclusively on conventional archival documents, from the etchings on metal plates to mitochondrial DNA. When he expressed interest in what I thought about his work as someone with professional historical training, I responded that historians had much to learn from his methods.

While Karanveer triangulated between digital tools, DNA, and family archives to dig up information about ancestral women, I encountered others using similar tactics to learn about more immediate ties. The overall structure of Ancestry foregrounds genealogical information gathered from state records. Still, some users, particularly those with diasporic pasts, use the platform to delve into affective histories suppressed in conventional archives. These were the pasts that I sensed haunting my own archival pursuits, made apparent as much through the absence as the presence of information. Yet some users foregrounded these suppressed emotions as they constructed their family archives on Ancestry, including Theresa Simmons.

When I came across Theresa Simmons's tree on Ancestry.com, I was immediately struck by how she wove emotional content into its branches, generally populated with dry references garnered from census, birth, death, and migration records. For example, in one photograph attached to the tree, she left a comment on her grim expression, noting, "Not a happy girl!" about a visit that her parents made to her foster home as a child. When I spoke to

Theresa, she explained that she only had periodic contact with her biological mother and father, although she had been close with her foster parents.[21] Her knowledge about her background was limited to a generic sense that she was Asian. She described wanting from a young age to know more but being told by her biological parents during occasional visits not to ask any questions. As Theresa explained, "When you get to your teenage years, you really want to know where you come from, even though I was really brought up happily." Her biological father, whom she had no contact with after turning eight, turned up on her doorstep after she was married and had her own children, but he still would not tell her where he came from. She had more regular contact with her biological mother, from whom she learned that while she was pregnant with Theresa, she discovered that Theresa's father was also expecting a child with another woman. After her mother passed, Theresa found some photographs and old diaries among her papers, including a photo of her mother's grandmother (Theresa's great-grandmother) with a note on the back, "from Kerala," now also part of her tree on Ancestry. She also found old diaries with addresses in Guiana and Kerala, but when she wrote letters to the addresses, she never received any replies.

Her first breakthrough came when her children convinced her to open a Facebook account, which helped her connect with more distant cousins who were more open to sharing information about the family. She explained, "I just messaged people. I would get one link, a message would come back, and that would lead to some others." Theresa also did a DNA test, which led to more connections and eventually allowed her to connect with her brother, whom she had known about but never met. By piecing together information, she now also knows that her father was born in British Guiana and lived in Trinidad before coming to the UK for work. On her mother's side, her grandfather migrated from Kerala to Singapore and later to Britain, and her grandmother was the child of an Afghan father and a Malay mother. But Theresa still longs to know more and expressed her frustration that many relatives refuse to share information. As she said, "Some of these [relatives] are still living, but they won't divulge any information to me. I don't want to intrude in any of their lives. All I want to do is build this tree so my family, we know, and we have a record. I don't necessarily want them to speak to me. I'd just like them to send me pictures."[22]

## Diversifying DNA Genealogy

As Karanveer's and Theresa's experiences suggest, for some family researchers DNA has become one tool among many that they use to trace their roots. For both, DNA tests were significant resources for stepping outside received narratives about their families' pasts—in Karanveer's case, against patriarchal lineages that excluded women, and in Theresa's, against her own exclusion from her family's past. Still, they used the tests alongside many other ways of engaging their pasts—from searching out local *patwari* record keepers in India to connecting with more distant relations identified using genetic testing services. Their experiences contrast with how DNA ancestry is typically marketed to the public as a definitive means of answering the question, "Who am I?" The services offer consumers a graphical representation that seems to provide authoritative insight into what percentage of one's ancestry can be traced to various regions, often corresponding to contemporary nation-states. This approach not only reinforces entrenched knowledge hierarchies favoring Western science but also perpetuates the misconception that populations from different areas are genetically and historically discrete and align with modern political boundaries and regimes of racial classification.[23] While claiming to celebrate diversity and mixed heritage, the results can reinforce ethno-nationalism and racism by repacking them in more up-to-date scientific frames—dynamics that White nationalists have been quick to exploit.[24] Problematic in any context, this imagery is deeply at odds with the mobile and intermixed histories that tie together the Indian Ocean. Yet from its earliest development, other groups have engaged with genetic genealogy with distinctly anti-racist and decolonial objectives.[25] In the United States, African Americans were among the earliest communities to develop platforms for using DNA to trace ancestral connections. They have used results from these tests to support legal claims for reparations against companies that made their fortunes by exploiting their enslaved ancestors.[26] Yet most research on DNA genealogy focuses on the United States and, within it, White, "native-born" Americans, even as these companies overtly market themselves as resources for diverse and increasingly global consumers.[27] Studies of their impacts, therefore, must look to broader geographies and consider not only the companies' problematic practices but also the subversive ways users deploy their products.

In the last decade, direct-to-consumer DNA test kits have exploded in popularity since the cost of testing, now around $100 per kit, has become more accessible to individuals in high-income countries. As of 2023, over 23 million people had used DNA testing kits marketed by Ancestry, the largest provider of these services, while over 12 million people had tested using 23andMe.[28] In the early 2020s, both businesses also attracted a massive surge of investment. Blackstone Inc. acquired Ancestry for $4.7 billion in 2020, and 23andMe reached almost $5 billion in market capitalization after going public in 2020.[29] But this success proved short-lived. In subsequent years, sales of DNA kits slowed while concerns mounted about how the resulting genetic data was being used, including being sold to pharmaceutical companies and mined by law enforcement.[30] Turbocharging these concerns, 23andMe experienced a catastrophic security breach in late 2023, in which the results of millions of users were stolen and sold on the dark web, leading the company's market value to collapse almost to zero. Especially disturbingly, the hackers may have specifically sought out the data of users identified as Chinese and Ashkenazi Jewish, suggesting how the platforms' population-based groupings can enable targeted attacks.[31] In March 2025, 23andMe declared bankruptcy, spurring a new flurry of concern about what would become of former users' private data.[32]

Yet with all its myriad problems, DNA testing has nonetheless become a critical element of how many roots researchers, particularly those in the United States and Britain, pursue their family pasts. Like Theresa and Karanveer, many of the individuals I connected with on Ancestry.com had used them. Their experiences were mixed, but also suggest that because the limits of these tests have been hyper-visible for consumers of non-European backgrounds, they are less likely to see them as singular or authoritative keys to their past. Despite the companies' efforts to reach broader markets, the number of people of Asian and African descent in their genetic datasets remains limited. This bias translates into less informative results for these groups since the tests work through comparison. For example, until recently, many testers with South Asian backgrounds received results that were either so general as to be of little use or outright inaccurate. For instance, in 2010, Arslan Zaidi, then a PhD student in genetics at Penn State, received a report from 23andMe indicating that his ancestry was 81% European. When he tested again in 2014 with the same company, his results showed that he was 92% South Asian.[33] Many purchasers understandably felt cheated. An Amazon review for 23andMe from November 2020 complained: "I just paid a 100 bucks to get to know I'm 100% Indian. . . . My neighbor's dog could have given me this information. . . . So many people are excited to find out about themselves with this product. Apparently their accuracy is limited to certain races only."[34]

The companies, however, have noted how such results hinder their efforts to meet investor pressure to capture ever-expanding markets. In 2019, both companies began refining their results to provide additional specificity concerning South Asian ancestry. 23andMe shifted from classifying the Subcontinent as a single origin to subdividing it into a motley map of seven regions of vastly different sizes and compositions, including Central Asia, Bangladesh/Northeast India, Central/Southern India, Gujarati Patel, Kannadiga/Tamil/Telugu/Sri Lankan, Malayali, and North India/South Pakistan.[35] This eclectic categorization likely reflected uneven sampling, with more specificity in areas where people using its services had ties, but also the confusion of mapping origin when national, linguistic, and regional boundaries have changed dramatically over time. During this period, AncestryDNA also started identifying regions within South Asia, such as Bengal and Punjab, and began offering information about the descent of South Asians who migrated to South Africa and the Caribbean.[36] At the same time, smaller, more specialized companies such as XCode Life actively recruited South Asians to diversify their dataset, offering free additional analysis of results from larger testing companies for some time.[37] As evidenced in the active Reddit boards dedicated to the topic, some consumers, however, continue to complain about confusing or uninformative genetic ancestry reports, which some feel reflect larger social scripts that tell South Asians that they are "'just' brown." For others, surprising results have sparked conversations about how "we're actually a lot more mixed than we think we are."[38] Some I spoke to also described being pleasantly surprised to receive updated results with more specificity from tests completed years ago.

Yet even as Ancestry and 23andMe have attempted to offer more refined results to non-European consumers, their relatively high cost and roots in the Global North undercut their self-projection as resources for tracing diverse heritage. Their services are not just unaffordable in the Global South but often met with justified wariness. Bio-colonialism is very much ongoing, as evidenced by gene hunters who, in recent decades, have harvested samples from "Indigenous" and other marginalized peoples using dubious consent protocols, if at all, and then profited off patenting their biomatter.[39] Massive data breaches are only likely to heighten such concerns. Thus, while AncestryDNA and 23andMe have expanded into international markets in recent years, with AncestryDNA shipping kits to over 128 countries, neither company operates in South Asia.[40] In India, which is potentially a sizeable market, regulations about the export of biological materials create significant barriers.[41] Some local Indian companies offer DNA testing services, but most are not primarily marketed for genealogical purposes. Instead, they focus on verifying immediate kinship relationships, particularly paternity, and providing health-related genetic information such as disease risk.[42] Similarly, neither AncestryDNA nor 23andMe offer services in Pakistan, Bangladesh, or Sri Lanka, although smaller local services exist. Recent developments suggest that emerging efforts to expand genetic testing services in the region will likely focus on healthcare and diagnostic purposes. Mukesh Ambani, by some measures the wealthiest man in Asia, recently acquired an India-based genetics company with plans to expand its services as part of his broader efforts to pursue data as the "new oil." There is little suggestion, however, that Ambani plans to develop the technology for genealogical purposes.[43]

The limited availability of genetic testing for genealogical purposes in India may reflect calculations about its potential marketability and the political risk of straying into controversial debates about India's diverse origins. Historians and archeologists have long battled efforts by the Hindu Right, often referred to as Hindutva, to push nativist histories that depict an essentialized Hindu nation that is finally throwing off the shackles of successive waves of foreign invasion. Since 2014, when the BJP, the political party most closely associated with the Hindu Right, swept national elections with Narendra Modi at its helm, this version of history has garnered increasing state support. Biologists have recently also been drawn into the fray, as work on genetics has become a new battleground in the history wars.[44] Hindutva groups are particularly concerned about research appearing in prestigious international science journals, including *Cell* and *Science*, which uses genetic data to support theories about Indo-Aryan migration. Originating in linguistic analysis of Indian languages, often spearheaded by European Orientalists, these theories posit that many Indians are descended from migrants who moved into the Subcontinent from Central Asia, Iran, and Eastern Europe thousands of years ago. For many supporters of Hindutva ideologies, these theories are a dangerous challenge to their belief that India, Hindus, and Hinduism share a single, territorially bounded history and are further tainted by their association with colonial knowledge. The mainstream press in India, over which the BJP government has exercised increasing control, has therefore sought to reframe new genetic findings in ways that seemingly refute arguments about ancient migration. Indian scientists, many of whom depend on government funding, have also been strong-armed into making public statements that support the party line. Some told me they avoid population genetics research altogether due to its political sensitivity.[45]

Yet corporations, national governments, and academic scientists do not monopolize knowledge about genetics and ancestry. It is misleading to suggest that those using such resources are mere pawns, although many have been misled. The roots researchers I spoke to who had used these tests were often both sensitive to their limits and creatively using them alongside other tools. Given the tests' weaknesses in analyzing South Asian descent, I heard repeatedly that the most interesting information was about matches to different regions and as a resource to explore family stories about mixed heritage, such as Farrah Jaufuraully.

Farrah Jaufuraully, a TV producer in her forties, was born and lives in the United Kingdom but traced her roots to Mauritius, which her parents had left in the 1960s. The family has traced their migration story back to her paternal great-great-grandfather, Jaufuraully (1823–1917), who migrated from Calcutta under a contract of indenture and married Madelon Sidonie. Growing up, Farrah heard stories about the family's mixed heritage, including speculation about why her mother's family had a Hindu name despite being Muslim, and commented that her curly hair was inherited from an African ancestor on her dad's side. When Farrah took a DNA test five years ago, she was therefore not surprised that it reported that her ancestry was part African. Recently, however, she received an updated report indicating that she had African ancestors on both her maternal and paternal sides.[46] Another Brit with Indian-Mauritian roots, Roshan also shared a story about comparing DNA test results to family stories about mixed heritage. His test results showed 1 percent Germanic ancestry, which he saw as potentially corroborating family stories about an Indian ancestor who had a child with a French plantation owner where she worked.[47] Neither Farrah nor Roshan took these results as definitive but instead read them alongside family stories, which had often been doubted. At a broader level, they interpreted them as supporting emerging diasporic identities that extend beyond conventional hyphenated connections to a singular homeland and host land. It is worth noting that Roshan did not take the label "Germanic" literally but rather interpreted it in light of stories he had heard about a French plantation owner.

Such stories now circulate among wider communities where test results sometimes bolster surprisingly decolonial and feminist interpretations of the past. Denise Abrahamse, who traced her roots to Tamil indentured migrants in South Africa, contributed a similar story to Brown History's Instagram account about receiving back DNA results that supported family memories. Growing up, she had been told that a British man raped her great-great-grandmother. To save her daughter from being killed as a "soiled" woman, her great-great-grandmother's mother decided that they should both flee, which eventually led the two women to enlist as indentured migrants. Denise's DNA test, which showed Irish/Northern England markers, confirmed the story. For Denise, the results, interpreted in the context of her family's oral history, provided a direct link between her own life and her ancestor's bravery in the past. Recounting that she also migrated from South Africa to the United States, Denise concluded: "Our trek across the world has not stopped I guess. Our bloodline resides in many parts of the world . . . I can only imagine how terrifying that decision and journey to a foreign land would have been for 2 Indian females at that time but it is a testament to the strength of the women through the generations of my family . . . mold breakers, dorward [sic] thinkers and risk takers has flown in our blood since then."[48] In contexts where oral histories within marginalized communities are still often viewed with suspicion, DNA tests can bolster inherited understandings of the past and give them new lives in the present. As I found so many times while working on this book, often these inherited narratives are passed down within families as a series of twisted and knotted threads, and a new perspective, as is sometimes offered by a DNA test result, can help a descendant to unravel this tangle and reweave it into their own story. When used with other ways of studying the past, DNA tests provide another layer in a family history collage—the multi-method and multi-media assemblages I have found helpful in presenting mobile pasts.

## Instagram Albums

While some individuals with links to the South Asian diaspora are creatively repurposing digital genealogy websites and DNA tests, many also clearly recognized the profound limits of these tools and have sought other alternatives. Some of the most innovative engagements with family history in Indian Ocean geographies unfold in spaces not explicitly designed for genealogy. The business of family history has emphasized textual and scientific knowledge—encouraging users to build trees through searches of archival documents primarily created by states and DNA datasets.[49] It is unsurprising that companies have emphasized these dimensions of family history research. They are easily marketed as providing users with information that might otherwise require time-consuming visits to distant archives or laboratory facilities. They thus can be sold to users as a value-added service that will open new doors to their family's past. Capitalism and racism also intersect since textual and scientific data are biased toward providing information to White, Euro-American families. Many of the individuals I spoke with were keenly aware of these dynamics. While some creatively repurposed platforms to archive different types of information, I also encountered many family trees that had been abandoned after adding a few relatives. I learned that some of these users, and others who had no interest in sites like Ancestry.com, were looking elsewhere to document their family histories. Turning to tools not specifically designed for family history research could be liberatory for these families. They no longer had to work against the grain of particular norms, such as the pressure to treat state documents as definitive sources. Instead, platforms like Instagram center visuality and memory in ways that facilitate alternative possibilities for exploring family histories.

For those unfamiliar with the platform, certain features of Instagram make it particularly conducive to these projects. Users of Instagram first see a series of images, which can be navigated by viewing different accounts, such as Brown History, or by navigating through different hashtags, such as #familyalbum. Accounts that feature historical family photos also often link to the personal accounts of the people who have contributed the photos, where they post a range of content, from other family photos to images of their current interests. These multiple modes of navigating content facilitate looking at images simultaneously within personal and shared frames of reference. Accounts exploring family photos also usually include accompanying text that provides context and commentary; other users often post responses. This foregrounding of images as the entry point into stories, which are simultaneously frequently profoundly personal and shared with wider audiences, has proven a popular means of engaging in new conversations about diasporic family pasts. These accounts bypass subscription services like Ancestry.com to create public platforms for histories that do not conform to state-backed narratives featured in textbooks and museum exhibits. These spaces have become particularly important in the context of state censorship of historical content, not just by authoritarian regimes, but also by democratic governments in India and the United States. Instagram has thus allowed amateur historians to write their own counter-histories even as its users note increasing vulnerability to manipulative algorithms and state surveillance of social media platforms, sometimes specially targeted at migrants.

While these accounts offer a range of content, posts that feature crowd-sourced family photographs and oral histories are among the most popular. The almost universal relatability of the form—who doesn't have a family album with stories attached to it?—makes these posts open to a range of contributors. Yet beneath their seemingly quotidian character, the posts have radical potential. By engaging with space and time through families' trajectories, they map South Asian pasts that traverse political, caste, religious, and racial borders.

As I would find during the year I spent in the United Arab Emirates, these spaces have also become particularly important in the Gulf. The massive diaspora in the region is the culmination of a half-century in which South Asians were critical to the region's economic development. According to UN statistics, India has had the largest diaspora in the world since 2015, and the top destination for Indians is the UAE, followed by the US and Saudi Arabia.[50] Yet, the experiences of Gulf South Asians, some of whose families have lived in the region for three or more generations, remain underrepresented in the literature on the South Asian diaspora, which centers on the experience of migrants to the US and Europe. Meanwhile, school curricula and museums in the Gulf most often narrate nationalistic histories in which the long-term contributions of South Asians are obscured by framing them as temporary guest workers.[51] Without official spaces for exploring their stories, sharing family photographs on Instagram, while seemingly innocuous, is decidedly radical.

While Instagram family albums have exploded in popularity recently, they have deeper roots. In 2010, Anusha Yadav started the *Indian Memory Project* (IMP) as a blog that evolved into a website archive and companion Instagram account. Anusha spends most of her time in Mumbai but also resists being territorially pinned down, describing the project as "based wherever the Founder-Editor may lay her hat/MacBook."[52] The account has featured old family photographs alongside narratives Anusha collected from contributors, sometimes written by family members directly or based on interviews. While not specifically diasporic, the project featured many photographs and stories of migration, both within the Subcontinent and beyond its borders. Anusha has also framed her work with reference to archival practices.[53] As part of her process, she assigns tags to the photographs she crowd-sources from personal archives, which can then be viewed by category. The frequency with which photographs are tagged with various categories shows that records of epochal events are interlaced with more quotidian measures of passing time in personal archives. For example, more posts are tagged with the category "hairstyle" than with either Partition or World War II.[54] Like any archive, the categorization reflects its creator's interests but also reorients assumptions about how history should be narrated. By centering everyday experiences and more intimate accounts of seismic events, IMP inspired others to build alternative archives from family collections and disseminate them via digital media. A more recent account, the Museum of Material Memory, archives family heirlooms through its Instagram account and website.[55]

In terms of its reach, *Brown History*, which Toronto-based Ahsun Zafar runs, dwarfs these other accounts. As of mid-2023, it had almost 700,000 followers, although Ahsun only began posting to the account in late 2017. A voracious reader, Ahsun started the account to share the information he was gathering through his own explorations of South Asian history. His geographies of exploration were at once global and rooted in the Subcontinent, or as he put it, "I was turning 30 and I just wanted to learn more about my place in the world. So I started to read more books about my roots." The beginning of the account also coincided with the seventieth anniversary of Partition, and Ahsun emphasized exploring its painful repercussions while framing posts in a way that would welcome audiences across the Indo-Pak border. Alongside stories of Partition migrations, *Brown History* also featured photographs of families whose migration trajectories followed a dizzying array of different paths within the Subcontinent, across South-South pathways linking Asia and Africa, and between the Global South and North and back again.[56] Moreover, in its very name, "Brown History," which sidesteps national affiliation and invites solidarities across different ethnicities, the account presents a mobile conception of diasporic identity.

Parallel with his efforts to rethink South Asian geographies, Ahsun has also posted content that offers alternative understandings of the intimate terrain of South Asian family life. Early on, he posted a photograph of a couple from the 1940s leaning in to exchange a kiss—defying taboos about public displays of affection.[57] Other photographs and narratives grappled with domestic violence, disability, and mental illness. Instagram's format, which invites an interplay between visuality and textuality, was crucial to how *Brown History* reoriented understanding of the past. One post, for example, featured a black-and-white photograph of a woman, seemingly attired like any young bride in all her finery to sit for an official studio portrait. The text, however, revealed a more subversive backstory. The subject, as a young woman, was married off and forced to spend "years enclosed within palatial walls of a mansion" in suburban Lahore. While pregnant with her first child and always regretful that her conservative in-laws had forbidden photography at her wedding, she snuck off in her finery, concealed beneath a burka, to take her own images.[58]

Often, *Brown History* told stories that weaved together suppressed geographies and forbidden intimacies. For example, a later post about the same woman revealed that several years later, she fled her in-laws, including leaving behind her children, to sit for another portrait: a passport ID. As her son narrated in the text accompanying the image: "Another studio portrait . . . another rebellion."[59] The intermingling of alternative intimacies and geographies has also made *Brown History* hospitable to stories about families of mixed heritage. In one post, a contributor described his father's journey from Multan to Florida, where he met his mother, a migrant from Columbia. The family later relocated to Dubai. The author summarized the terrains that shaped his childhood: "At home, we spoke Spanish, Urdu, and English. Being South Asian/Latinx and Muslim born and raised in a country that we weren't able to call home was a constant reminder of the nation as an imagined community."[60]

As this post suggests, *Brown History* was especially empowering for individuals whose diasporic journeys did not track traditional South-North trajectories, including families who moved between South Asia and the Gulf, sometimes with intermediate stops. In March 2019, Ayesha Saldanha, an Indian writer and Arabic translator who grew up in the UK before living in Bahrain for over a decade, set up the Instagram account *Gulf ⇄ South Asia* to feature such stories. As reflected in the two-way arrows, Ayesha explicitly sought content that reflected both the movement of South Asians to the Gulf and Khaleejis (people from the Gulf) to South Asia. She was inspired by her research on the Bahraini poet Ebrahim Al-Arrayedh, born in Bombay.[61] Within weeks of its creation, the account was already attracting positive press coverage in both South Asia and the Gulf, evidence of the deep hunger for spaces for sharing the experience of migrating between the two regions.[62] As Priyanka Sacheti, who wrote two early articles about the account for publications in India and Pakistan, and contributed her own photos to *Gulf ⇄ South Asia*, explained: "Sometimes we are really hungry to read about ourselves. . . . Our experience is very distinct, and we don't read enough about it."[63]

Another contributor, Aathma Nirmala Dious, put it this way:

> We don't have the concept of hyphenated identity here, like Indian-American, Indian-European. Here it's a completely different thing. I go with saying I'm Malayali from Abu Dhabi. I have an issue with identifying with

> the Indian-thing as a whole, especially pertaining to recent politics. And I say I'm from Abu Dhabi because that's all I really know. I was born there, brought up there. I only recently moved to Dubai two years back. I'm still very much an Abu Dhabi girl.

In choosing which photos to submit to the account, she remembers searching for images that showed her family within the city's urban landscape, which was so central to her identity.[64]

For her post, Priyanka contributed a childhood photograph from her family home in Muscat, Oman's capital, in which she is standing in front of built-in bookshelves filled with framed baby photos, travel souvenirs, and statues of Ganesh (see Figure 5.1).[65] Priyanka is dressed in Indian festive wear for Diwali, which she described as one of her favorite parts of the holiday since she usually wore jeans and t-shirts. She recalled that her parents would host up to a hundred guests, filling their home with friends, whereas "traditionally [they would have] celebrated with . . . family back home." In addition to conveying her memories of these parties, the photograph also captured her deep attachment to the faculty house on the campus of Sultan Qaboos University. She grew up in the home and returned even as an adult until her parents retired and moved to Dubai in 2020 after three decades in Oman. Yet even after they moved, as Priyanka explained, her home on the SQU campus is "still my house in my mind."[66]

The photograph resonated deeply with others following the *Gulf ⇄ South Asia* account. The comments chimed in with recognition: "The feelings of every gulfie kid 💔" and "You managed to put in words what every gulfie kid feel [sic] when they have to leave the place where their heart and memories belong to." The affectionate term "gulfie," which is neither national nor ethnic, is particularly striking here, suggesting affective ties to a place rooted in quotidian experiences of space and material surroundings—from architecture to food. In one comment, a follower even recognized the bookshelves in Priyanka's photograph as part of the standard furnishing in the SQU campus houses, although she had not named the university in her original post.

When I asked Priyanka what it felt like to see these comments pop up, she related: "For me, it was a sense of kinship. It was affinity. It was a feeling of, may our tribe increase! . . . Sometimes, when I share Oman Chips [a popular snack] on my stories, people will come and say oh this reminds us of home! . . . It is this kind of kinship. This sense that someone knows what it feels like. . . . This bonding experience." As she elaborated, Priyanka has sometimes found it challenging to connect with her family in India, having lived an itinerant lifestyle that took her from Oman to the UK and the US before settling more recently in Bangalore, where much of her husband's family is based. Friends and relatives in Bangalore find some of her habits baffling, such as her preference for Coco Pops, a chocolate-flavored American cereal marketed to children, over parathas, a buttery South Asian flatbread. "They are like, there are so many hot breakfasts, why would you want to have boring cereal? And I'm like, this is the only way I know how to have breakfast! I know it is such a tiny, mundane thing, but it is a constant battle." Against this backdrop, the more fluid geographies of social media have provided Priyanka with an alternative network of diasporic kin—"strangers who you've often never met, but with whom you bond."

Priyanka's comments are reminiscent of Benedict Anderson's argument about the role of print capitalism in fostering the nation as an "imagined community," an idea also invoked in the previously mentioned contribution to *Brown History*.[67] Much has been made of the power of social media in remaking how nations operate as affective communities.[68] What is striking about Priyanka's comments is that she points to the equally transformative impact of social media on the family as an imagined community, opening up new modes of imaging kinship beyond normative biological and legal relations. By reassembling one's family photos while forging new bonds rooted in shared diasporic experiences, accounts like *Gulf ⇄ South Asia* reimagine the family album—and the family along with it. It is, therefore, unsurprising that the medium has been particularly appealing for diasporic families. Many of these families have for generations been reworking kinship relationships in the context of shifting geographies, alternative modes of communication, and the imperative to bond across traditional boundaries—with social media just the latest iteration.

While Priyanka framed her experience as diasporic, when I reached out to others whose photographs appeared on *Gulf ⇄ South Asia*, some were not sure whether the label accurately described them. Many grew up in the Gulf but now live in India or Pakistan. Some had not directly contributed to the account, but Ayesha had reposted their photographs from elsewhere. Some of these contributors spoke instead of a broader wanderlust and a willingness to uproot in search of better opportunities. Others articulated a sense of dislocation born of repeated moves. Sometimes, when they returned "home," they no longer felt comfortable in the place where they were legal citizens. Their ambivalence about labeling these experiences "diasporic" reflects how heritage and cultural engagements with diaspora based in the United States and Europe travel globally, where they marginalize other ways of being diasporic. Images of diaspora in the Global North foreground one-way migrations, while actual migration patterns, both past and present, are often multi-sited and circular. When such routes do feature in popular media, they are frequently flattened into unidimensional narratives, as was the case of many stories about the exploitation of South Asian laborers in the months leading up to the 2022 World Cup in Qatar.

Instagram offered a space to exhibit other migration experiences, which conformed to neither the stereotype of the Silicon Valley tech professional nor the impoverished oil-rig worker. For example, the account borrowed a photograph from the personal feed of Manju Sara Rajan, who grew up in Dubai and now works as a writer and designer in India, including serving as the CEO of the Kochi Biennale Foundation. Manju was quite surprised when I reached out to her about the post on *Gulf ⇄ South Asia*. She did not realize it had migrated off her personal account, where she had posted the photograph after the death anniversary of her brother.[69] The image was also not immediately recognizable as one with links to the Gulf. It showed two framed family portraits, including one of her parents and brother, soon after arriving in the Gulf in the 1970s. The image showed the portraits sitting on a wooden chest, with a small statue of a Buddha in front and surrounded by a handful of red seeds. Manju explained that the image captured her itinerant past, in which the Gulf was just one stop among many. The wooden chest was an antique meat safe, a cupboard lined with perforated metal to allow air circulation before refrigerators were standard, which reminded Manju of her grandmother's kitchen in Kerala. The Buddha was a memento from the years she spent living in Southeast Asia, from 1996 to 2003, after leaving Dubai and before returning to India. The red seeds reminded her of her childhood in Kerala, where she would collect them, a pastime she also passed on to her kids. But she noted that they were also commonly found in Africa, tying local childhoods to global contexts.[70]

As Manju's photograph suggested, even those who had been back in India for years or moved elsewhere felt that their time in the Gulf had left an imprint, although one often interwoven with other cultural influences. *Gulf ⇄ South Asia* created a vital space for reflecting on these ties, even when bittersweet. Neetha Kurup, who shared a photograph of a family trip to Wild Wadi, a popular amusement park in Dubai, told me that when she was pregnant, she "constantly dreamed about Dubai, specifically the 2-bedroom flat in Deira I grew up in and my classroom in Our Own English High School." Yet she also expressed hesitance about moving back, particularly "when I remember the precariousness of their [her parents'] situation, having to tolerate sexism and/or racism in their jobs because they felt they had no other option due to their visas being at the mercy of their employers."[71] The importance of domestic spaces to Neetha's reflections also suggests how ties to "home," not as a country of origin but as a space of comfort, provide an alternative imaginary of belonging to those associated with nationality or citizenship.

While perhaps universal to migrants, these themes of temporariness versus permanence and mobility versus attachment also have particular significance in the Gulf. Many immigration regimes privilege migrants deemed highly skilled and fast-track them to permanent residency or citizenship. Still, temporality and status have become particularly closely intertwined in the Gulf.

I personally encountered this valuation during my first days in the UAE, when I was instructed to attend an official lecture at the *Tawjeeh* (guidance) Office at the Ministry of Human Resources and Emiratisation. Apparently, as a visiting humanities research scholar, I was classified among workers in skill levels three to five, including receptionists, storekeepers, mechanics, laborers, and domestic workers—who required extra guidance. Although I initially felt that this was a slight against my humanities PhD, I suspect it had more to do with my short-term contract.[72] On arrival, I was ushered into a classroom equipped with a large screen and individual desks, each with its own headphones. We were told to put on the headphones and select from several language options. An animated video soon commenced, featuring a young man who traveled to the UAE to work. Interspersed with the story of his journey through the "land of achieving your dreams," the video offered information about the labor contract, advice on saving money, and warnings against going on strike. Notably, at the end of the video, the fictional migrant returned home to open his own shop with the money he had saved. The message was clear: for states like the UAE the "ideal" unskilled or semi-skilled migrant is single, works for a period of years in the country, and lives frugally, often in a dormitory provided by their employer, before returning to a home and family elsewhere. Clearly, the "Emiratisation" of such "human resources" was meant to be strictly circumscribed, even as the government was introducing a new "Golden Visa," designed to retain foreign talent on a long-term basis. One's temporality—short-term, long-term, or for a small number of citizens, permanent—is officially determined according to hierarchies of skill, although in practice, it often, if not always, maps onto North/South geographies and racialized bodies.[73]

In the Gulf, having a history is, therefore, a privilege from which many South Asians feel excluded. Some members of the South Asian diaspora with whom I spoke pushed back against this storyline by pointing to the centuries-old trade links between India and the Gulf. Others cited their own families, who had lived, for multiple generations, in the region. In many families, however, these stories had only been shared with close friends and relatives or even suppressed within families themselves. Aathma related how, as a child, she had thought that her grandfather lived in India and had merely visited the family in Abu Dhabi, where her parents worked as professionals. As an adult, however, she realized her grandfather had his own Gulf itinerary, working as a tailor in Oman, Qatar, and Abu Dhabi until Aathma was around four years old. Reflecting, Aathma thought: "If I had known . . . I might have had an earlier sense of stability within the region, which I did not have until recently." Aathma noted that greater awareness of such personal histories is critical. Even as many in her family have transitioned to white-collar professions, "the lack of any permanency within the Gulf as migrants remains the same and that is still a struggle."[74]

Speaking about the importance of projects like *Gulf ⇄ South Asia,* Aathma explained that third-generation families like hers are pushing for more openness about these histories even as much fear remains. For her parents' generation, "Their first priority is our safety, so for them, it's either we keep quiet and stay within the lines, or we leave." But Aathma insisted that greater openness about stories like her grandfather's is essential for young adults like herself and, eventually, their children. She explained: "If we stay here long term, then are we actually allowed to tell our stories the way it is, or are we going to have to constantly self-censor? If we create families here, and the generations continue, are we going to do the same thing over and over again?" For Aathma, telling stories about the past was crucial to envisioning different futures. While Instagram accounts like *Gulf ⇄ South Asia* were doing crucial work in this regard, she was also concerned about their impermanence. Ayesha has not posted new content to the account since January 2022. Although the account remains accessible, the lack of ongoing engagement raises questions about its future. Aathma mused:

> If the app goes down, we are going to have an issue. . . . It will be quite devasting if we lose something as intensive as this because there is no official government archive being kept, or I as an expat, I don't have access to the government archives or anything like that. I don't even know if there's an archive beyond our legal papers being kept here of our stories. That's something to think about long term. Can the archive stretch beyond social media and become something a lot more concrete, if we are supposed to stabilize ourselves and our narratives in the region?[75]

## Diasporic Archives

When speaking with Aathma, I wondered what such a diasporic archive might look like. I agree with her that Instagram is a problematic medium, even as it has empowered highly creative projects in recent years. The landscape of Instagram is already shifting, with the platform prioritizing income-generating accounts in a way that often buries content from feeds such as *Gulf ⇄ South Asia,* which is non-profit. Aathma told me that she now prefers to circulate much of her own commentary on TikTok. She finds its algorithms are more effective at pushing out content to diverse viewers in Dubai and Abu Dhabi, not just people who share particular affinities, for example to the South Asian community. She gets more critical comments on TikTok from people who think only citizens of the UAE should describe themselves as "from Dubai," but this creates opportunities for shifting people's mindset about migration and belonging. Yet, TikTok ultimately shares many of the same structural biases as Instagram, and within a few years, both platforms, like Friendster or Myspace, may be obsolete. This is hardly a good strategy for long-term archiving of diasporic pasts, even if it generates important new conversations. The underlying emphasis on revenue, which is a common denominator across most of these platforms, is also deeply troubling. Accounts like *Brown History*, which also has a commercial website that sells art and a subscription-based Substack newsletter, may fare better in this environment. Still, we should all be wary of the corporatization of history, even if one cannot blame creators for trying to make a living. Monetizing historical knowledge, which is already a problem within academia, where much research remains locked behind subscription paywalls, is only likely to reinforce existing imbalances in whose diasporic experiences are represented and whose remain marginal. Already rendered more vulnerable by the relentless drive to capitalize culture, increasing state surveillance of social media, including by ascendant, anti-migrant regimes, may sound the death knell for these platforms as spaces for alternative diasporic expression.

The impermanence of digital archives is hyper visual, as I learned while frantically revising this chapter to incorporate the latest rise and fall of different companies and platforms, even as I knew my revisions would themselves be quickly out-of-date. Yet the seeming permanence and stability of traditional archives can themselves be a mirage, which serves to bolster certain stories about migration while marginalizing others. We saw this, for example, in the last chapter in the title of the exhibit, "Once British Always British," which emphasized the permanence of national identities even as the exhibit itself subtly altered the archival materials it used to construct its narrative. Demanding that such traditional archives, with their associated mythologies, make more room for diasporic histories can serve essential purposes in terms of writing histories that support citizenship—undergirding efforts by migrants to achieve permanent legal status in adopted homelands. The fact that this pathway to citizenship is currently closed to South Asians in many Gulf states gives this desire for archival permanence and stability added salience. When you are officially limited to being temporary, demanding a stable place to store your past is a claim to having a right to a future in the region, both for yourself and your children.

But having spent many years working in state repositories, in which the biodata of colonial migrants has indeed been filed away for a century or more, I see both the power and limits of such archival strategies of permanence and stability for conveying diasporic histories. As should now be clear, many diasporic journeys were circuitous as they wove across landscapes that looked less like conventional maps with clear borders than layered collages of variegated political, economic, cultural, and religious authority. Decolonization reordered these landscapes, but diasporic circuits have remained multi-sited and circular—and geographies of belonging have only become more, rather than less, complex with the opening of digital vistas. Today, traces of these journeys can be found in archives, but often, they spill out from the logic of the nation-states that remain the dominant custodians of official histories. We, therefore, can and should turn to archives to unearth rich raw material—details of passages, snapshots of migrants, records of deaths, and receipts for the transmission of material assets. However, configuring this data into diasporic histories requires reorganizing them into continually shifting assemblages.

For me, working with families greatly aided my efforts to create such historical collages. Families have helped me to connect archival data points into narratives, even as material from the archives has also deepened my analysis of family memories—as was the case with Angamma/English Mary's story from Chapter 3. Family researchers have suggested strategies for reassembling materials born out of colonial violence into intimate memorials. I opened the book with one such example, the indentured ID photograph of Gowsee that now hangs alongside his Indo-Mauritian-British descendants, but other examples abound. The role of movement in these acts of archival collage show the overlap between centering mobility as a key feature of diasporic history and how we approach research. Just as diasporic families repeatedly uprooted and re-rooted themselves in new landscapes, moving records or information extracted from them into assemblages allows us to rework the past into an ever-shifting present. These processes can happen through physical collage—as in the brilliant art of Renluka Maharaj, whose work I discussed in the introduction. With paint, rhinestones, fabric, and gold leaf, she overlays colonial photographs of indentured laborers with color, texture, and radiance—transforming them from static artifacts into mobile legacies that can bridge the past and present. Yet, for many others, digital tools have made these processes of re-routing and collaging more accessible. Once glued into an album, physical photographs may be difficult to move. However, their digital reincarnations can be endlessly shared, rearranged, and edited. Regardless of which mediums they deploy, practitioners of these methods rely not on archival permanence and stability but on mobility and adaptability. They work with knowledge born out of *jahaji* roots, which weave across land and water, periodically dug and divided, only to emerge with a new vibrance. Or as Ruth D'Souza, one of my interviewees, put it: "migrating for better prospects is ingrained in our DNA."[76]

# Conclusion

## UPROOTING HISTORY

WHILE WORKING on this book, I found myself explaining that it was a family history but with the caveat that it was not *my* family history. Many of the people I interviewed did not believe me. Before telling me about their families, they wanted to know about mine. When I talked about being married into a family that traces their roots through Kerala and the Gulf, they nodded with understanding—okay, that's why you are interested in our stories. My motivations are more complex, interweaving personal and professional interests. Yet, those convinced that I was also trying to understand my family were right, but not just because I married into a "South Asian" diasporic family. Much of my work on this book has overlapped with a period when I became a mother, altering how I moved through the world. These shifts were compounded by experiencing early motherhood during the COVID-19 pandemic. My experience during this period pushed me to rethink family and mobility through a more deeply feminist lens, foregrounding gendered bodies as central to both.

In contrast, I completed the initial research for some chapters before having children and with a generous research fellowship from the Social Science Research Council. Unlike many academic fellowships tethered to a particular university or a single nation, it provided funding with no residential requirement. At the time, it felt like I was embodying the ideal lifestyle for a global historian—able to fly unburdened between archives in London, Natal, Delhi, Singapore, and Hong Kong. While I remain deeply grateful for this opportunity, I now realize that it encouraged me to experience mobility as a rootless condition, untethered from place or familial attachments.

Coming soon after my return, pregnancy and motherhood felt like the opposite. It became more physically challenging to move my body across long distances, including missing a flight while security agents tested my pumped breast milk for explosives. Around this time, I realized that Janbai and Caroline nursed infants (or supervised wet nurses) on extended oceanic journeys, making my struggles seem minor. But Janbai's and Caroline's journeys must have been far easier than that of the single mother Ponnamma, who traveled alongside Angamma's family on the Castleton from Madras to Natal with two infants. Our experiences of motherhood and mobility were profoundly shaped by class and race. Still, there were underlying resonances in the tethering responsibilities of caring for dependents—of moving from place to place while pulling our roots and branches along with us.

As I contemplated these journeys, my own and those of my historical subjects, I sometimes also griped about being stuck at home due to pandemic restrictions and the burdens of infant care. But my world was still in motion. At a macro level, I observed time and space remapped as a microscopic virus tore across borders in a matter of weeks. At a micro level, every aspect of my daily routine shifted—from worrying about locating necessities like formula and diapers I had previously taken for granted to learning to teach online. I was physically stationary but caught in a whirlwind of change—a condition that reminded me that family members who were left at home, historically disproportionately women, children, and the elderly, were as much a part of diasporic families as those who physically traveled abroad. Like those who traveled, they learned to navigate new regimes of communication and finance as they waited for letters and remittances to trickle in. They took on new responsibilities for managing reconfigured households just as their relations forged new intimate bonds abroad. Thinking about mobility through a gendered lens made me more aware of both the embodied, physical experiences of migration and their role in reshaping how people experienced the world, even when they remained in one place. Many who "stayed at home" were women who appear only as stray hints in colonial records. They were the woman Sher Dilkhan omitted from his will, which gave all his property to an unborn son, and "Golam Fattyma," the wife in India that Jan Mahomed named on his Application for a Document of Identity. Sitting in one place, rereading the materials I had previously collected rather than racing between archives, made me more attuned to their fleeting, ghostly presences, which were too easy to miss when plowing through hundreds of dossiers before quickly moving on to the next archive.

During the pandemic, I also spent a lot of time gardening—an outdoor activity that seemed safe and which my daughter and I both enjoyed—digging up and dividing my perennials while she rolled in the mud. Scholars of the Indian Ocean are prone to aquatic metaphors, but I found myself thinking with roots and dirt. While water makes bodies feel more buoyant, soil weighs us down. Yet, unlike trees, many plants cannot thrive perpetually rooted in one place. They must be periodically uprooted, divided, and transplanted—a laborious process through which gardens produce ever-shifting beauties. Perennial roots are more akin to threads than the underground edifice of roots depicted in most family trees. They are meant to be untangled from one patch of earth and woven into another tapestry of earth and living matter, which makes each season's garden unique. As roots or threads, these relations to the past are the tethered mobility I saw echoed in the experience of many diasporic families—connected, even burdened, by the past but in ways that required constant movement and remaking. Thinking with perennials also helped me appreciate the ghosts that haunt family histories. These are plants that seem to die back every season only to re-emerge a few months later—just as in families, the ties between generations complicate the ethical boundaries historians and archivists attempt to draw between what we owe the living and the dead.

My point is not to exceptionalize the intellectual insights of motherhood, botany, or weaving (a hobby I have yet to embrace). Instead, I want to underline how thinking with gendered bodies immersed in earth and water (just as Thamboosamy's body was carried on board a yacht before being entombed) transforms how we approach family and mobility. It is to appreciate how gendered bodies touch the past—not as an abstraction but through what we materially make, with the heir*looms* we inherit, but also those torn from our grasp. These ways of engaging the past allow us to draw more women into diasporic histories that are too often told as stories of men. They also allow us to see different types of kinship relations than those recorded in family trees or mapped by ethno-nationalist affinities. They reveal ties that bound women to women and men to men outside of normative regimes of blood and legal relations. These are the threads that linked Asian and African seamen when they borrowed each other's hats to pose for ID photographs. They are the kinship bonds forged on the Instagram account *Gulf ⇄ South Asia* through sharing nostalgic cravings for "gulfie" snacks.

Thinking in this way "uproots" the who, what, where, when, and how of writing histories of diasporic families. It draws in new subjects, geographies, temporalities, and modes of research. Yet many of these methods are deeply familiar even as they are hived off from academic scholarship. We already know how to flip through albums and appreciate the intimacy of wearing an inherited heirloom against our skin—but we often fail to see how they relate to what we have come to know as History.

Working with students helped me to see these connections. Early on, one of my best decisions was to develop an undergraduate seminar that would overlap with my research for this book. The class invited students to explore their family histories, using methods I was simultaneously experimenting with in my research. When I first brought the idea up with colleagues, however, several expressed concern. One warned that students and other faculty might view a family history and roots research seminar as not academically serious.

Their comments reflected more widespread attitudes among academic historians who see roots research as an amateur pursuit, with little to teach professional historians about their craft. One colleague joked that I was proposing a "G-rated" course in histories of gender and sexuality, although I reject approaches to family history that reinforce normative conceptions of conjugal relations. Initially, I heeded such advice and taught the course under the more academic title of "Family and Empire." However, many of the books on the syllabus featured historians writing family histories, and my students found thinking about roots research as a serious mode of engaging with the past exciting. Several raised questions that have become central to the book.[1]

The palatable pleasure my students took in the class emboldened me to rename the seminar "Family History." I also redesigned it to meet the requirements for my department's capstone course on historical research methods—widely considered by students and faculty alike our most rigorous offering. The class gave me space to think with my students about heirlooms and albums as sources and explore the landscapes of digital genealogy. These methods became critical springboards for class assignments, such as asking students to write a historical analysis of an object from their childhood home. Many other instructors found the research capstone challenging, with students often seeming discouraged and intimidated by "professional" historical methods. In contrast, I found that teaching research through family history bypassed the intimidation factor, even as I was able to guide students through challenging methods—from reading census records to conducting oral-history interviews.

Although I no longer found it necessary to justify the seriousness of family history as a method, my students in these seminars challenged me in new ways. Many were first- and second-generation Americans, some of whose families jumped at the opportunity to document their journeys, while others were more hesitant. In working with their parents and grandparents, the students had to develop their own ethics, which went far beyond drafting consent forms. Many had a deep desire to know about their ancestors' stories. Some found their relatives, however, did not want to pass on the burdens of the past to the next generations. Some students disagreed and felt that they had a right to know about their parents' and grandparents' struggles as a crucial context for their own lives. But these students also found that respecting their relatives' silences was essential to building trust, a precondition for ongoing conversations. Observing these family dramas unfold, I developed a deeper appreciation for the role of relationship building to responsibly engaging with the past. It was in this back-and-forth between different generations as they negotiated their collective claims to the past that I saw a different vision of what historical ethics might mean beyond the academy's reductive emphasis on bureaucratic and legalistic protocols. I came to emulate this emphasis on cultivating ongoing conversations as I came to work more intimately with the different families who populate the book's chapters.

These questions became more urgent after the Black Lives Matter movement. While I think students often wondered about my position as a White historian who studies South Asia, when I again taught Family History in the Fall of 2020, I found that students felt more empowered to ask these questions openly. While at times uncomfortable, these conversations made me think more deeply about how my family history informs my work—from childhood memories of being told stories about how my Jewish grandparents fled pogroms to struggles as an adult to figure out how I belong within the South Asian family into which I married. Being pushed by my students has also made me more thoughtful about what I owe the subjects whose family stories populated the previous pages—both living and dead. Sometimes, this has meant recognizing that I do not have a right to tell their stories, pulling back, as I did when encountering the will in Chapter 2. Ultimately, when I knew that a family preferred a story to be untold, I tried to honor those wishes. But I do not see this as a one-size-fits-all ethical formula—sometimes, it may be appropriate, even imperative, for historians to betray the wishes of descendants. I have also grappled with cases in which families disagreed—a pattern of fissures within families that material and immaterial inheritances often bring to the fore. Yet there is still much to learn from thinking about how writing history can be shaped by an ethics of care—which is deeply contingent on the relationships in which a historian's work is entangled. We should feel accountable not only to our professional colleagues, but also to those who share intimate connections with our work, including the ghosts who rifle through our archival documents.

At a time when we constantly hear about the decline of the humanities, family history offers rich opportunities to make our work relevant to the larger public and to interrogate our own methods. As the rapid spread of artificial intelligence threatens to uproot how we teach writing and research, family history provides opportunities to teach students to tap personal connections with the past and develop their unique narrative voices. ChatGPT cannot write our family histories. However, in many professional spaces, I continue to find that colleagues hesitate to engage with family history and popular modes of engaging with the past more broadly. Many of my colleagues who work on South Asian history are enthusiastic followers of the Instagram account *Brown History* and greatly admire its work, particularly with family photographs and oral histories. However, I encountered awkward laughs when I mentioned using Instagram in my research. How could I be doing serious scholarship by scrolling through photos on my phone and sending DMs? At times, I felt somewhat afraid to own up to the unexpected directions that my research path had taken. Yet, if I had been running keyword searches on a digitized newspaper database, which required a costly subscription and was therefore only accessible to academics at wealthy research institutions, no one would have questioned the seriousness of my work. Again, undergraduates, in this case, two research assistants with whom I worked at New York University in Abu Dhabi, helped dispel my fears about conducting Instagram research.

I take these awkward laughs as symptomatic of entrenched professional gatekeeping. Historians want more people to read our books. However, we remain far less inclined to open two-way conversations that recognize methods and arguments honed outside academia as relevant to our work. As I found early in my career, historians sometimes write off family history by treating it as inherently conservative—tracing a straight line from elitist practices of ancestral genealogy to vanilla-flavored stories about White, heteronormative families. While plenty of such narratives circulate within roots research, my experiences engaging with family researchers rarely fit these stereotypes. Instead, I found many who were excavating radical pasts—including of racial and gender violence—using methods that deeply unsettled my professional training. Learning that families often found my queries about personal collections of letters and diaries insensitive to their ancestors' limited literacy, I instead began asking how they connected with their pasts—leading me to pay more attention to pictures and objects, or material memories of lost heirlooms.

These families also repeatedly drew me out of my professional comfort zone of writing about the past and into the present. They asked polite but unsettling questions about the value of my work. In one particularly memorable conversation, I was asked what I saw my research contributing to the families whose past I was using, particularly given my propensity to lapse into citing obscure historians and theorists. Since that conversation, I have tried to share my archival sources with families by searching out descendants. I have taken this as a challenge to write a more accessible book so families can tell me what I got wrong. But it has also made me think more deeply about my honest answer during that earlier conversation: I am not sure how many people will read my book, but I hope to reach many more in my classrooms. It was my students who first gave me the courage to take this work seriously, and it is to them that I owe my greatest debts.

# ACKNOWLEDGMENTS

FOLLOWING THE trails of the remarkable families that peopled the pages of this book has taken many years and journeys. My greatest debts are to the families that shared their stories with me, whose names, with permission, are cited in the chapters themselves. I have tried to write a book that does justice to their generosity in sharing their past and the trust they placed in me to tell one version of their stories. I ask their forgiveness for my shortcomings and hope our conversations will continue long after the book is published. As I have learned while working on this book, family histories are never finished, and this book is just one of many retellings.

I also owe a tremendous debt to my students, whose research with their own families was deeply inspirational for my work on this book. I thank the dozens of students who have enrolled in my "Family History" course over the years. Sergio Infante and Barbara Shi deserve special acknowledgment for deeply provocative conversations about ethics. I also benefitted enormously from the input of my graduate students, Avigyan Banerjee, Cherene Aniyan Puthethu, and Yuntian (Christopher) Xuan, who taught "Family History" with me and commented on draft chapters.

I have benefitted from working in remarkable archives, and even more importantly, with archivists and librarians who shared their enthusiasm for preserving dusty legacies. These include the staff of the Arkib Negara Malaysia, the National Archives of Singapore, the Zanzibar National Archives, the Gandhi-Luthuli Documentation Centre, the National Archives of South Africa (Pietermaritzburg), The National Archives (Kew), the National Archives of India (Delhi), the British Library, the National Archives and Records Administration (College Park and Chicago), the Peabody Essex Museum, and the Tower Hamlets Local History Archives. In Zanzibar, Omar Sheha facilitated access to the archives and was a hospitable host. In Pietermaritzburg, Zama Thenjwayo shared her remarkable expertise in navigating their collection and its importance as a resource for family researchers. Paul Johnson at The National Archives was incredibly patient with me over the many months it took to obtain the images for Chapter 4.

Multi-sited research poses challenges, and I have only been able to write this book because many showed remarkable generosity in sharing their expertise and local knowledge. In Kolkata, when I was just beginning to think about this book, Sreemati Mitter hosted me in her multi-generational bungalow, whose story was also an inspiration for this book. In Kuala Lumpur, Wilbert Wong provided help locating relevant public-history projects, including the Facebook Group Malaysian Heritage and History Club. Dear family friends, Valsa Auntie and Mon Uncle, were intrepid hosts, cheerfully accompanying me to visit dreary cemeteries and crematoriums. The staff at the Sri Maha Mariamman Temple graciously answered my odd queries. In South Africa, Goolam Vahed introduced me to the collections at the Gandhi-Luthuli Documentation Centre and shared his incredible knowledge about their history. In Maryland, Hannah Groch-Begley helped navigate the US National Archives. At the TNA, Nicholas Sprenger helped dig into maritime records. In London, Deborah, Tom, and Alice listened with tireless enthusiasm to my many reports from the field. In Abu Dhabi, Zaina Awan and Aliza Safeer worked as student assistants while sharing their expertise as children of the South Asian-Gulf diaspora.

Many institutions have supported this research, both materially and intellectually. Sugata Bose and Ayesha Jalal inspired me from the beginning of my PhD to think about South Asia's connections to the wider Indian Ocean. I began work on this project during a post-doctoral fellowship at the Centre for History and Economics at Cambridge University. The circle of scholars that orbit CHE provided much of the inspiration for this work. I am deeply grateful to Emma Rothschild, Sunil Amrith, Tim Harper, William O'Reilly, Iza Hussin, Inga Huld Markan, Rachel Leow, Fei Hsien Wang, Catherine Evans, Fahad Bishara, Aditya Balasubramanian, Diana Kim, and Kalyani Ramnath for their feedback at multiple CHE workshops and afternoon teas. At Yale, the History Department and South Asian Studies Council helped nurtured this project, and I am particularly grateful to Rohit De, Steven Pincus, Francesca Trivellato, and Kalyanakrishnan Sivaramakrishnan for helping me to conceptualize it as a book. The Social Science Research Council, through its InterAsia Program, supported a vital year of multi-continental research. During this time, Engseng Ho pushed me to think more deeply about haunting as method, advice that proved transformative. At Rutgers, this book grew to maturity, inspired by my amazing colleagues. Chie Ikeya, Seth Koven, Judith Surkis, Tamara Sears, Zeynep Gürsel, and Kristin O'Brassill-Kulfan were particularly influential in shaping my thinking. I also benefitted enormously from faculty fellowships connected to the projects, "Life and Death" at the Rutgers Center for Historical Analysis and "Knowing Otherwise: Haunting, Conjuring, and Spectral Encounters" at the Institute for Research on Women. After several exhausting years during the pandemic, the Humanities Research Fellowship at NYU Abu

Dhabi provided a vital opportunity to spend a year in the Gulf, during which I wrote most of the manuscript. I am grateful to Martin Klimke and Alexandra Sandu for myriad support in facilitating my research. Nathalie Peutz, Zekeria Ahmed Salem, Saqer Almarri, Peter Kitlas, Susan Abraham, Marwa Koheji, Burak Sayim, and Ada Petiwala provided a year of non-stop intellectual engagement. Conversations with Michele Bambling about albums deeply shaped Chapter 4. Raya Lakova's and Israa Mahgoub's suggestions about digital archiving and family history in the UAE transformed Chapter 5. Masha Kirasirova and Maurice Pomerantz were wonderful scholarly companions and opened their hearts to me and my family. We miss them, Sasha, Susu, Deepika, and Sara.

I received feedback on various elements of the project during presentations at the Association for Asian Studies, Annual Conference on South Asia, American Society for Legal History, Law and Society Association, DelVal British Studies Group, University of Wisconsin, University of Pittsburg, InterAsian Academy, Harvard University, University of Pennsylvania, University of Chicago, Columbia University, University of the Witwatersrand, Princeton University, Cambridge University, Hong Kong University, the National University of Singapore, and Delhi University. I am particularly grateful to Mou Banerjee, Isabel Hofmeyr, Nurfadzilah Yahaya, James Pickett, and Anupama Rao for invitations to present this work and comments that pushed it in new directions. Many others provided invaluable feedback that I am not able to adequately acknowledge here.

The team at Princeton University Press has shown great faith in this project over the many years that it took for it to come to fruition. I am grateful to Brigitta van Rheinberg and Eric Crahan for advocating for the book during its early stages of development and to Priya Nelson and Emma Wagh for seeing it through to completion. The anonymous reviewers provided a critical roadmap for revision that inspired me with new energy to make this a better book. I am indebted to Kathleen Cioffi for her skill in shepherding the book through production. I am also grateful to Katherine Wiley for her editorial support and critical input as an Africanist and anthropologist—her talented editing improved every page.

My deepest thanks go to my beloved Johan and Lily. Johan somehow managed to juggle the roles of adventurous travel companion, sharp intellectual critic, and loving cheerleader during the many years it took to complete the book. Lily, I started this book before you existed, but it has only come into being in this form because you taught me to live and love in new ways.

# NOTES

## Introduction: Worldly Afterlives

1. My fictionalized account of Gowsee's photographic encounter draws on research that Kathleen Harrington-Watt conducted for her dissertation, "'Still We Live On': The Transfiguration of Colonial Indentured Labour Photographs in Mauritius" (PhD Dissertation, University of Canterbury, 2016). Details such as Gowsee's arrival date in Mauritius are based on archival research conducted by Caitlin Golaup using these same records.

2. The following discussion draws on an interview with Kyriaki Anagnostopoulou and Caitlin Golaup on April 14, 2023 and a follow-up conversation over email with Caitlin Golaup on April 21, 2023.

3. The only other comparable, but much smaller, project that I have been able to locate is another nineteenth-century project in the Seychelles involving photographs of formerly enslaved Africans. Yvette Christiansë, "Coming into Visibility in the Indian Ocean," *History of Photography* 45, no. 3–4 (2021): 231–44.

4. The Facebook Group is by invitation only, but its frontpage, which includes Gowsee's indenture photograph, can be viewed at https://www.facebook.com/groups/495513475152467, accessed January 16, 2025.

5. In crafting the opening, I drew inspiration from Saidiya Hartman's theorization of critical fabulation in "Venus in Two Acts," *Small Axe* 12, no. 2 (June 2008): 1–14. I have also benefited richly from the theorization of archival profusion in Anjali Arondekar, *Abundance: Sexuality's History* (Durham: Duke University Press, 2023).

6. These numbers are for migrants from India between 1840 and 1940 and are based on the analysis of the demographer Kingsley Davis, who drew on data from the colonial census. *The Population of India and Pakistan* (New York: Russell and Russell, 1951). For further analysis of these statistics, see Adam McKeown, "Global Migration, 1846–1940," *Journal of World History* (2004): 155–89; Sunil S. Amrith, *Migration and Diaspora in Modern Asia* (Cambridge: Cambridge University Press, 2011) and *Crossing the Bay of Bengal: The Furies of Nature and the Fortunes of Migrants* (Cambridge, MA: Harvard University Press, 2013).

7. In considering the entangled histories of South Asia, the Indian Ocean, and British Empire, I build on a large body of work inspired by the pioneering scholarship of Sugata Bose, *A Hundred Horizons: The Indian Ocean in the Age of Global Empire* (Cambridge: Harvard University Press, 2006); Thomas R. Metcalf, *Imperial Connections: India in the Indian Ocean Arena, 1860–1920* (Berkeley: University of California Press, 2007).

8. Mike Davis, *Late Victorian Holocausts: El Niño Famines and the Making of the Third World* (London: Verso Books, 2002).

9. Clare Anderson, *Convicts: A Global History* (Cambridge: Cambridge University Press, 2022); Anand A. Yang, *Empire of Convicts: Indian Penal Labor in Colonial Southeast Asia* (Oakland: University of California Press, 2021).

10. Gopalan Balachandran, *Globalizing Labour?: Indian Seafarers and World Shipping, c. 1870–1945* (New Delhi: Oxford University Press, 2012); Kate Imy, *Faithful Fighters: Identity and Power in the British Indian Army* (Stanford: Stanford University Press, 2019).

11. Crispin Bates, "Some Thoughts on the Representation and Misrepresentation of the Colonial South Asian Labour Diaspora," *South Asian Studies* 33, no. 1 (2017): 9. On the dominant, but often neglected, migration around the Bay of Bengal, see Amrith, *Crossing the Bay of Bengal.*

12. Claude Markovits, *The Global World of Indian Merchants, 1750–1947: Traders of Sind from Bukhara to Panama* (Cambridge: Cambridge University Press, 2000); Johan Mathew, *Margins of the Market: Trafficking and Capitalism across the Arabian Sea* (Oakland: University of California Press, 2016); Fahad Ahmad Bishara, *A Sea of Debt: Law and Economic Life in the Western Indian Ocean, 1780–1950* (Cambridge: Cambridge University Press, 2017).

13. Rozina Visram, *Ayahs, Lascars and Princes: The Story of Indians in Britain 1700–1947* (London: Routledge, 2015); Arunima Datta, *Waiting on Empire: A History of Indian Travelling Ayahs in Britain* (Oxford: Oxford University Press, 2023); Shikha Chakraborty "'Nurses of Our Ocean Highways': The Precarious Metropolitan Lives of Colonial South Asian Ayahs," *Journal of Women's History* 32, No.2 (Summer 2020): 37–64. On the global circulation of Indian performers, and efforts to regulate their movements, see "Proposed legislation for the protection outside of India of native Indian artisans and performers," Oct. 1895–Dec. 1901, India Office Records, British Library [hereafter IOR], L/PJ/6/584, File 2076.

14. On the circular nature of much migration in the Indian Ocean, see Amrith, *Crossing the Bay of Bengal*, 28.

15. Since 2015 the UN has described India as having the world's largest diaspora, as measured by people born in India who are living outside its borders. United Nations, Department of Economic and Social Affairs, Population Division, *International Migration 2020: Highlights* and *International Migration Report 2015: Highlights*. These statistics, however, do not account for the descendants of migrants in previous generations, for which comparative data is much more difficult to compile.

16. Avery F. Gordon, *Ghostly Matters: Haunting and the Sociological Imagination*, new edition (2008; Minneapolis: University of Minnesota Press, 1997), 6. I also draw on the large corpus of work inspired by Jacques Derrida's concept of hauntology, as developed in *Specters of Marx: The State of Debt, the Work of Mourning, and the New International*, trans. Peggy Kamuf (New York: Routledge, 1994).

17. For a helpful overview of some of the theoretical interventions related to ghosts and haunting, and their relevance for South Asian historiography, see Margrit Pernau, *Emotions and Temporalities* (Cambridge: Cambridge University Press, 2021).

18. Interview with Esha Pillay by Bava Dharani, November 21, 2022, https://girmit.world/portfolio-item/learning-about-indenture/, accessed December 14, 2022.

19. María del Pilar Kaladeen, Sumayya Vally, Gitan Djeli, and Shivanjani Lal, "Living the Legacy of Indenture from Mauritius to Guyana from South Africa to Fiji," *The Funambulist* 43 (August 18, 2022), https://thefunambulist.net/magazine/diasporas/living-the-legacy-of-indenture-from-mauritius-to-guyana-from-south-africa-to-fiji, accessed July 1, 2024.

20. Iain Walker and Martin Slama, "The Indian Ocean as a Diasporic Space: A Conceptual Introduction," *The Journal of Indian Ocean World Studies* 4, no. 2 (2021): 76–90.

21. Isabel Hofmeyr, "The Black Atlantic Meets the Indian Ocean: Forging New Paradigms of Transnationalism for the Global South–Literary and Cultural Perspectives," *Social Dynamics* 33, no. 2 (2007): 18.

22. While I was working on this book, spreadsheets containing this information were available for download from https://scnc.ukzn.ac.za/doc/ship/shipndx.html but have since been removed. I work much more extensively with these materials in Chapter 3. See also Crispin Bates and Marina Carter, "Remigration of Indian Subalterns in the Colonial Indian Ocean," *Journal of Colonialism and Colonial History* 22, no. 1 (2021); Reshaad Durgahee, *The Indentured Archipelago: Experiences of Indian Labour in Mauritius and Fiji, 1871–1916* (Cambridge: Cambridge University Press, 2022), especially Chapter 4 on "Subaltern Careering."

23. Kalyani Ramnath, *Boats in a Storm: Law, Migration, and Decolonization in South and Southeast Asia, 1942–1962* (Stanford: Stanford University Press, 2023), 19.

24. Amrith, *Migration and Diaspora in Modern Asia*, 57.

25. Engseng Ho, *The Graves of Tarim Genealogy and Mobility across the Indian Ocean* (Durham: Duke University Press, 2006); Sunil Amrith, "Tamil Diasporas Across the Bay of Bengal," *The American Historical Review* 114, no. 3 (2009): 547–72.

26. Sana Aiyar, *Indians in Kenya: The Politics of Diaspora* (Cambridge, MA: Harvard University Press, 2015).

27. Rachel Leow, "Beyond Diaspora's Horizons: Mass Deportations to China and an Alternative to the Diaspora Paradigm," *Inter-Asia Cultural Studies* 24, no. 4 (2023): 587–89. I draw inspiration from Leow's effort to adopt a "rhizomatic" frame (via fungus) as an alternative to the family tree but draw on other botanical metaphors.

28. On roots in oceanic as well as terrestrial contexts, see Elizabeth DeLoughrey, *Routes and Roots: Navigating Caribbean and Pacific Island Literatures* (Honolulu: University of Hawaii Press, 2017). I also borrow from Nurfadzilah Yahaya the idea of fluid landscapes as a frame for thinking both about the role of water in shaping Indian Ocean geographies and the fluidity of continually shifting regimes of governance employed by states and by families. *Fluid Jurisdictions: Colonial Law and Arabs in Southeast Asia* (Ithaca: Cornell University Press, 2020).

29. As of July 2024, there were 1.1 million posts using the hashtag "diaspora." The next most common was #africandiaspora with 477,000 posts.

30. Rogers Brubaker, "The 'Diaspora' Diaspora," *Ethnic and Racial Studies* 28, no. 1 (2005): 1–19.

31. Mitra Sharafi, *Law and Identity in Colonial South Asia: Parsi Legal Culture, 1772–1947* (New York: Cambridge University Press, 2014); Yahaya, *Fluid Jurisdictions*; Ramnath, *Boats in a Storm*.

32. I build on a small but growing body of scholarship that looks at the entanglement of Indian migration and settler colonialism, particularly in South Africa. See Neilesh Bose, "New Settler Colonial Histories at the Edges of Empire: 'Asiatics,' Settlers, and Law in Colonial South Africa," *Journal of Colonialism and Colonial History* 15, no. 1 (2014); Nienke Boer, *The Briny South: Displacement and Sentiment in the Indian Ocean World* (Durham: Duke University Press, 2023).

33. Radhika Mohanram, *Imperial White: Race, Diaspora, and the British Empire* (Minneapolis: University of Minnesota Press, 2007); James Belich, *Replenishing the Earth: The Settler Revolution and the Rise of the Angloworld* (Oxford: Oxford University Press, 2011).

34. Maia Ramnath, *Haj to Utopia: How the Ghadar Movement Charted Global Radicalism and Attempted to Overthrow the British Empire* (Berkeley: University of California Press, 2011); Sana Aiyar, "Anticolonial Homelands Across the Indian Ocean: The Politics of the Indian Diaspora in Kenya, ca. 1930–1950," *The American Historical Review* 116, no. 4 (2011): 987–1013.

35. I draw inspiration, however, from a few creative efforts to think Indian diaspora and empire together, including Sukanya Banerjee, *Becoming Imperial Citizens: Indians in the Late-Victorian Empire* (Durham: Duke University Press, 2010); Ashwin Desai and Goolam Vahed, *The South African Gandhi: Stretcher-Bearer of Empire* (Stanford: Stanford University Press, 2016). Neither book is concerned with the afterlives of such diasporic and imperial entanglements in the post-colonial period. In rethinking empire through the lens of mixed heritage and diasporic families, I also draw inspiration from Maya Jasanoff, "Border-Crossing: My Imperial Routes," in *History Workshop Journal* 64, no. 1 (2007): 372–81.

36. On the power and subversive potential of Victoria as an imperial symbol, see Sarah Carter and Maria Nugent, eds., *Mistress of Everything: Queen Victoria in Indigenous Worlds* (Manchester: Manchester University Press, 2016).

37. This is a vast literature, but my own thinking has been particularly influenced by the following works: Ann Laura Stoler, *Carnal Knowledge and Imperial Power: Race and the Intimate in Colonial Rule* (Berkeley: University of California Press, 2002); Durba Ghosh, *Sex and the Family in Colonial India: The Making of Empire* (Cambridge: Cambridge University Press, 2006); Mrinalini Sinha, *Specters of Mother India: The Global Restructuring of an Empire* (Durham: Duke University Press, 2006); Ritu Birla, *Stages of Capital: Law, Culture, and Market Governance in Late Colonial India* (Durham: Duke University Press, 2008); Rachel Sturman, *The Government of Social Life in Colonial India: Liberalism, Religious Law, and Women's Rights* (Cambridge: Cambridge University Press, 2012); Judith Surkis, *Sex, Law, and Sovereignty in French Algeria, 1830–1930* (Ithaca: Cornell University Press, 2019); Durba Mitra, *Indian Sex Life: Sexuality and the Colonial Origins of Modern Social Thought* (Princeton: Princeton University Press, 2020); Guo-Quan Seng, *Strangers in the Family Gender, Patriliny, and the Chinese in Colonial Indonesia* (Ithaca: Cornell University Press, 2023); and Chie Ikeya, *InterAsian Intimacies across Race, Religion, and Colonialism* (Ithaca: Cornell University Press, 2024).

38. Amrith, *Migration and Diaspora in Modern Asia*, 47; Adam McKeown, "Chinese Emigration in Global Context, 1850–1940," *Journal of Global History* 5, no. 1 (2010): 112. It is worth noting that many women, however, migrated locally in the context of marriage, a point that gender historians have emphasized is often overlooked in studies of migration and mobility. Sucheta Mazumdar, "What Happened to the Women: Chinese and Indian Male Migration to the United States in Global Perspective," *Asian/Pacific Islander American Women: A Historical Anthology*, eds. Shirley Hune and Gail M. Nomura (New York: NYU Press, 2003): 58–76.

39. For accounts that foreground mobile men across different temporalities, see Philip Curtin, *Cross Cultural Trade in World History* (Cambridge: Cambridge University Press, 1984); K. N. Chaudhuri, *Trade and Civilization in the Indian Ocean: An Economic History from the Rise of Islam to 1750* (Cambridge: Cambridge University Press, 1985); Engseng Ho, *Graves of Tarim* and "Inter-Asian Concepts for Mobile Societies," *The Journal of Asian Studies* 76, no. 4 (2017): 907–28.

40. Ikeya, *InterAsian Intimacies*, 13.

41. Scott Reese, "The Myth of Immobility: Women and Travel in the British Imperial Indian Ocean, *Journal of World History* 33, no. 2 (June 2022): 301–20; Rachel Leow, "The Patriarchy of

Diaspora: Race Fantasy and Gender Blindness in Chen Da's Studies of the Nanyang Chinese, *Twentieth-Century China* 47, no. 3 (October 2022): 243–65; Samia Khatun, "The Book of Marriage: Histories of Muslim Women in Twentieth-Century Australia," *Gender & History* 29, no. 1 (2017): 8–30; Sucheta Mazumdar, "What Happened to the Women."

42. Hollian Wint, "Keeping it in the Family? Her-and His-stories among Gujarati Business Communities in the Nineteenth Century Indian Ocean," *Perspectives of Female Researchers: Interdisciplinary Approaches to the Study of Gujarati Identities* (2016): 173–88.

43. See (among others) Emma Rothschild, *The Inner Life of Empires: An Eighteenth-Century History* (Princeton: Princeton University Press, 2011); Rebecca J. Scott and Jean M. Hébrard, *Freedom Papers: An Atlantic Odyssey in the Age of Emancipation* (Cambridge: Harvard University Press, 2012); Chandra Mallampalli, *Race, Religion and Law in Colonial India: Trials of an Interracial Family* (Cambridge: Cambridge University Press, 2011). My use of micro-history and subaltern biography was also shaped by Clare Anderson, *Subaltern Lives: Biographies of Colonialism in the Indian Ocean World, 1790–1920* (Cambridge: Cambridge University Press, 2012).

44. See (among others) Mira Kamdar, *Motiba's Tattoos: A Granddaughter's Journey from America into her Indian Family's Past* (New York: Plume, 2001); Gaiutra Bahadur, *Coolie Woman: The Odessey of Empire* (Chicago: University of Chicago Press, 2013); Alison Light, *Common People: In Pursuit of My Ancestors* (Chicago: University of Chicago Press, 2014); and Hazel V. Carby, *Imperial Intimacies: A Tale of Two Islands* (London: Verso Books, 2019).

45. For a recent roundtable exploring the need for a more robust exchange between historians and family researchers, see C. Anderson, T. Birch, S. Cox, N. Couronne, C. Crockett, and L. Paterson, "Genealogies of Enslavement and Convictism: Family Histories and their Legacies in Barbados, Mauritius, and Australia," *Family & Community History* 26, no. 3 (2023): 111–36.

46. Tina M. Campt, *Image Matters: Archive, Photography and the African Diaspora in Europe* (Durham: Duke University Press, 2012); *Listening to Images* (Durham: Duke University Press, 2017); Tiya Miles, *All That She Carried: The Journey of Ashley's Sack, A Black Family Keepsake* (New York: Random House Trade Paperbacks, 2022).

47. Alondra Nelson, *The Social Life of DNA: Race, Reparations, and Reconciliation after the Genome* (Boston: Beacon Press, 2016).

48. Marisa J. Fuentes, *Dispossessed Lives: Enslaved Women, Violence, and the Archive* (Philadelphia: University of Pennsylvania Press, 2016).

49. Estate of Said Tasselm (d. 1893), The National Archives of Britain at Kew [hereafter TNA], FO 847/2; Estate of Narang Singh (d. 1914), TNA, FO 1092/307, 324.

50. My method of looking at photographs with families draws on Zeynep Devrim Gürsel, "Looking Together as Method: Encounters with Ottoman Armenian Expatriation Photographs," *Visual Anthropology Review* 39, no. 1 (2023): 200–229.

51. Sumathi Ramaswamy's and Aanchal Malhotra's interdisciplinary projects have deeply inspired my work with such materials. Christiane Brosius, Sumathi Ramaswamy, and Yousuf Saeed eds., *Visual Homes, Image Worlds: Essays from Tasveer Ghar, The House of Pictures* (New Delhi: Yoda Press, 2015); Aanchal Malhotra, *Remnants of a Separation: A History of the Partition through Material Memory* (New Delhi: HarperCollins India, 2017). I have also been inspired by the brilliant analysis of paintings in Ghosh, *Sex and the Family in Colonial India* and of photographs in marriage advertisements in Rochona Majumdar, *Marriage and Modernity: Family Values in Colonial Bengal* (Durham: Duke University Press, 2009).

52. E. A. Gait, Census of India, 1911, vol. 1, Part 1., Report, 292. The report did, however, note that the measure of literacy used was the ability to read and write, and that many Indians, who would not be deemed literate by this measure, were in fact able to read a limited canon of religious texts.

53. *Oxford English Dictionary*, s.v. "heirloom (n.)," June 2024, https://doi.org/10.1093/OED/6945855455.

54. These works have most recently been exhibited in a solo show, Suchitra Mattai, "Myth from Matter," National Museum of Women in the Arts, September 20, 2024–January 15, 2025, Washington, D.C. See also quotes from Mattai in Salomé Gómez-Upegui, "Suchitra Mattai's Woven Sculptures Give Voice to Women Around the World," *WMagazine*, September 25, 2024, https://www.wmagazine.com/culture/suchitra-mattai-artist-interview; Kriston Capps, "The Vivid Thread of Memories by the Yard," *The New York Times*, December 27, 2024, https://www.nytimes.com/2024/12/27/arts/design/mattai-textiles-museum-women-washington.html.

55. For a discussion of letter writing in the context of indenture, see Ashutosh Kumar, *Coolies of the Empire: Indentured Indians in the Sugar colonies, 1830–1920* (Cambridge University Press, 2017), 31–38; Marina Carter, *Voices from Indenture: Experiences of Indian Migrants in the British Empire* (London: Leicester University Press, 1996). For example, I found multiple references to letters that were found on dead bodies. See Julia Stephens, "Stuck at Home: Rethinking Mobility and Immobility in Histories of Asian Migration," in AHR History Lab, "On Transnational and International History," *The American Historical Review* 128, no. 1 (2023): 311–17.

56. Clifford Geertz, *The Interpretation of Cultures: Selected Essays* (New York: Basic Books, 1973), 452.

57. Gaiutra Bahadur, "Postcards from Empire," *Dissent* 62, no. 2 (2015): 49–58.

58. Quoted in Mansi Shah, "Renluka Maharaj Steps Into the Shoes of Her Ancestors to Create Her Vibrant Art," *Elle India*, October 6, 2021, https://elle.in/article/renluka-maharaj-steps-into-the-shoes-of-her-ancestors-to-create-her-vibrant-art/.

59. Renluka Maharaj, "Bhumi's Daughters," Project for Empty Space, October 1, 2022–January 21, 2023, Newark, NJ, https://www.projectforemptyspace.org/renlukamaharaj.

60. Jacques Derrida, *Right of Inspection* (New York: Monacelli Press, 1998), n.p.

61. Madhavi Thampi, "Indian Soldiers, Policemen and Watchmen in China in the Nineteenth and Early Twentieth Centuries," *China Report* 35.4 (1999): 40337.

62. Will of Sher Dilkhan, Records of the British Consulate in Tientsin, TNA, FO 678/2885.

63. Derrida repeatedly returns to this quote from *Hamlet* in *Specters of Marx: The State of the Debt, the Work of Mourning and the New International*, translated by Peggy Kamuf (New York: Routledge, 1994).

64. https://discovery.nationalarchives.gov.uk/details/r/C17208842. The case from 1929 involved the estate of Thamboosamy Pillai (d. 1902), which is discussed in more detail in Chapter 1. As far as I could ascertain, all parties named in the case are dead.

65. Lee White, "Oral History Research Excluded from IRB Oversight," January 19, 2017, https://www.historians.org/research-and-publications/perspectives-on-history/january-2017/oral-history-research-excluded-from-irb-oversight.

66. Anonymization is common in the life sciences for which IRB protocols were originally designed. Groups such as the Oral History Association have developed alternative ethical

guidelines that allow for naming when researchers follow protocols that ensure that subjects have consented to be interviewed and cited by name. This is a major disciplinary contrast with anthropology, in which scholars have typically anonymized their subjects. This practice, however, is also evolving among anthropologists as some question the ethics of not crediting subjects by name for their contributions to research. For the purposes of the IRB, the distinction between historical and ethnographic studies is that the latter "gather information from individuals in order to understand the beliefs, customs, and practices, not only of those individuals, but also of the community or group to which they belong." See "Oral History, The Protection of Human Subjects in Research and Institutional Review Board Oversight," July 2020, https://oralhistory.org/information-about-irbs/. Given the dense networks of interdisciplinary exchange between historians and anthropologists, these distinctions are often more complex on the ground. On these evolving discussions, see Erica Weiss, "Pseudonyms as Anti-Citation," in "Rethinking Pseudonyms in Ethnography," edited by Carole McGranahan and Erica Weiss, *American Ethnologist* website, 13 December 2021, https://americanethnologist.org/features/collections/rethinking-pseudonyms-in-ethnography/pseudonyms-as-anti-citation.

67. Light, *Common People*; Jerome De Groot, "Digital Public History: Family History and Genealogy," *Handbook of Digital Public History* (2022): 369.

68. Sandra Ponzanesi, "Digital Diasporas: Postcoloniality, Media and Affect," *Interventions* 22, no. 8 (2020): 977–93.

69. "Welcome to Brown History Newsletter," July 24, 2021, https://brownhistory.substack.com/p/coming-soon.

70. Paul Knevel, "Public History: The European Reception of an American idea?," *Levend Erfgoed* 6 (2009): 8.

71. Thomas Cauvin, "The Rise of Public History: An International Perspective," *Historia Crítica* 68 (2018): 3–26.

72. Paul Ashton and Alex Trapeznik, eds., *What is Public History Globally?: Working with the Past in the Present* (London: Bloomsbury Publishing, 2019), 6.

73. Laith Ulaby, "On the Decks of Dhows: Musical Traditions of Oman and the Indian Ocean World," *The World of Music* 1, no. 2 (2012): 43–62; Jim Sykes and Julia Byl, eds., *Sounding the Indian Ocean: Musical Circulations in the Afro-Asiatic Seascape* (Oakland: University of California Press, 2023).

74. I am grateful to Kristin O'Brassill-Kulfan, who is the series editor for the Routledge series "Global Perspectives on Public History," for thinking through these dynamics with me.

75. Pedro Machado, "Memory, Memorialization, and 'Heritage' in the Indian Ocean," in *Reimagining Indian Ocean Worlds*, Smriti Srinivas, Bettina Ng'weno, and Neelima Jeychandran, eds. (London: Routledge, 2020), 149–64; Burkhard Schnepel and Tansen Sen, eds., *Travelling Pasts: The Politics of Cultural Heritage in the Indian Ocean World* (Leiden: Brill, 2019).

76. I use the term "mixed" rather than multiracial in the book to foreground the multiple ways in which families incorporated different forms of diversity, including religious, socioeconomic, linguistic, national, racial, and ethnic background. For much of the period discussed in the book, the boundaries separating these different categories were also far more fluid than implied by their contemporary use. I also find that "mixed" rather than "multi" better captures how diasporic families fostered new hybrid identities and habits that went beyond the mere

accumulation of multiple heritages. I recognize that historically the idea of being "mixed" was sometimes used as a way of denigrating such families. Still, I chose, as a historian and a member of a multi-generational "mixed" family, to reclaim a positive meaning for this word.

77. United Nations, Department of Economic and Social Affairs, Population Division, *International Migration 2020: Highlights*, available online at https://www.un.org/en/desa/international-migration-2020-highlights.

## Chapter 1. Cosmopolitan Graves

1. The role of diasporic Asian capitalists like Thamboosamy in the development of colonial cities such as Kuala Lumpur remains under-researched and often constricted by frameworks that primarily view them as colonial compradors. I have benefitted greatly from the pioneering research published in Sivachandralingam Sundara Raja's article, "Thamboosamy Pillai and the Colonial Elite of British Malaya," *Journal of the Malaysian Branch of the Royal Asiatic Society* 94, no. 1 (2021): 101–17.

2. "The Late Mr Thamboosamy Pillay," *The Singapore Free Press and Mercantile Advertiser*, July 31, 1902, 70.

3. David Arnold, *Burning the Dead: Hindu Nationhood and the Global Construction of Indian Tradition* (Oakland: University of California Press, 2021), 3.

4. Similar customs are described in a contemporary context in Isabelle Nabokov, "Deadly Power: A Funeral to Counter Sorcery in South India," *American Ethnologist* 27, no. 1 (2000): 154.

5. "The Funeral of the Late Mr Thamboosamy Pillay," originally published in the *Malay Mail*, reprinted in *The Singapore Free Press and Mercantile Advertiser*, August 7, 1902, 4. While this description draws heavily on newspaper reporting, the displays of Chinese fireworks were a feature that descendants narrated to me during oral history interviews. Contemporary ethnographic research among Tamil Hindus in Singapore describes similar rituals. Siti Hazariah Binte Abu Bakar, "Changing Funerary Practices of the Tamil Hindus in Singapore," in *Indian Diaspora: Socio-Cultural and Religious Worlds*, ed. Pratap Kumar (Leiden: Brill, 2015), 248, ft. 17.

6. Scholars have long considered cremation an almost uniform feature of Hindu death rituals as prescribed in Vedic texts. Recent scholarship recognizes a more diverse range of funerary practices in India, but often consider them "subaltern" practices associated with lower-caste groups, women, children, and *sadhus* (religious ascetics). Amy L. Allocco has argued that the existing emphasis on cremation in the scholarship contrasts sharply with the far more diverse practices she has encountered while conducting fieldwork in Tamil Nadu with lower and middle-caste Hindus, most of whom were buried rather than cremated. "Bringing the Dead Home: Hindu Invitation Rituals in Tamil South India," *Journal of the American Academy of Religion* 89, No. 1 (March 2021): 123.

7. Ho, *The Graves of Tarim*; Arnold, *Burning the Dead*.

8. My work draws inspiration from Joshua Comaroff's work on ghosts and haunting in the landscapes of Singapore. See "Ghostly Topographies: Landscape and Biopower in Modern Singapore," *Cultural Geographies* 14, no. 1 (2007): 56–73.

9. For a deeper exploration of the connections between Malaya's plantations and urban civic spaces, see Lynn Hollen Lees, *Planting Empire, Cultivating Subjects: British Malaya, 1786–1941* (Cambridge: Cambridge University Press).

10. I draw inspiration from scholarship on the Indian Ocean that has shown that paying greater attention to water opens creative new ways of studying the past. Isabel Hofmeyr, "The Complicating Sea: The Indian Ocean as Method," *Comparative Studies of South Asia, Africa and the Middle East* 32, no. 3 (2012): 584–90; Isabel Hofmeyr, *Dockside Reading: Hydrocolonialism and the Custom House* (Durham: Duke University Press, 2021); Renisa Mawani, *Across Oceans of Law: The Komagata Maru and Jurisdiction in the Time of Empire* (Durham: Duke University Press, 2018); Dilip M. Menon, Nishat Zaidi, Simi Malhotra, and Saarah Jappie, eds., *Ocean as Method: Thinking with the Maritime* (New York: Routledge, 2022).

11. Yahaya, *Fluid Jurisdictions*.

12. On this deeper history of the region's cosmopolitan culture, see Ronit Ricci, *Islam Translated: Literature, Conversion, and the Arabic Cosmopolis of South and Southeast Asia* (Chicago: University of Chicago Press, 2011). For the evolution of this cosmopolis in the shadows of European imperial expansion, see Michael Francis Laffan, *Under Empire: Muslim Lives and Loyalties Across the Indian Ocean World, 1775–1945* (New York: Columbia University Press, 2022).

13. Iza R. Hussin, *The Politics of Islamic law: Local Elites, Colonial Authority and the Making of the Muslim State* (Chicago: University of Chicago Press, 2016), 83–86.

14. For example, in 1891 the first census of the state of Selangor (where Kuala Lumpur was located) divided its population into "Europeans," "Eurasians," "Chinese," "Malays and Other Natives of the Archipelago," "Tamils and Other Natives of India," and "Other Nationalities." Charles Hirschman, "The Meaning and Measurement of Ethnicity in Malaysia: An Analysis of Census Classifications," *The Journal of Asian Studies* 46, no. 3 (1987): 562.

15. The relationship between shifting regimes of ethnic and linguistic categorization, and the deeply internally diverse and intermixed populations they sought to divide, is illustrated beautifully in Rachel Leow, *Taming Babel: Language in the Making of Malaysia* (Cambridge: Cambridge University Press, 2018).

16. Joel S. Kahn, *Other Malays: Nationalism and Cosmopolitanism in the Modern Malay World* (Singapore: Singapore University Press, 2006); Jaclyn Ling-Chien Neo, "Malay Nationalism, Islamic Supremacy and the Constitutional Bargain in the Multi-ethnic Composition of Malaysia," *International Journal on Minority & Group Rights* 13 (2006): 95–118; and Tamir Moustafa, *Constituting Religion: Islam, Liberal Rights, and the Malaysian State* (Cambridge: Cambridge University Press, 2018).

17. Rajesh Rai, *Indians in Singapore, 1819–1945: Diaspora in the Colonial Port-City* (New Delhi: Oxford University Press, 2014), 8.

18. Anand A. Yang, *Empire of Convicts: Indian Penal Labor in Colonial Southeast Asia* (Oakland: University of California Press), 186.

19. "He Built the Sri Mariamman Temple," *The Straits Times*, November 6, 1983, 18.

20. Vina Jie-Min Prasad & Jaime Koh, "Raffles Institution," https://www.nlb.gov.sg/main/article-detail?cmsuuid=a4e62a93-b5e8-44e0-950b-be94c1b4f01a, accessed September 15, 2022.

21. Mitra Sharafi, "A New History of Colonial Lawyering: Likhovski and Legal Identities in the British Empire," *Law & Social Inquiry* 32, no. 4 (2007): 1059–94.

22. "Report of his having received an application from the Treasurer for three months leave of absence. Recommends Mr. Tambusamy Pillai to act as Treasurer," January 1887, Arkib Negara Malaysia, Kuala Lumpur (hereafter ANMKL), file KL 181/87.

23. "Re: Metalling of Java Road," June 1883, ANMKL, PWD 763/83; "Application for a loan of ($600)," June 1883, ANMKL, MISC 866/83; "Enclosing the audit report," January 1884, ANMKL, TRY 119/84; "K. Thamboosamy Pillay, Chief Clerk, Treasury, to J. P. Rodger, Acting British Resident, Selangor," April 24, 1884, ANMKL, TREASURY 2042/84. See also Raja, "Thamboosamy Pillai and the Colonial Elite of British Malaya," 101–17.

24. "Application for 200 acres of land on Petaling road and 600 acres on the 10 M.S. Damansara Road," March 1884, ANMKL, 567/84.

25. "K. Thamboosamy Pillay to J. P. Rodger," April 24, 1884, ANMKL, TREASURY 2042/84.

26. "Re cheque of $6000 in favour of the Manager Chartered Mercantile Bank Singapore, requesting him to pen a credit for the amount with the branch of his bank at Nagapatnam on behalf of Mr. Thambusamy Pillay," January 1889, ANMKL, KL114/87; "Re Mr. Thambusamy Pillay proceeding to India for the purpose of recruiting labourers," January 1889, ANMKL, KL 115/87.

27. Systems of labor recruitment in Malaya developed along somewhat different patterns than those in the Caribbean, Pacific, and South Africa. Under the *kangani* system, which formally replaced indenture after 1910, foremen were sent back to their home regions to recruit fellow workers. See Arunima Datta, *Fleeting Agencies: A Social History of Indian Coolie Women in British Malaya* (Cambridge: Cambridge University Press, 2021), 30; Kernial Singh Sandhu, *Indians in Malaya: Some Aspects of their Immigration and Settlement (1786–1957)* (Cambridge: Cambridge University Press, 2010).

28. "Forwards & recommends acceptance of the resignation of his Chief Clerk," August 1889, ANMKL, TRY 3967/89.

29. "Recommends 4 month's leave of absence to be allowed to his Chief Clerk," June–July 1889, ANMKL, TRY 1864/89.

30. "Schedule of Tenders for Railway loading and unloading contract for 1893. Forwards recommending Thamboosamy Pillay's," December 1892, ANMKL, 1117/1892.

31. "States that Syed Mohamed has applied for payment of $846.60 due to him by Govt. through his attorney K. Thamboosamy Pillai," April 1890, ANMKL, KLANG 1812/90.

32. The 1891 census listed Singapore's population as 67% Chinese, 20% Malay, and 9% Indian. Saw Swee-Hock, "Population Trends in Singapore, 1819–1967," *Journal of Southeast Asian History* 10, no. 1 (1969): 41. For the same year, census data from Kuala Lumpur indicated the population as 79% Chinese, 14% Malay, and 6% Indian. Prem Kumar Raja, *Ruling the Margins: Colonial Power and Administrative Rule in the Past and Present* (New York: Routledge, 2015), 34–35. Colonial census data, however, is notoriously problematic as a measure of what were often fluid ethnic boundaries.

33. Barbara Watson Andaya, "The 'Knowledge Economy' and Tin Mining in 19th Century Malaya," *Economic Histories of Malaya*, https://www.ehm.my/publications/articles/the-knowledge-economy-and-tin-mining-in-19th-century-malaya, accessed September 15, 2022.

34. "Mining land at Simpah recommends an application for 100 acres, from Messers. Thamboosamy, Loke Yew, Wong Chi Siew and Oh Joo Kiong," June 1893, ANMKL, CHINESE SECRETARIAT, 3616/1893.

35. Raja, "Thamboosamy Pillai," 105–7.

36. Ummadevi Suppiah and Sivachandralingam Sundara Raja, "Chettiar Capital and the Emergence of the Chinese Bourgeois in British Malaya," *Kajian Malaysia* 35, no. 1 (2017): 10–11.

37. "Regarding appointment of Mr. Tambusamy Pillay as a member of the Sanitary Board," January 1894, ANMKL, RESIDENT 162/1894.

38. "Tamboosamy Pillai," *The Straits Budget*, July 30, 1902, 2.

39. Cecilia Leong-Salobir, *Food Culture in Colonial Asia: A Taste of Empire* (London: Routledge, 2011), 106.

40. Cecilia Y. Leong-Salobir, "'Mem' and 'Cookie': The Colonial Kitchen in Malaysia and Singapore," in *Cooking Cultures: Convergent Histories of Food and Feeling*, ed. Ishita Banerjee-Dube (Cambridge: Cambridge University Press, 2016), 90–91.

41. "Selangor Padre Who Was Everyone's Friend," *The Straits Times*, 7 October 1934, 15.

42. "A Malay Wedding," *Selangor Journal*, vol. IV, no. 2, 23–25.

43. "The Wedding," *Selangor Journal*, vol. IV, no. 16, 269–70.

44. Dharm Navaratnam, "Victoria Institution, 125 years of excellence," *Malay Mail*, August 14, 2018.

45. Vadivella Belle Carl, *Thaipusam in Malaysia: A Hindu Festival in the Tamil Diaspora* (Singapore: ISEAS Publishing, 2017), 185–88; "Ask permission to utilize certain part of the Batu Caves for the purpose of making it into a place of religious workshop for the Chinese," February 1889, ANMKL, MISC 686/89. On regional identity and cosmopolitanism in shaping working-class culture in Malaya, see Amrith, "Tamil Diasporas across the Bay of Bengal."

46. On the paucity of scholarship on InterAsian intimacies, and the use of legal records to study such relations, see Chie Ikeya, "Colonial Intimacies in Comparative Perspective: Intermarriage, Law and Cultural Difference in British Burma," *Journal of Colonialism and Colonial History* 14, no. 1 (2013).

47. Lenore Manderson, "Migration, Prostitution and Medical Surveillance in Early Twentieth-Century Malaya," in *Migrants, Minorities & Health: Historical and Contemporary Studies*, eds. Lara Marks and Michael Worboys (London: Routledge, 1997), 67.

48. *K. T. Ganapathy Pillay* v *Alamaloo and another* (Selangor) [1929] UKPC 18, Record of Proceedings, Privy Council Cases with the Judgements, Social Science Collections, the British Library, 26.

49. Rajat Kanta Ray, "Asian Capital in the Age of European Domination: The Rise of the Bazaar, 1800–1914," *Modern Asian Studies* 29, no. 3 (1995): 449–554; Bose, *A Hundred Horizons*, 77.

50. On the use of labor recruiters in Southeast Asia, often referred to as *kangani*, and the contrast with systems of indenture elsewhere, see Crispin Bates, "Representations and Misrepresentations of the Colonial South Asian Diaspora," in *Global Indian Diaspora: Charting New Frontiers*, eds. Brinsley Samaroo, Primnath Gooptar, Kumar Mahabir (London: Routledge, 2021), vol. 1, 29.

51. Johan Mathew, *Margins of the Market*; Yahaya, *Fluid Jurisdictions*; Bishara, *Sea of Debt*; Itamar Toussia Cohen, "Parsi Capital and Imperial Infrastructure: Shipping and Shopping in the Port of Aden, 1840–1888," *Journal of Global History* (2023): 1–21.

52. Fahad Bishara and Hollian Wint, "Into the Bazaar: Indian Ocean Vernaculars in the Age of Global Capitalism," *Journal of Global History* 16, no. 1 (2021): 44–64.

53. For the foundational role of linguistic and literary frameworks to engagements with cosmopolitanism and vernacularism, see Sheldon Pollock, "The Cosmopolitan Vernacular," *The Journal of Asian Studies* 57, no. 1 (1998): 6–37. Subsequent scholarship has tried to root cosmopolitanism in non-European geographies and imaginaries by adding various modifiers,

including vernacular, rooted, coloured, and oceanic cosmopolitanism. See Homi K. Bhabha, *The Location of Culture* (1994; London: Routledge, 2012), ix–xxv; K. A. Appiah, "Cosmopolitan Patriots," *Critical Inquiry* 23, no. 3 (1997): 617–39; Nico Slate, *Colored Cosmopolitanism* (Cambridge, MA: Harvard University Press, 2012); Dilip M. Menon and Nishat Zaidi, eds., *Cosmopolitan Cultures and Oceanic Thought* (New York: Routledge, 2023); Sugata Bose and Kris K. Manjapra, eds., *Cosmopolitan Thought Zones: South Asia and the Global Circulation of Ideas* (Houndmills, Basingstoke, Hampshire: Palgrave Macmillan, 2010). For an argument against using cosmopolitanism altogether in these contexts, see Nile Green, "The Waves of Heterotopia: Toward a Vernacular Intellectual History of the Indian Ocean," *The American Historical Review* 123, no. 3 (2018): 846–74.

54. J.S. Furnivall, *Colonial Policy and Practice: A Comparative Study of Burma and Netherlands India* (Cambridge: Cambridge University Press, 1948), 304. For pointing to the need for a richer reading of the nature of "market" interactions, I am indebted to Sunil Amrith, "Tamil Diasporas Across the Bay of Bengal," *The American Historical Review* 114, no. 3 (2009): 547–72.

55. Thomas W. Laqueur, *The Work of the Dead: A Cultural History of Mortal Remains* (Princeton: Princeton University Press, 2015), 305–9.

56. Brenda S. A. Yeoh, *Contesting Space in Colonial Singapore: Power Relations and the Urban Built Environment* (Singapore: National University of Singapore, 2013), 281–311.

57. "The Chinese Dead," *The Straits Budget*, 28 July 1896, 2.

58. "Applies for a piece of land in some suitable locality for the cremation of deceased Sikhs," April 1890, ANMKL, POLICE 2340/90; "Cremation Ground for Sikh, Forwards tracing shewing block of land measured for," December 1893, ANMKL, SURVEY 6987/1893.

59. "The Humble Memorial of the under signed Tamils of Jaffna, Ceylon, now residing in the State of Selangor," April 9, 1896, ANMKL, MISCELLANEOUS 2027/1896.

60. Tomoko Masuzawa, *The Invention of World Religions* (Chicago: University of Chicago Press, 2012).

61. "The humble Memorial of the undersigned, Representatives of the Chitty Community residing in Kuala Lumpur," April 11, 1896, ANMKL, MISCELLANEOUS 2076/1896.

62. "Crematorium for Jaffna Tamils. Reports selection of a piece of land," June 1896, ANMKL, LANDS 3284/1896,.

63. "Cremation Ground, Kuala Lumpur," 1897, 4978/1897, ANMKL; "Licensed Burial and Burning Grounds in the Kuala Lumpur District," March 1890, 1612/1900, ANMKL; "Re: Fees charged for cremation by the Selangor Ceylon Tamils' Association," September 1907, 5218/1907, ANMKL.

64. "Music at Funerals," *The Straits Budget*, March 12, 1931, 5.

65. "Render Unto Caesar," *Malaya Tribune*, June 18, 1914, 6.

66. "Matters of Indian Interest: Hindu Funeral Processions," *The Singapore Free Press and Mercantile Advertiser*, October 29, 1931, 12.

67. Arnold, *Burning the Dead*, xi.

68. "A Semi-Christian Funeral," *Eastern Daily Mail and Straits Morning Advertiser*, February 8, 1906, 2; "A Desirable Innovation," *Eastern Daily Mail and Straits Morning Advertiser*, February 7, 1906, 2.

69. "Tamil Funerals," *Eastern Daily Mail and Straits Morning Advertiser*, February 15, 1906, 2.

70. "Selangor Padre."

71. Interview with Namasivayam, Kuala Lumpur, January 20, 2023.

72. Reports from Malacca suggest that embalming was very common among wealthy Chinese merchants who passed away while in residence there. "A Chinese Funeral," *Malacca Weekly Chronicle and Mercantile Advertiser,* September 15, 1888, 2. On Chinese diasporic practices of embalming, see also Elizabeth Sinn, "Returning Bones," Chapter 7 of *Pacific Crossing: Californian Gold, Chinese Migration, and the Making of Hong Kong* (Hong Kong: Hong Kong University Press, 2013), ft. 14.

73. "Embalming the Sultan of Johore," reprinted from the *Pall Mall Gazette* in *The Straits Times*, July 8, 1895, 3.

74. Siti Hazariah Binte Abu Bakar, "Betwixt and Between: Social Marginalization and Ritual Specialization of Tamil Hindu Undertakers in Contemporary Singapore," MA Thesis, McGill University, 2016.

75. Interview with Valuppillai, son of Pandarapillai, November 22, 1983, interviewed by Pitt Kuan Wah, Communities of Singapore (Part 2), National Archives of Singapore, Accession Number 000339, Reel 19, 139.

76. Hussin, *The Politics of Islamic Law*, 83–86.

77. Amrith, "Tamil Diasporas and the Bay of Bengal," 547–72; Sunil Amrith, "Islam's Eastern Frontiers: Tamil, Chinese, and Malay Worlds," in *Oceanic Islam: Muslim Universalism and European Imperialism*, eds. Sugata Bose and Ayesha Jalal (London: Bloomsbury India, 2020), 57–86.

78. Joel S. Kahn, *Other Malays: Nationalism and Cosmopolitanism in the Modern Malay World* (Singapore: Singapore University Press, 2006).

79. "Chitty Community in Melaka on a Quest to Obtain Bumiputera Status," *New Straits Times*, September 9, 2017, https://www.nst.com.my/news/nation/2017/09/277963/chitty-community-melaka-quest-obtain-bumiputera-status, accessed January 6, 2025.

80. Neo, "Malay Nationalism, Islamic Supremacy and the Constitutional Bargain."

81. Andrew Clinton Willford, *Cage of Freedom: Tamil Identity and the Ethnic Fetish in Malaysia* (Ann Arbor: University of Michigan Press, 2006); for the interlinked but distinct evolution of Tamil identities in India and Southeast Asia during an earlier period, see Darinee Alagirisamy, "The Self-Respect Movement and Tamil Politics of Belonging in Interwar British Malaya, 1929–1939," *Modern Asian Studies* 50, no. 5 (2016): 1547–75.

82. Ramnath, *Boats in a Storm*.

83. I am particularly grateful to Wilbert Wong, who wrote his PhD dissertation on colonial Malaya, for his helpful suggestions about how to connect with local heritage groups in Kuala Lumpur.

84. "Will of K. Thamboosamy Pillay," *K. T. Ganapathy Pillay* v *Alamaloo and another*, Record of Proceedings, 23.

85. "Petition by Alamaloo, widow of K. Thamboosamy Pillai, praying that her mother's burial ground may remain undisturbed," September 1926, ANMKL, SEL Sec 3110/1926. Despite the file name, which was added by a colonial official, I think that the grave was that of Thamboosamy Pillai's mother, not Alamaloo's mother. Thamboosamy's full name was Kayaroganam Thamboosamy Pillai, and the family followed the practice of a son adopting his father's name before his own, often abbreviated as an initial. The letter submitted by Alamaloo's lawyer described the woman as the wife of Kayaroganam and grandmother of her son Ganapathy.

86. "KL indebted to Thambusamy for Batu Caves," *Malaysian Post*, n.d. The date of the article was cut off in the clipping that Santa shared with me.

87. J. M. Gullick, *Josephine Foss and the Pudu English School: A Pursuit of Excellence* (Petaling Jaya: Pelanduk Publications, 1988), 147.

## Chapter 2. In-Laws

1. Sections of this chapter were previously included in my article, Julia Stephens, "Material Modernities: Tracing Janbai's Gendered Mobilities Across the Indian Ocean," *Modern Asian Studies* 58, no. 2 (2024): 386–420. Copyright Cambridge University Press, reprinted with permission.

2. The history of abolition and emancipation in Zanzibar is highly complex, with legislation progressively outlawing slave transport, trade, and the legal status of slavery between 1873 and 1897. Tharia owned slaves early in his career and was also instrumental in negotiating the treaties that gradually restricted slavery in Zanzibar, for which he was knighted in 1890. Gaurav Desai, *Commerce with the Universe: Africa, India, and the Afrasian Imagination* (New York: Columbia University Press, 2013), 108. He was also a significant financial backer of one of the most important slave and ivory traders in the region, Tippu Tip. Hollian Wint, "Financing the Indian Ocean Slave Trade," *Oxford Research Encyclopedia of African History* (2022); https://oxfordre.com/africanhistory, accessed November 26, 2024.

3. See Chandra Mallampalli, *Race, Religion and Law in Colonial India: Trials of an Interracial Family* (Cambridge: Cambridge University Press, 2011); Rachel Sturman, *The Government of Social Life in Colonial India*; Nandini Chatterjee, *The Making of Indian Secularism: Empire, Law and Christianity, 1830–1960* (New York: Palgrave Macmillan. 2011); Teena Purohit, *The Aga Khan Case: Religion and Identity in Colonial India* (Cambridge, MA: Harvard University Press, 2012); Eleanor Newbigin, *The Hindu Family and the Emergence of Modern India: Law, Citizenship and Community* (Cambridge: Cambridge University Press, 2013); Stephens, *Governing Islam*. On the role of women as bearers of national and religious identities, see Partha Chatterjee, *The Nation and its Fragments: Colonial and Postcolonial Histories* (Princeton: Princeton University Press, 1993); Lata Mani, *Contentious Traditions: The Debate on Sati in Colonial India* (Berkely: University of California Press, 1998).

4. For the Ismailis, see S. T. Lokhandwalla, "Islamic Law and Ismaili Communities," *Indian Economic and Social History Review* 4, no. 2 (1967): 155–76; Amrita Shodhan, *A Question of Community: Religious Groups and Colonial Law* (Kolkata: Samya, 2001).

5. While this chapter explores these struggles with reference to Janbai and Tharia's family, Hollian Wint has traced a wide range of litigation among merchant families straddling the coasts of eastern Africa and western India. These cases feature in her forthcoming book *Mobile Households: Intimate Economies Across the Indian Ocean, c. 1860–1964*. Similar patterns of litigiousness also emerge in recent work on diasporic families in the Indian Ocean, including Nurfadzilah Yahaya's *Fluid Jurisdictions* and Kalyani Ramnath's *Boats in a Storm*.

While this chapter touches on how discourses of religious reform and revival shaped debates within the Topan family, I explore these questions in more depth in a separate article. Stephens, "Material Modernities."

6. On the role of smaller Muslim minorities, including the Bohras, Memons, and Khojas, see Michael O'Sullivan, *No Birds of Passage: A History of Gujarati Muslim Business Communities, 1800–1975* (Cambridge: Harvard University Press, 2023). While I find much to appreciate in O'Sullivan's work, I am less convinced of the utility of framing these groups through the lens of "Muslim capitalism," particularly given how much they resembled other non-Muslim trading diasporas. For these groups, see Mircea Raianu, *Tata: The Global Corporation that Built Indian Capitalism* (Cambridge: Harvard University Press, 2021); Cohen, "Parsi Capital and Imperial Infrastructure"; Stein, "Protected Persons?".

7. My work echoes recent scholarship by Wint, Yahaya, and Ramnath cited previously. See also my earlier article, Julia Stephens, "An Uncertain Inheritance: The Imperial Travels of Legal Migrants, from British India to Ottoman Iraq," *Law and History Review* 32 (November 2014): 749–72.

8. For an example of reporting about the Topan's legal battles in Zanzibar in the press in Bombay, see "Tippo Tib's Claim Upon Sir Tharia Topan," *The Times of India*, September 24, 1895, 6.

9. Records of the case include both the published judgment and records of proceedings before the Privy Council, which include evidence, testimony, and decisions from the lower courts. For the judgment, see *Sala Mohommed Jafferbhoy and another* v *Dame Janbai* (Bombay) [1897] United Kingdom Privy Council 17, http://www.bailii.org/uk/cases/UKPC/1897/1897_17.html, accessed September 6, 2022. Hereafter cited as Judgment. For larger records reviewed by the Privy Council, see *Sala Mahomed Jafferbhoy and Alli Mahomed Jafferbhoy* v. *Dame Janbai*, Record of Proceedings, Privy Council Cases with the Judgements, Social Science Collections, British Library, PP.1316* (1897), Box 349G, 175. Hereafter cited as Record of Proceedings.

10. Sturman, *The Government of Social Life in Colonial India*; Stephens, *Governing Islam*.

11. Legal historians would refer to this as "forum shopping," in which litigants pursue their interests through multiple judicial and extra-judicial forums, opting at any given point to litigate in the forum which was most likely to produce an outcome in their favor but also using their advantage in one forum to exert pressure in another. Mitra Sharafi, "The Semi-Autonomous Judge in Colonial India: Chivalric Imperialism Meets Anglo-Islamic Dower and Divorce Law," *The Indian Economic & Social History Review* 46, no. 1 (2009): 57–81.

12. This has been one of the most resounding contributions of a new generation of legal histories of South Asia and the Indian Ocean. For a survey of some of these contributions see Mitra Sharafi, "South Asian Legal History," *Annual Review of Law and Social Science* 11 (2015): 309–36; Renisa Mawani and Iza Hussin, "The Travels of Law: Indian Ocean Itineraries," *Law and History Review* 32, no. 4 (2014): 733–47; Mahmood Kooria and Sanne Ravensbergen, "The Indian Ocean of Law: Hybridity and Space," *Itinerario* 42, no. 2 (2018): 164–67.

13. Farouk Topan, conversation with author, June 23, 2015. My conversations with Farouk have continued throughout the progress of this book, and we are currently discussing the possibility of working together to publish his father's biography of Tharia, which I read also as a narrative of his mother.

14. Edward Simpson, *Muslim Society and the Western Indian Ocean: The Seafarers of Kachchh* (London: Routledge, 2006); Chhaya Goswami, *Globalization Before its Time: The Gujarati Merchants from Kachchh* (Gurgaon: Portfolio, Penguin, 2016).

15. Purohit, *The Aga Khan Case*.

16. Purohit, *The Aga Khan Case*; Nile Green, *Bombay Islam: The Religious Economy of the West Indian Ocean, 1840–1915* (Cambridge: Cambridge University Press, 2013), 155–78.

17. "Biography of Sir Tharia Topan, Knight," Books I and II.

18. Abdul Sheriff, *Slaves, Spices and Ivory in Zanzibar: Integration of an East African Commercial Empire into the World economy, 1770–1873* (Athens: Ohio University Press, 1987); Seema Alavi, *Sovereigns of the Sea: Omani Ambition in the Age of Empire* (New Delhi: Penguin Books, 2023).

19. Hollian Wint, "'From *Desh* to *Desh*': The Family Firm as Trans-Local Household in the Nineteenth Century Western Indian Ocean," *Journal of World History* (June 2023): 198.

20. Gijsbert Oonk, "South Asians in East Africa (1880–1920) with a Particular Focus on Zanzibar: Toward a Historical Explanation of Economic Success of a Middlemen Minority," *African and Asian Studies* 5, no. 1 (2006): 12; Bishara, *A Sea of Debt*, 55.

21. Sharif, *Slaves, Spices, & Ivory*, 107.

22. Shizuo Katakura, "Introduction of British Consular Jurisdiction to Zanzibar: Indian Merchants in a Judicial Transition," in *Re-searching Transitions in Indian History*, eds. Radhika Seshan and Shraddha Kumbhojkar (London: Routledge, 2018), 134–43; Bishara, *Sea of Debt*, 154.

23. The historian Ranajit Guha, the founder of Subaltern Studies, a collective of scholars of South Asia who focused on new modes of studying non-elite subjects, is generally credited with pioneering reading colonial archives "against the grain." In a seminal essay on peasant insurgency, Guha provided a model of such analysis, which he compared to "read[ing] from a distorting mirror." "The Prose of Counterinsurgency," in *Selected Subaltern Studies*, eds. Ranajit Guha and Gayatri Spivak (Oxford: Oxford University Press, 1988), 45–85.

24. For works citing the manuscript see, Frederick Cooper, *Plantation Slavery on the East Coast of Africa* (New Haven: Yale University Press, 1977); M. Reda Bhacker, *Trade and Empire in Muscat and Zanzibar: The Roots of British Domination* (London: Routledge, 1994); Margaret Frenz, "Doing Well but Also Doing Good? East African Indian Merchants and Their Charitable Work, c. 1850–1920," in *Knowledge and the Indian Ocean: Intangible Networks of Western India and Beyond*, ed. Sara Keller (Cham, Switzerland: Palgrave Macmillan, 2019), 173–88.

25. Biography of Sir Tharia Topan, "First Attempt to Write Biography."

26. For a deeper discussion of religious debates within the Khoja-Ismaili community, which delves more into the valences of this accusation of fanaticism, see my article "Material Modernities."

27. Tharia had a daughter and two sons from his first marriage, but no children from his second wife.

28. Biography of Sir Tharia Topan, Book VI, 13–14.

29. The biography does not provide dates for these births, but in Tharia's will, which was dated January 1886, he listed the ages of his living children as follows: Musa (43); Nanbai (37); Jafar (35); Fatma (19); Khadija (16); Mohamed Medi (10); Mohamed Ali (6); and Beuba (1). Mohamed Hussein was born in February 1886. Janbai and Tharia's eldest daughter, Jainab, passed away in 1885.

30. Biography of Sir Tharia Topan, Book X, 10–12; Book XI, 9.

31. Ibid., Book XII, 4; Jeremy Prestholdt, *Domesticating the World: African Consumerism and the Genealogies of Globalization* (Berkeley: University of California Press, 2008), 110–11.

32. Biography of Sir Tharia Topan, Book XII, 2-12.

33. Ibid. The "value" of ceremonial celebrations in building social reputation is a well-established theme in anthropological studies. See for example Nancy D. Munn, *The Fame of Gawa: A Symbolic Study of Value Transformation in a Massim (Papua New Guinea) Society* (Cambridge: Cambridge University Press, 1986).

34. The biography does not mention Beuba's birth, but Tharia listed her age as one and a quarter in his will (dated January 1886), suggesting she was born before the family traveled to Bombay in 1885.

35. Biography of Sir Tharia Topan, Book XIII, 5–7.

36. Record of Proceedings, 24.

37. Record of Proceedings, 24–25.

38. Letter from Tharia to Moosa, November 6, 1890, reprinted in Record of Proceedings, 185.

39. Letter from Tharia to Moosa, January 16, 1890, reprinted in Record of Proceedings, 175; Letter from Tharia to Moosa and Jaffer, October 10, 1890, reprinted in Record of Proceedings, 184.

40. Record of Proceedings, 88.

41. Ibid., 236.

42. Ibid., 241.

43. Ibid., 228.

44. Judgement, 7. For a similar pattern of splitting legal subjects into different frames for judging "economic" and "domestic" relations, see Julia Stephens, *Governing Islam*, 57–69.

45. Sharafi, "The Semi-Autonomous Judge in Colonial India."

46. Judgement.

47. "Lady Janbai and Her Mehtas," *The Times of India*, February 17, 1898, 3; "Lady Janbai's Case," *The Times of India*, June 16, 1898, 3.

48. "Serious Charges Against a Tutor," *The Times of India*, February 16, 1895, 3.

49. "A Consent Decree. Nusserwanji Maneckji Cooper vs. Mahomed Mehdi Tharia Topan," *The Times of India*, August 7, 1895, 3.

50. "Matrimonial Case," *The Times of India*, January 6, 1912, 10; "Post-Nuptial Difficulty," *The Times of India*, September 3, 1912, 8.

51. "Mother and Son: Suit No. 27 of 1913," *The Times of India*, July 28, 1913, 10.

52. Record of Proceedings, 28–30. Tharia was not alone in warning his descendants to avoid the courts. Another Indian migrant, Iqbal al-Daulah, a cousin of the Nawab of Awadh who spent much of his life in Ottoman Iraq, cautioned his heirs: "British courts are uncertain, stock in trade of bribery, wrong, delay . . . the seekers of redress, are captives of the paw of the Court officials." Stephens, "An Uncertain Inheritance."

53. Biography of Sir Tharia Topan, Book XVII, 6–8.

54. For additional analysis of cases involving Khoja women who engaged colonial courts in Zanzibar, see Wint, "'From *Desh* to *Desh*,'" 187–216.

55. Biography of Sir Tharia Topan, Part II, Chapter 1, 11. The presence of slaves in the Topan household is in some tension with legal provisions restricting Indian ownership of slaves, which were stricter than those applied to the Sultan of Zanzibar's subjects. These policies, however, were sporadically enforced. Moreover, as much of the historiography on slavery in the Indian Ocean has emphasized, abolition and emancipation often did not end practical relations of enslavement, particularly for women and children working in households. Elke E. Stockreiter,

*Islamic Law, Gender and Social Change in Post-Abolition Zanzibar* (Cambridge: Cambridge University Press, 2015), 203–39.

56. George Granville Putnam, *Salem Vessels and Their Voyages* (Salem, MA: The Essex Institute, 1924), 111–12. On Tharia's relationships with Salem merchants, see Joshua Sidney Chamberlin Morrison, "Cut from the Same Cloth: Salem, Zanzibar, and the Consolidation of the Indo-Atlantic World, 1790–1875," PhD Dissertation, University of Virginia, 2021, 205–7.

57. Frederick Clifton Pierce, *Batchelder, Batcheller Genealogy* (Chicago: W.B. Conkey Company, 1898), 304; US. Census of 1920 and 1930. While Nathan and Caroline had six children, only one of their sons had children, who were born in New Zealand, far away from their aunt Minnie, who lived with her other spinster sisters in Salem and taught music until her death in 1936.

58. I am indebted to Susan Bean, the retired curator of South Asian art at the PEM, for sharing some of her impressions of the bracelet with me. Email correspondence with the author, January 22, 2020.

59. Jeremy Prestholdt, "On the Global Repercussions of East African Consumerism," *The American Historical Review* 109, no. 3 (2004): 755–81; Chhaya R Goswami, "Professor JC Jha Memorial Prize Essay: The Ivory Trade at Zanzibar and the Role of Kutchis," in *Proceedings of the Indian History Congress* vol. 67 (2006): 921–35. The trade between Zanzibar and Salem waned during and after the American Civil War, but ties between merchants in the two places remained, as evinced in gifts exchanged between the Topans and Batchelders.

60. For example, a recent PhD dissertation on Salem-Zanzibar ties makes no mention of Janbai or Caroline. Morrison, "Cut from the Same Cloth."

61. Letter from Tharia to Moosa and Jaffer, April 19, 1889, reproduced in the Record of Proceedings, 190.

62. Historians of the genre have argued that the very flatness and uniformity of the photographs were essential to their ability to assimilate their subjects into global cultures of consumption. Prita Meier, "The Surface of Things: A History of Photography from the Swahili Coast," *The Art Bulletin*, 101, no. 1 (2019): 48–69; Christopher Pinney, "Notes from the Surface of the Image: Photography, Postcolonialism, and Vernacular Modernism," in *Photography's Other Histories*, eds. Christopher Pinney and Nicholas Peterson (Durham: Duke University Press, 2003), 202–20.

63. Christopher Pinney, *Camera Indica: The Social Life of Indian Photographs* (London: Reaktion Books, 1997).

64. Xavier Courouble, "Swahili Coast: Exploration by French Captain Charles Guillain, 1846–1848. Part 3, Encounters and Partnerships," blog post, May 13, 2015, https://blog.library.si.edu/blog/2015/05/13/guillain3/#.Yl2lI5PMLrD, accessed April 18, 2022.

65. Meier, "The Surface of Things."

66. Siddhartha Ghosh, "Zenana Studio: Early Women Photographers of Bengal," from *Taking Pictures: The Practice of Photography by Bengalis*, translated by Debjani Sengupta, *Trans Asia Photography* 4, no. 2 (2014). While Ghosh's account is based on practices in Bengal, techniques of photography circulated widely. Raja Deen Dayal, one of the most prominent Indian photographers in the nineteenth century, opened a "zenana studio" in Hyderabad in 1892, which was surrounded by a high wall and where he employed a British woman photographer, Mrs. Kenny Levick, to manage the studio. Malavika Karlekar, *Visual Histories: Photography in the Popular Imagination* (New Delhi: Oxford University Press, 2013), 15; Gayatri Sinha, "Women Artists in

India: Practice and Patronage," in *Local/Global: Women Artists in the Nineteenth Century*, edited by Deborah Cherry and Janice Helland (London: Routledge, 2006), 69–70.

67. H. F. Plate, Portrait of Emily Ruete in Omani dress, Leiden University Libraries, Or. 27.135 D 1 http://hdl.handle.net/1887.1/item:2365279, accessed April 13, 2022.

68. Kate Roy, "Only the 'Outward Appearance' of a Harem? Reading the Memoirs of an Arabian Princess as Material Text," *Belphégor: Littérature Populaire et Culture Médiatique* 13–1 (2015): 12. The photograph was omitted from the earliest English translation of the memoir, which was published in 1888, but later appeared in a 1907 version. Notes on the verso of the framed photograph (previously cited) indicate that copies were also held privately in Zanzibar.

69. "Indienne, Zanzibar," The Humphrey Winterton Collection of East African Photographs: 1860–1960, Northwestern University Libraries, https://dc.library.northwestern.edu/items/3ab423cc-14ca-4524-8bde-7e3a04aa8f36, accessed April 18, 2022. I have also discussed these three photographs with Prita Meier, who has worked extensively on photography in Zanzibar. We both found the overlap striking even as we came across the three photographs independently during our respective research.

70. Record of Proceedings, 24, 39.

71. There has been surprisingly little research on jewelry as a gendered asset. For some observations from Orissa, see Nilika Mehrotra, "Gold and Gender in India: Some Observations from South Orissa," *Indian Anthropologist* 34, no. 1(2004): 33.

72. Biography of Sir Tharia Topan, Part II, Chapter 1, 11.

73. Interview with Karanveer Sahota, December 20, 2022. This interview is discussed in more depth in Chapter 5.

## Chapter 3. Jahaji Roots

1. María del Pilar Kaladeen refers to this as "cultural amnesia," processes of forgetting that she has written about concerning her own family's histories of indenture in the Caribbean. Maria Pilar Kaladeen, "Invisible Windrush: How the Stories of Indian Indentured Labourers from the Caribbean were Forgotten," *The Conversation*, June 6, 2023, https://theconversation.com/invisible-windrush-how-the-stories-of-indian-indentured-labourers-from-the-caribbean-were-forgotten-206330, accessed January 6, 2025. For additional contributions to an emerging scholarship on indenture and memory studies, see Jack Webb, Rod Westmaas, Maria del Pilar Kaladeen, and William Tantam, eds. *Memory, Migration and (de) Colonisation in the Caribbean and Beyond* (London: University of London Press, 2020).

2. My own work draws on the scholarship on indenture in Natal, particularly the rich archival research and oral histories found in Ashwin Desai and Goolam Vahed, *Inside Indian Indenture: A South African Story* (Cape Town: HSRC Press, 2010).

3. Ranjanithevi Moodley, "The Circumstances Surrounding the Arrival from India of My Grandfather, Mr. Pungavanam Moodley, to South Africa," 1984, Gandhi-Luthuli Documentation Centre, University of KwaZulu-Natal. Although I have chosen to center the history of one family, as recorded in Ranjanithevi's paper and a digital family tree, this chapter is informed by my reading of 136 student papers written at the University of Durban, Westville (UDW) in the early 1980s and which are now archived at the Gandhi-Luthuli Documentation Centre. (I have not included in this sample projects for "passenger" Indians, who paid for their own transport

to South Africa.) Some, although not all of these papers, were digitally available at https://scnc.ukzn.ac.za/doc/B/Roots/Roots_ndx.htm, but were removed as of December 2024. Ranjanithevi's paper was not part of this digital collection. I will refer to the student papers by the author's names and titles, along with "Roots Project."

4. Desai and Vahed, *Inside Indian Indenture*, 438.

5. Pungavanun Moodley, https://www.geni.com/people/Pungavanun-Moodley-53200/6000000024731726160, accessed February 21, 2023.

6. Early examples of this work, which includes research on indenture within and beyond India, include Samita Sen, "Unsettling the Household: Act VI (of 1901) and the Regulation of Women Migrants in Colonial Bengal," *International Review of Social History* 41, no. S4 (1996): 135–156; Samita Sen, "'Without his consent?': Marriage and Women's Migration in Colonial India," *International Labor and Working-Class History* 65 (2004): 77–104; and Piya Chatterjee, *A Time for Tea: Women, Labor and Post/Colonial Politics on an Indian Plantation* (Durham: Duke University Press, 2001). This work has been deepened by more recent scholarship, particularly Bahadur, *Coolie Woman*; Datta, *Fleeting Agencies*.

7. Indrani Chatterjee, *Gender, Slavery and the Law in Colonial India* (Oxford University Press, 1999).

8. Desai and Vahed, *Inside Indian Indenture*, 104.

9. Hugh Tinker subsequently adopted this phrase as the title for his canonical history of indenture, *A New System of Slavery: The Export of Indian Labour Overseas, 1830–1920* (London: Oxford University Press, 1974), xiv.

10. Rachel Sturman, "Indian Indentured Labor and the History of International Rights Regimes," *The American Historical Review* 119, no. 5 (2014): 1439–65.

11. On the centrality of these periodic "inquiries" to the perpetuation of indenture, see Radhika Mongia, *Indian Migration and Empire: A Colonial Genealogy of the Modern State* (Durham: Duke University Press, 2018).

12. The implementation of these policies can be traced through the annual reports of the Protector of Indian Immigrants in Natal. For further examples of letters and remittances as a link between migrants and kin in India, see also Ashutosh Kumar, *Coolies of the Empire: Indentured Indians in the Sugar Colonies, 1830–1920* (Cambridge University Press, 2017), 31–38; Marina Carter, *Voices from Indenture*.

13. "Disposal of the Estate of Indian Immigrants Dying Intestate and without Heirs in the Colonies," NAI, Home, Revenue and Agriculture Department/ Emigration/July 1880/Nos. 25–30.

14. On South Africa as early pioneer in the development of systems of identification, and their entanglement with policies of racial segregation, see Keith Breckenridge, *Biometric State: The Global Politics of Identification and Surveillance in South Africa, 1850 to the Present* (Cambridge: Cambridge University Press, 2014).

15. Goolam Vahed, "The Protector, Plantocracy, and Indentured Labour in Natal, 1860–1911," *Pacific Historical Review* 87, no. 1 (2018): 101–27.

16. Thembisa Waetjen and Goolam Vahed, "Passages of Ink: Decoding the Natal Indentured Records into the Digital Age," *Kronos* 40, no. 1 (2014): 45–73. For many years the Excel spreadsheets were available for download at https://scnc.ukzn.ac.za/doc/SHIP/shipndx.html. This site, however, was inactive in 2024. Information organized by individual indenture numbers remains available at https://gldc.ukzn.ac.za/printable-shipslist/, accessed December 3, 2024.

17. On *jahaji bahin* as a de-colonial, feminist analytic, see Joy Mahabir and Mariam Pirbhai, eds., *Critical Perspectives on Indo-Caribbean Women's Literature* (New York: Routledge: 2013), 1; Brinda Mehta, "Jahaji-bahin Feminism: A De-Colonial Indo-Caribbean Consciousness," *South Asian Diaspora* 12, no. 2 (2020): 179–94.

18. Desai and Vahed, *Inside Indian Indenture*, 22.

19. Report of the Protector of Immigrants for the Year 1883, National Archives of South Africa, KwaZulu-Natal Provincial Archives, Pietermaritzburg (hereafter NAB), Indian Immigration Department (hereafter II).

20. Bahadur explores different reasons that single women entered indenture in her book *Coolie Woman.*

21. On the global context for Indian famines during this period, and the role of colonial policies in their making, see Davis, *Late Victorian Holocausts.*

22. Some scholarly studies of indenture have dismissed the possibility that migrants were outright kidnapped, but many others have noted that such capture likely occurred, although perhaps its frequency was later overemphasized by Indian nationalists who campaigned for the end of indenture. The most sophisticated scholarship on the topic now emphasizes the diversity of reasons that migrants ended up bound to contracts of indenture. Desai and Vahed, *Inside Indenture*, 48. Some families also recount oral histories in which their ancestors described being kidnapped. See, for example, the contribution to Instagram account *Brown History*, discussed in Chapter 5.

23. Rule 77, Act XXI of 1883. This legislation represented an increase from legislation enacted in 1860, which prescribed one woman for every four men. David Pradhan, "Normativised Misogyny: A Socio-Legal Critique of Colonial Indentured Labour," in *Indentured and Post-Indentured Experiences of Women in the Indian Diaspora*, ed. Amba Pande (Singapore: Springer, 2020), 43; Mongia, *Indian Migration and Empire*, 88.

24. For additional details on the recruitment of women, see Sen, "'Without his consent?'"

25. These deaths were reported in the annual "Report of the Protector of Immigrants, for the Year 1883," NAB, II.

26. "Walter Bisset Applies for the Lease of 250 Acres Situated in Lower Umzimkulu for Coffee Planting," 1883, NAB, Survey General's Office (SGO), III/1/50.

27. Statistics prepared in 1890 indicated that the mortality rate for Indians in Natal was 16 per thousand. Maureen Tayal, "Indian Indentured Labour in Natal, 1890–1911," *The Indian Economic & Social History Review* 14, no. 4 (1977): 519–47.

28. "Report on Heavy Mortality in the Year 1906 among Indian Laborers on the Tonga Sugar Cos. Estate," quote in Tayal, "Indian Indentured Labour," 527.

29. Estates of Deceased Indian Mangathoyi, No. 905335, NAB, II 10/1/5, Ref. No. 2742 /1905.

30. George A. Grierson, "Report on Colonial Emigration from the Bengal Presidency," February 25, 1883, 23, copy cited from BL, IOR/V/27/820/35.

31. For examples of how migrants creatively engaged with bureaucratic regimes of paperwork in another context, see Ramnath, *Boats in a Storm.*

32. R. Singh, Untitled [Bio of Durga Gur Bux Singh], Roots Project, 11.

33. Girls over the age of thirteen and boys over the age of sixteen were taxed. Desai and Vahed, *Inside Indian Indenture*, 357–58.

34. On Gandhi's failure to push for a more radical platform in India, and his general apathy towards indentured migrants and their descendants, see Desai and Vahed, *The South African Gandhi*.

35. https://www.sahistory.org.za/article/natives-land-act-1913, accessed January 9, 2025.

36. Thomas Blom Hansen, *Melancholia of Freedom: Social Life in an Indian Township in South Africa* (Princeton: Princeton University Press, 2012), 29–35.

37. G. C. Oosthuizen, ed., *Challenge to a South African University: The University of Durban-Westville* (Cape Town: Oxford University Press), 32–52.

38. Uma Dhupelia-Mesthrie, "'A Blast from the Past': The Teaching of South African History at an Apartheid University, 1960s–1980s," *South African Historical Journal* 42 (May 2000): 54.

39. S. Bhana, "Student Perception of History," *Problems in History Teaching at the Tertiary Level*, ed. S. Bhana (Durban: Institute for Social and Economic Research, 1985), 71. The volume is the published proceedings of a conference held at the University of Durban-Westville in 1984.

40. Dhupelia-Mesthrie, "A Blast from the Past," 50.

41. Nienke Boer, *The Briny South: Displacement and Sentiment in the Indian Ocean World* (Durham: Duke University Press, 2023), 132–53.

42. Charu Gupta, "'Innocent' Victims/'Guilty' Migrants: Hindi Public Sphere, Caste and Indentured Women in Colonial North India," *Modern Asian Studies* 49, no. 5 (2015): 1345–77; Amba Pande, "Women and Indenture: Revisiting Indian Discourses," in *Kala Pani Crossings, Gender and Diaspora*, eds. J Misrahi-Barak J, R Tyagi, and H Kalpana (Abington, England: Routledge India, 2024), 52–66.

43. Rina Agarwala, *The Migration-Development Regime: How Class Shapes Indian Emigration* (New York: Oxford University Press, 2022).

44. Pallavi Rastogi, *Afrindian Fictions: Diaspora, Race, and National Desire in South Africa* (Columbus: Ohio State University Press, 2008), 4.

45. This account is based on an unpublished memoir that Bhana shared with his former student and friend, Uma Dhupelia-Mesthrie. "Writing in the Twenty-First Century about Indian South Africans: Revisiting Agendas and Reflecting on Foundational Writings: Inaugural Surendra Bhana Memorial, 10 November 2018, Presented at the 1860 Heritage Centre, Durban," *Journal of Natal and Zulu History* 34, no. 1 (2021): 166–77.

46. S. Bhana, "Student Perception of History," 92. It is worth nothing that Bhana used the term "black" here when answering a question about why there was such a high level of student interest in History at UDW, whose student body was predominantly Indian. I read this as a critical counter-discourse to Apartheid logics which would have differentiated between Black and Asian students.

47. Ibid., 68, 72.

48. Ibid., 75–77.

49. Norvella P. Carter, Warren Chalklen, and Bhekuyise Zungu, "Re-Rooting *Roots*: The South African Perspective," in *Reconsidering Roots: Race, Politics and Memory*, eds. Erica L. Ball and Kellie Carter Jackson (Athens: University of Georgia Press, 2017), 165–82.

50. Selva Govender, "The Arrival and Settlement of My Grandfather in South Africa," [1983], Roots Project, 1.

51. Ibid.

52. S. Budden, "A Research into One's Roots," [n.d.] Roots Project, 9.

53. Waetjen and Vahed, "Passages of Ink," 58.

54. Boer, *Briny South,* especially chapters 3 and 5.

55. On the role of settler-colonial logics in shaping diverse facets of law in South Africa, see Neilesh Bose, "New Settler Colonial Histories at the Edges of Empire: 'Asiatics,' Settlers, and Law in Colonial South Africa," *Journal of Colonialism and Colonial History* 15, no. 1 (2014).

56. https://abr.business.gov.au/ABN/View?id=27956294068, accessed March 1, 2023.

57. Moodley, "The Circumstances Surrounding the Arrival From India of My Grandfather," Roots Project, 7–8.

58. Ibid., 9.

59. Ibid., 19.

60. Ibid., 22.

61. Ibid., 23–4.

62. Ibid., 3.

63. D. Maharaja, "Indian Immigration with Special Emphasis on Mr Ganga Reddy," Roots Project, 17–18.

64. B. E. Francis, "The Indian Immigrant and his Contribution to the Sugar Industry in South Africa," Roots Project, 6.

65. L. Nasaree, "An Indentured Laborer—A Study," Roots Project, 2–3.

66. Desai and Vahed, *Inside Indian Indenture,* 199.

67. Devarakshanam Betty Govinden, *A Time of Memory: Reflections on Recent South African Writing* (Pretoria: University of South Africa Press, 2008).

68. Anneline's profile and links to her family research can be found at https://www.geni.com/people/Anneline-Moodley/6000000022798420450. The following pages draw on an interview I conducted with her on January 3, 2023. In addition to this conversation, we also traded many WhatsApp messages as both of our research and writing continued to progress. Anneline also credits her cousin Joe Matthias, who is also active on Geni.com, for providing crucial information that aided in building her own tree.

69. For examples of how roots research has been at the forefront of public efforts to engage histories of indenture in South Africa, see https://1860heritagecentre.wordpress.com/, accessed January 6, 2025.

70. "The Story of English Mary," uploaded by Anneline Bernice Moodley, https://www.geni.com/photo/view?album_type=photos_of_me&id=6000000024747265243&photo_id=6000000067984394839&position=0, accessed July 5, 2018. I have corrected a couple of typos in the text. After sharing information from my research, Anneline updated some of the profiles in her tree to include names and numbers from the Ships List so this story is now listed under the profile "Angamma Narrainan (30128)," accessed February 15, 2023.

71. Report of the Protector of Immigrants for the Year 1887, NAB, II.

72. Gabeba Baderoon "The African Oceans—Tracing the Sea as Memory of Slavery in South African Literature and Culture," *Research in African Literatures* 40, no. 4 (2009): 89–107. On the pressure to disassociate Indian indenture from African enslavement in the context of Mauritius, see Mathieu Claveyrolas, "With or Without Roots: Conflicting Memories of Slavery and Indentured Labor in the Mauritian Public Space," in *Politics of Memory: Making Slavery Visible in the Public Space,* ed. Ana Lucia Araujo (New York: Routledge, 2013), 54–70. On the broader need for connective histories linking slavery and indenture, see Lowe, *Intimacies of Four Continents.*

73. Édouard Glissant, *Caribbean Discourse: Selected Essays* (Charlottesville: University of Virginia Press, 1989), 67. I am indebted to Elizabeth M. DeLoughrey for drawing my attention to the rich theorization of Oceanic roots in the literature on the Caribbean. *Routes and Roots.*

74. Desai and Vahed, *Inside Indian Indenture*, 343.

75. Dr. Devi Moodley Rajab, "In Celebration of a Mother at 106," May 8, 2021, https://www.facebook.com/groups/1326540524106022/permalink/4014992875260760.

76. Renluka Maharaj, *Through Space and Time*, 2021, mixed media on pigmented ink print, 36 × 60 inches. I viewed the art via Maharaj's Instagram feed, posted on October 30, 2024, https://www.instagram.com/renlukamaharaj/p/DBxEbE_Mznt/.

77. "The Victoria Connection," Victoria and Albert Museum, https://www.vam.ac.uk/articles/the-victoria-connection?srsltid=AfmBOooqD-6lwewTinqb2sQ5zg2l4olo_Oh3luA-C1OMVCPlAluYrxy9B, accessed January 6, 2025.

78. Homi Bhabha, "Of Mimicry and Man: The Ambivalence of Colonial Discourse," *October* 28 (Spring 1984): 125–33.

79. Boer, *Briny South*, 132.

80. Bahadur, *Coolie Woman*; Amitav Ghosh, *Sea of Poppies* (New Delhi: Viking, 2008).

81. Kasturi Chetty, Kaliani Lyle, and Sanusha Naidu, "From Indenture to Matriarch: Rajwantia's Journey," https://www.thestoryofrajwantia.com/. Interview with Kaliani Lyle, January 27, 2023. Lyle published excerpts from our conversation on her website, https://www.thestoryofrajwantia.com/post/conversations-with-julia-stephenson-about-roots-research, accessed May 24, 2023.

82. D. Chetty, "Trace the Origins of Your Ancestor(s)," [1983], Roots Project, 7, 9.

83. Gordon, *Ghostly Matters*, 6.

84. G M, Naidoo, "Circumstances Surrounding the Arrival of my Grandfather Gorly Kanniah into Natal in June 12 1900," [1983], Roots Project, ii.

85. Albie Sachs, "Archives, Truth, and Reconciliation," *Archivaria* (2006): 14.

86. Sean Carey, "Caste Matters in Mauritius," Blog Post on *Anthropologyworks*, https://anthropologyworksdotcom.wordpress.com/2011/07/02/caste-matters-in-mauritius-3/, accessed August 24, 2018.

87. "Access Policy to the MGI Indian Immigration Archives," http://online.fliphtml5.com/ogvv/fsvs/#p=3, accessed February 21, 2023.

88. This phrase is quoted from the work of Krishna Gubili, who has traced his great-grandfather's history of migrating from India to Natal. *Viriah* (Chennai: Notion Press, 2018), 16.

89. Kimberlé W. Crenshaw, Andrea J. Ritchie, Rachel Anspach, Rachel Gilmer, and Luke Harris, "Say Her Name: Resisting Police Brutality Against Black Women" (2015), https://scholarship.law.columbia.edu/faculty_scholarship/3226/, accessed January 9, 2025.

## Chapter 4. Seamen's Album

1. Hassan Abdulrazzak, "The Fireman," A Tamasha Digital Production for The National Archives, posted June 9, 2021, https://www.youtube.com/watch?v=LYTayxRZ778, accessed January 6, 2025.

2. Laura Tabili, *"We Ask for British Justice": Workers and Racial Difference in Late Imperial Britain* (Ithaca: Cornell University Press, 1994).

3. Holger Weiss, *A Global Radical Waterfront: The International Propaganda Committee of Transport Workers and the International of Seamen and Harbour Workers, 1921–1937* (Boston: Brill, 2021). The biography of the seaman-turned-leftist activist Amir Haider Khan also provides a first-person account of maritime politics during the period. *Chains to Lose Life and Struggles of a Revolutionary: Memoirs of Amir Haider Khan* (Karachi: Pakistan Study Centre, 2007).

4. Caroline Adams, *Across Seven Seas and Thirteen Rivers: Life Stories of Pioneer Sylhetti Settlers in Britain* (London: Tower Hamlets Arts Project, 1987), xiv.

5. In the introduction to his seminal work on Indian seafarers, G. Balachandran also discussed Jan Mohamed using records from The National Archives (UK) and India Office Records, including those suggesting that he was the same John whose citizenship was cancelled by US courts in 1925. Balachandran, however, does not examine photographs of Jan or materials from the US, and thus did not encounter some of the "mismatches" in his/their stories and pictures which have inspired this chapter. G. Balachandran, *Globalizing Labour? Indian Seafarers and World Shipping, c. 1870–1945* (New Delhi: Oxford University Press, 2012), 1–3.

6. While much of this project was organized during the pandemic, and exhibited online, I was able to see the physical installation of "The 1920s: Beyond the Roar" at TNA in May 2022 just before it closed in June 2022. Additional videos describing both the wider 1920s project and the "Once British Always British" offshoot were released by TNA on YouTube. Both mention Jan Mahomed, but not his potential American connections. "Behind the Scenes: Making 'Once British Always British'," posted January 12, 2022, https://www.youtube.com/watch?v=yzl87vz-ma7I; and "The 1920s: Beyond the Roar: Exhibition Tour," posted March 14, 2022 https://www.youtube.com/watch?v=AHaCVbsDxWQ, accessed January 6, 2025. Interestingly, the only mention of the links to the US denaturalization case are made in a student graphic novel featuring Jan Mahomed's story. Micah N., "The Adventures of Jan Mahomed," in *Seafarers' Stories* (2022), https://cdn.nationalarchives.gov.uk/documents/education/seafarers-stories-ebook.pdf, accessed January 6, 2025.

7. The title of this section plays on similar wording used in the article on John published in SAADA, which was entitled "Measured by a Hat." The full quote published in a story in the *LA Times* was, "His love for the country of his adoption, he insists, cannot be measured by a hat." "Prophet Heads His Ancestors," *Los Angeles Times*, February 11, 1925, 2.

8. John Mohammad Ali, Naturalization Petition, Detroit, Michigan, USA, January 11, 1921, Michigan, U.S., Federal Naturalization Records, 1887–1931, downloaded from Ancestry.com.

9. "Mohammad Ali," c. 1910–1919, Redpath Chautauqua Collection, MSC0150, University of Iowa, digitalized at South Asian American Digital Archive, https://www.saada.org/item/20111208-527 [hereafter cited as Chautauqua pamphlet].

10. Marriage of Emily F Lambourne and John M Ali, January 10, 1906, Detroit, Michigan, Michigan, U.S., Marriage Records, 1867–1952, downloaded from Ancestry.com.

11. Emma F Lambourne, 1891 England Census, downloaded from Ancestry.com.

12. John M Ali, 1910 United States Federal Census, downloaded from Ancestry.com.

13. It is unclear whether Roosevelt actually used this phrase or whether it was subsequently erroneously credited to him or paraphrased. The phrase though was commonly used to describe the shows. Charlotte Canning, *The Most American Thing in America: Circuit Chautauqua as Performance* (Iowa City: University of Iowa Press, 2005), 238, ft. 100.

14. Chautauqua pamphlet.

15. Ibid.; "A Lady Reviews Chautauqua," in *The Redwood Gazette*, July 27, 1910, 2.

16. J Mohammad Ali, 1920 United States Federal Census, downloaded from Ancestry.com.

17. John Mohammed Ali, Declaration of Intention to Naturalize, January 18, 1918, Michigan, U.S., Federal Naturalization Records, 1887–1931, downloaded from Ancestry.com.

18. John Mohammad Ali, U.S., World War I Draft Registration Cards, 1917–1918, downloaded from Ancestry.com.

19. Jan or John or Ali John Mohamed, Aliens Branch, December 1929, TNA, HO 45/13750.

20. *United States* v. *Ali*, 7 F.2d 728 (E.D. Mich. 1925), https://law.justia.com/cases/federal/district-courts/F2/7/728/1509701/, accessed January 6, 2025.

21. "An Introduction to South Asian American History," *SAADA*, https://www.saada.org/resources/introduction, accessed January 6, 2025.

22. Vivek Bald, *Bengali Harlem and the Lost Histories of South Asian America* (Cambridge: Harvard University Press, 2013).

23. Maia Ramnath, *Haj to Utopia: How the Ghadar Movement Charted Global Radicalism and Attempted to Overthrow the British Empire* (Berkeley: University of California Press, 2011).

24. Kris Manjapra, *M. N. Roy: Marxism and Colonial Cosmopolitanism* (London: Routledge, India, 2010), 33.

25. *United States* v. *Bhagat Singh Thind*, 261 U.S. 204 (1923), https://supreme.justia.com/cases/federal/us/261/204/, accessed January 6, 2025.

26. I am indebted to Zeynep Devrim Gürsel for multiple conversations about photography, legal, and popular contestations of citizenship and race. For her work on similar cases involving Armenian-Americans, see "Classifying the Cartozians: Rethinking the Politics of Visibility Alongside Ottoman Subjecthood and American Citizenship," *photographies* vol. 15, no. 3 (2022): 349–80. On the importance of visuality and photography to these cases, see also Sherally Munshi, "'You Will See My Family Became So American': Toward a Minor Comparativism," *The American Journal of Comparative Law* 63, no. 3 (2015): 655–718.

27. Joan M. Jensen, *Passage from India: Asian Indian Immigrants in North America* (New Haven: Yale University Press, 1988), 259–60.

28. Kritika Agarwal, "Uncertain Citizenship: Race, Empire, and the Denationalization of Asian Americans in Twentieth-Century United States," PhD Dissertation, University of Buffalo, State University of New York, 2015. In the wake of the *Thind* case, pending naturalization cases for persons from other parts of Asia and the Middle East were also challenged. On Armenian efforts to prove their "whiteness" in the aftermath of *Thind*, see Gürsel, "Classifying the Cartozians." What set apart the Indian cases, however, was the decision by the Department of Justice to pursue a large-scale effort to retroactively revoke the citizenship of persons who had naturalized before *Thind*.

29. Jensen, *Passage from India*, 259–64.

30. Kritika Agarwal, "Living in a Gilded Cage: Vaishno Das Bagai's Disillusionment with America," August 6, 2014, https://www.saada.org/tides/article/living-in-a-gilded-cage, accessed January 6, 2025.

31. John Mohammad Ali, June 28, 1923, INS Reference 1525-C1621908, U.S. Subject Index to Correspondence and Case Files of the Immigration and Naturalization Service, 1903–1959, downloaded from Ancestry.com. Federal records from the prosecution of the case can be found in File 38–636, (Naturalization) Litigation Case Files and Enclosures, 1907–1978, US National

Archives and Records Administration (hereafter NARA), College Park, MD, Record Group 60, Entry A1-COR 38, Box 381, Shelf location: 230/14/35/3.

32. Case file for *US* v. *John Muhammed Ali*, Equity Case 614, Records of the US District of the Eastern District of Michigan, NARA, Chicago, Record Group 21.

33. In several cases the government claimed that it could not locate the person and simply published a subpoena in a local newspaper. When the person failed to appear within sixty days, the courts treated their absence as a de facto "confession" and cancelled their citizenship. Agarwal, "Uncertain Citizenship," 101.

34. "Sakharam Pandit: High Caste Brahmin Teacher and Lecturer from India," 1910, Redpath Chautauqua Collection, MSC 0150, University of Iowa, digitized at https://www.saada.org/item/20111208-530.

35. "Prophet Heads his Ancestors," *Los Angeles Times*, February 11, 1925, 2.

36. "A Sheik in Distress," *The Detroit Free Press*, February 3, 1925, 3.

37. "Prophet Heads his Ancestors."

38. Ibid.

39. Hsu-Ming Teo, *Desert Passions: Orientalism and Romance Novels* (Austin: University of Texas Press, 2012), 87–143.

40. "Prophet Heads His Ancestors."

41. "A Sheik in Distress."

42. *United States* v. *Ali* 7 F.2d 728 (E.D. Mich. 1925).

43. Case file for *US* v. *Ali*, Equity Case 614, NARA, Chicago, Records of District Courts of the United States, Record Group 21.

44. Agarwal, "Uncertain Citizenship," 57.

45. Jensen, *Passage from India*, 260. As discussed in the following section, this issue was raised with respect to Jan/John, and the British officials reviewing his case differed on their interpretation of whether he "reverted" to British nationality after losing his US citizenship.

46. Meg Hacker, "When Saying 'I do' Meant Giving Up Your U.S. Citizenship," *Prologue* (Spring 2014): 56–61. The wife of Taraknath Das, Mary Keating Das, publicized the impact of *Thind* on the white wives of the men who were denaturalized. See her article, "A Woman without a Country," *Nation* 123, no. 3187 (August 4, 1926): 105–6. On her role in protesting the *Thind* decision, and lobbying Congress to pass legislation restoring citizenship to those naturalized before 1923, see Agarwal, "Uncertain Citizenship," 79–93.

47. Sucheng Chan, "Asian American Economic and Labor History," in *The Oxford Handbook of Asian American History*, eds. David K. Yoo and Eiichiro Azuma (New York: Oxford University Press, 2013), 306.

48. 1930 United States Federal Census, downloaded from Ancestry.com.

49. It was official British policy *not* to issue passports to colonial seamen purportedly because passports were "too easily disposed of for cash." "Colonial merchant seamen: standardization of certificates of national identity, 1949–1960," TNA, HO 213/1621.

50. British officials continuously complained that seamen traded and forged their paperwork. "Registration and control of coloured seamen," 1930–1931, TNA, HO 45/14299.

51. Balachandran, *Globalizing Labour?*, 36.

52. Laura Tabili, "The Construction of Racial Difference in Twentieth-century Britain: The Special Restriction (Coloured Alien Seamen) Order, 1925," *Journal of British Studies* 33, no. 1 (1994): 64.

53. Balachandran, *Globalizing Labour?*, 5.

54. Laura Tabili was instrumental in challenging the idea that resistance to the presence of colonial seafarers was largely a bottom-up manifestation of popular, working-class racism. Tabili, *"We Ask for British Justice."*

55. Jacqueline Jenkinson, *Black 1919: Riots, Racism and Resistance in Imperial Britain* (Liverpool: Liverpool University Press, 2009).

56. Lucy Bland, "White Women and Men of Colour: Miscegenation Fears in Britain After the Great War," *Gender & History* 17, no. 1 (2005): 29–61.

57. Tabili, "The Construction of Racial Difference," 72.

58. "Certificates of nationality for coloured seamen, 1930–1936," TNA, DO 35/131/6.

59. "Jama, Mohamed: issue of special seaman's Certificate of Nationality," 1934, TNA, HO 382/26.

60. "Identity papers of seamen in lieu of passports," 1934–1935, TNA, CO 323/1262/16.

61. "Nationality and Naturalisation (including Certificates of British Origin): Special Certificates of Nationality (Coloured Seamen): Controversial cases, 1931–1934," TNA, HO 45/15774.

62. The following description of Jan's travails in Britain is based on TNA, HO 45/13750.

63. For details about this collection, see https://discovery.nationalarchives.gov.uk/details/r/C14990, accessed January 6, 2025.

64. W. J. Killingback, "The Work of the Registry of Shipping & Seamen and of the Mercantile Marine Offices," unpublished manuscript, c. 1945, TNA, Main Library, Call number 387.20216 *.

65. Kenneth Chapman, *Peace, War, and Friendships: Life Ashore and Afloat in the 1930s and 1940s* (East Hoathly: Barham Press, 2006), 75.

66. "Issue of certificates of identity to British Seamen," 1940, BL, IOR/L/PJ/7/3790.

67. In the 1939 register, Esther is listed as single and living with two children in South Shields. A note on the register indicated that she was married in 1943, and her last name is amended to "Ali." Ref: RG101/2693B/006/1 Letter Code: FCAB, downloaded from findmypast.co.uk.

68. Mohamed Ali, TNA, BT 372/50/13, R124667.

69. Maung Aung Sein, TNA, BT 372/127/51, R166967.

70. Suna Meah, TNA, BT 372/148/100, R175479.

71. Mohamed Mottassim, TNA, BT 372/200/144, R195170 and Surcoom Ali, TNA, BT 372/200/145, R195171.

72. Pakianadar Swaminathan, TNA, BT 372/144/121, R173853.

73. Heloise Finch-Boyer, "Lascars through the Colonial Lens: Reconsidering Visual Sources of South Asian Sailors from the Twentieth Century," *Journal for Maritime Research* 16, no. 2 (2014): 246–63; Daniel Davies, "Serving the Empire: P&O, Design, Identity and Representation (1837–1969)," PhD dissertation, Middlesex University, 2017.

74. Harry Furniss, *P & O Sketches in Pen and Ink* (London: Studio of Design & Illustration Supply Agency, c.1898), 6–8.

75. The butcher shop was a collaboration between Nawab Ali and his wife and Taslim Ali, another former seaman. "Taslim Ali," *Making Britain Database* https://www.open.ac.uk/researchprojects/makingbritain/content/taslim-ali, accessed October 31, 2022.

76. Nawab Ali Oral History Interview, Papers of Caroline Adams, Tower Hamlets Local History Library & Archives, P/ADM1/2. An edited version of this interview (which omits some

of the discussion of clothing found in the original) was published in Adams, *Across Seven Seas*, 67–94.

77. Herman Melville, *Billy Budd, and Other Prose Pieces* (London: Constable and Company, 1924), 5; Stephen Matterson, *Melville: Fashioning in Modernity* (London: Bloomsbury Academic & Professional, 2014).

78. Charles Baudelaire, "The Dandy," in *The Painter of Modern Life and Other Essays* (1863), translated by Jonathan Mayne (London: Phaidon Press, 1995), 26–29.

79. Jan Mohamed, CR2, TNA, BT348, R976527, downloaded from findmypast.co.uk.

80. "Alleged Theft of Suitcase in Nottingham," *The Nottingham Evening Post*, December 14, 1931, 6.

81. Balachandran, *Globalizing Labor?*, 3, and BL, IOR/L/PJ/12/645.

82. "Stories of the Town," *Lewiston Evening Journal*, August 9, 1946, 16.

83. "John Mohammad Ali Allison," August 2, 1947, District Court, Eastern District of New York, US Naturalization Records Indexes, 1794–1995, accessed via Ancestry.com.

84. John Lambourne Allison, Report of the Death of an American Citizen, May 17, 1954, accessed via Ancestry.com.

85. "John Allison, Federal Telecommunication Engineer," *The Herald-News* (Passaic, New Jersey), June 2, 1954, 30. The reference to the "first Caliph of Mohammed" is somewhat unclear, possibly indicating that the family was descended from Abu Bakr, the first caliph and father-in-law of the Prophet, rather than to Muhammad himself.

86. Anthony Williams, "Williams Family Tree," https://www.ancestry.com/family-tree/tree/161083382?cfpid=282103258677&dtid=100, accessed January 6, 2025.

87. On the eugenic connection, see Francis Galton, *Life History Album* (London: Macmillan and Co., 1884).

88. When providing me with a digital copy of the photograph, the TNA's imaging team removed the photograph from the plastic sleeve, so the new reddish-orange thread is not visible in the image reproduced in Figure 4.5.

89. See, for example, the contributions to the special issue of the journal *Past & Present*, "Global History and Microhistory," 242, no. 14 (November 2019).

90. Carlo Ginzburg and Carlo Poni, "The Name and the Game: Unequal Exchange and the Historical Marketplace," in *Microhistory and the Lost People of Europe*, eds. Edward Muir and Guido Ruggiero, trans. Eren Branch (Baltimore: John Hopkins University Press, 1991), 1–10; Carlo Ginzburg, *Threads and Traces: True False Fictive*, trans. Anne C. Tedeschi and John Tedeschi (Berkeley: University of California Press, 2012), 1.

91. Rothschild, *The Inner Life of Empires*, 277–8; Francesca Trivellato, "Is There a Future for Italian Microhistory in the Age of Global History?," *California Italian Studies* 2, no.1 (2011).

92. Durba Ghosh, "Decoding the Nameless: Gender, Subjectivity, and Historical Methodologies in Reading the Archives of Colonial India," in *A New Imperial History: Culture, Identity, and Modernity in Britain and the Empire, 1600–1840*, ed. Kathleen Wilson (Cambridge: Cambridge University Press, 2004), 297–316.

93. "Rogue's Yarn," in *The Oxford Companion to Ships and the Sea*, eds. I.C.B. Dear and Peter Kemp (Oxford: Oxford University Press, 2006).

94. Carlo Ginzburg, "Family Resemblances and Family Trees: Two Cognitive Metaphors," *Critical Inquiry* 30, no. 3 (2004): 539.

95. Ibid., 556.

96. Natalie Zemon Davis, *The Return of Martin Guerre* (Cambridge, Harvard University Press, 1983), 67.

## Chapter 5. Digital Genealogy

1. My own efforts to think more deeply about digital and DNA genealogy were inspired by the work of Nelson, *The Social Life of DNA*; and Jerome De Groot, *Consuming History: Historians and Heritage in Contemporary Popular Culture*, 2nd ed. (London: Routledge, 2016).

2. Interview with Esha Pillay by Bava Dharani, November 21, 2022, https://girmit.world/portfolio-item/learning-about-indenture/, accessed December 14, 2022.

3. I am indebted to Noora Jabir for this insight, which draws on her research while an undergraduate at New York University, Abu Dhabi.

4. United Nations, Department of Economic and Social Affairs, Population Division, *International Migration 2020: Highlights*, available online at https://www.un.org/en/desa/international-migration-2020-highlights, accessed January 6, 2025.

5. Jerome de Groot, "Ancestry. com and the Evolving Nature of Historical Information Companies," *The Public Historian* 42, no. 1 (2020): 8–28; on the need for more research on how users of these sites perceive them and their role in reshaping history, see Paul Knevel, "Genealogy from Below," *National Council on Public History*, August 14, 2015, https://ncph.org/history-at-work/genealogy-from-below/, accessed January 6, 2025.

6. Matt Matsuda, "Genetic Drift: Pacific Pasts and Futures," in *Pacific Futures*, eds. Warwick Anderson, Miranda Johnson, and Barbara Brooks (Honolulu: University of Hawai'i Press, 2018), 52. See also Matt Matsuda, *Genealogies, Genomes, and Histories in the Pacific: Genetic Drift* (Cham, Switzerland: Palgrave Macmillan, 2023); and Nelson, *The Social Life of DNA*. Both Matsuda and Nelson point to the creative ways in which the very populations who have been exploited by genetic sciences have repurposed this knowledge to promote anti-racist and decolonial projects.

7. Leo A. Goodman, "Snowball Sampling," *The Annals of Mathematical Statistics* (1961): 148–70. For historians, the equivalent might be locating one relevant file and then pulling the other files that it cites or which cite it, information that is often included on the cover of archival files.

8. Maya Jasanoff, "Our Obsession with Ancestry Has Some Twisted Roots," *The New Yorker*, May 2, 2022; Carolina Johnsson Malm, "Genealogy and the Problem of Biological Essentialism," September 10, 2015, National Council on Public History, https://ncph.org/history-at-work/genealogy-and-biological-essentialism/, accessed January 6, 2025.

9. Jasanoff, "Our Obsession with Ancestry."

10. https://www.ancestry.com/corporate/about-ancestry/company-facts, cited April 11, 2023; https://pro.similarweb.com/#/digitalsuite/websiteanalysis/overview/website-performance/*/999/3m?webSource=Total&key=ancestry.com, cited April 11, 2023.

11. https://www.ancestry.com/offers/subscribe, cited April 11, 2023.

12. Bruce Falconer, "Ancestry.com's Genealogical Juggernaut," *Bloomberg*, September 20, 2012, https://www.bloomberg.com/news/articles/2012-09-20/ancestry-dot-coms-genealogical-juggernaut#xj4y7vzkg.

13. This analysis is based on data provided by the analytics company SimilarWeb on their website in March 2023.

14. Jerome de Groot, "Ancestry.com and the Evolving Nature of Historical Information Companies," *The Public Historian* 42, no. 1 (2020): 17–28.

15. "Kal Penn Reacts to Family History in Finding Your Roots," https://www.youtube.com/watch?v=7M3h4wyV3ss, posted November 1, 2021.

16. A list of these sites can be found at the bottom of the Ancestry.com website. The list included in the text was based on the sites listed in March 2023.

17. https://pro.similarweb.com/#/digitalsuite/websiteanalysis/audience-geography/*/999/3m?key=ancestry.com&webSource=Total, cited March 27, 2023.

18. https://www.ancestry.com/search/places/asia/india/, cited April 11, 2023.

19. https://www.familysearch.org/en/wiki/India,_Hindu_Pilgrimage_Records_-_FamilySearch_Historical_Records, cited April 11, 2023.

20. The following discussion is based on an interview that I conducted with Karanveer Sahota on December 20, 2022. His family tree can also be found https://www.ancestry.com/family-tree/tree/47164097?cfpid=6707946539&dtid=100, accessed January 6, 2025.

21. Interview with Theresa Simmons, January 4, 2023.

22. Ibid.

23. Amina Zarrugh, and Luis Romero, "Genetic Racialization: Ancestry Tests and the Reification of Race," *Social Problems* 20 (2023): 1–17.

24. Aaron Panofsky, Kushan Dasgupta, and Nicole Iturriaga, "How White Nationalists Mobilize Genetics: From Genetic Ancestry and Human Biodiversity to Counterscience and Metapolitics," *American Journal of Physical Anthropology* 175, no. 2 (2021): 387–98.

25. For examples of decolonial projects that engage with genetic genealogy in other oceanic contexts, see Matsuda, *Genealogies, Genomes, and Histories in the Pacific*.

26. Nelson, *The Social Life of DNA*.

27. For an example of a study deploying this limited sampling approach, see Wendy D. Roth, Şule Yaylacı, Kaitlyn Jaffe, and Lindsey Richardson, "Do Genetic Ancestry Tests Increase Racial Essentialism? Findings From a Randomized Controlled Trial," *PLoS One* 15, no. 1 (2020).

28. These numbers are provided by both companies in the "About Us" sections of their websites and reflect published statistics as of March 2023, https://www.ancestry.com/corporate/about-ancestry/company-facts and https://www.23andme.com/about/.

29. "Blackstone Completes Acquisition of Ancestry®, Leading Online Family History Business, for $4.7 Billion," December 4, 2020, https://www.blackstone.com/news/press/blackstone-completes-acquisition-of-ancestry-leading-online-family-history-business-for-4-7-billion/. Data on the stock price of 23andMe is taken from Yahoo Finance.

30. Sarah Zhang, "Big Pharma Would Like Your DNA," *The Atlantic*, July 28, 2018; Sarah Zhang, "The Messy Consequences of the Golden State Killer Case," *The Atlantic*, October 1, 2019.

31. "23andMe Breach Targeted Jewish and Chinese Customers, Lawsuit Says," *New York Times*, January, 26, 2024.

32. Max Eddy, "23andMe Just Filed for Bankruptcy. You Should Delete Your Data Now," *New York Times*, March 25, 2025.

33. Michael Keller, "How Ancestry Test Results Became Browner," *The Juggernaut*, September 8, 2020, https://www.thejuggernaut.com/genetic-ancestry-testing.

34. https://www.amazon.com/gp/customer-reviews/R3CLU29CZ3405H/ref=cm_cr_getr_d_rvw_ttl?ie=UTF8&ASIN=B01LZ5K87Z, posted November 14, 2020.

35. "23andMe Tests New Ancestry Breakdown in Central and South Asia," April 3, 2019, https://blog.23andme.com/articles/central-and-south-asia.

36. https://support.ancestry.com/s/article/List-of-AncestryDNA-Regions?language=en_US, cited March 29, 2023.

37. https://www.xcode.life/the-south-asian-genome-project/. The free analysis was later discontinued.

38. https://www.reddit.com/r/ABCDesis/comments/tgms8s/best_ancestry_test_for_south_asians/, cited March 29, 2023.

39. Mark Munsterhjelm, *Forensic Colonialism: Genetics and the Capture of Indigenous Peoples* (Montreal: McGill-Queen's University Press, 2023). These examples are reminiscent of the famous case of Henrietta Lacks but suggest that such practices are ongoing.

40. https://support.ancestry.com/s/article/Countries-Where-AncestryDNA-is-Available; https://eu.customercare.23andme.com/hc/en-us/articles/204712980-What-Countries-Do-You-Ship-To-#:~:text=Our%20EU%20services%20are%20available,Netherlands*. These results date to March 2023.

41. Website accessed March 2023; site subsequently removed. More recently, the Government of India has launched an online portal for gaining permission to export human biological samples. https://www.icmr.gov.in/transfer-of-human-biological-material#:~:text=ICMR%20under%20Department%20of%20Health,research%20by%20Indian%20companies%2Forganizations, accessed December 12, 2024.

42. https://www.dnaforensics.in/, accessed December 12, 2024; https://www.xcode.in/faqs/, accessed March 2023. While Xcode does market its services primarily as "genetic testing kits for health and wellness," and it does not provide family relationship matches, it does provide information about regional ancestry. As of late 2024, Xcode's website had been taken down.

43. Saritha Rai and P R Sanjai, "Asia's Richest Man Mukesh Ambani to Foray Into Genome Testing with $145 Kit," March 2, 2023, https://www.bloomberg.com/news/articles/2023-03-02/mukesh-ambani-s-firm-will-offer-genome-tests-for-145-to-detect-disorders-early.

44. Banu Subramaniam, *Holy Science: The Biopolitics of Hindu Nationalism* (Seattle: University of Washington Press, 2019).

45. Shoaib Daniyal, "Two New Genetic Studies Upheld Indo-Aryan Migration. So Why Did Indian Media Report the Opposite?," *Scroll.in*, September 12, 2019, https://scroll.in/article/936872/two-new-genetic-studies-upheld-aryan-migration-theory-so-why-did-indian-media-report-the-opposite.

46. Interview with Farrah Jaufuraully, December 13, 2022.

47. Interview with Roshan, December 19, 2022.

48. https://www.instagram.com/p/CMXzky9Hn6J/, posted March 14, 2021.

49. de Groot, "Ancestry.com and the Evolving Nature of Historical Information Companies," 11.

50. United Nations, Department of Economic and Social Affairs, Population Division, *International Migration 2020: Highlights* and *International Migration Report 2015: Highlights*.

51. Neha Vora, *Impossible Citizens: Dubai's Indian Diaspora* (Durham: Duke University Press, 2013).

52. @indianmemoryproject; https://www.indianmemoryproject.com/about/, accessed January 6, 2025.

53. Anusha Yadav interviewed in Mallika Bhagat, "Indian Memory Project: Tracing India's History Through Pictures," *Outlook*, August 3, 2022, https://www.outlookindia.com/travel/indian-memory-project-tracing-india-s-history-through-pictures-news-219524.

54. https://www.indianmemoryproject.com/tag/hair-styles/.

55. @museumofmaterialmemory; https://museumofmaterialmemory.com/

56. Ciaran Thapar, "Brown History, the Instagram Spotlighting South Asia's Hidden Stories," *AnOther*, October 3, 2022, https://www.anothermag.com/design-living/14413/brown-history-instagram-south-asia-partition-ahsun-zafa-interview.

57. Ibid.

58. https://www.instagram.com/p/B7ZpavXHvEV/, posted January 17, 2020.

59. https://www.instagram.com/p/B-YAED3HRbO/, posted March 31, 2020.

60. https://www.instagram.com/p/CEwmj24H4Sf/, posted September 5, 2020.

61. Priyanka Sacheti, "On a New Instagram Account, Indians and Pakistanis are Sharing Their Memories of Living in the Gulf," *Scroll.in*, April 25, 2019, https://scroll.in/magazine/920009/on-an-instagram-account-indians-and-pakistanis-are-sharing-their-memories-of-living-in-the-gulf. Sacheti also published the same story in the Pakistani newspaper *Dawn*, https://www.dawn.com/news/1479188.

62. Anna Zacharias, "Nostalgic Photos that Challenge the Stereotypes of migration Between the Gulf and South Asia," *The National UAE*, May 29, 2019, https://www.thenationalnews.com/arts-culture/art/nostalgic-photos-that-challenge-the-stereotypes-of-migration-between-the-gulf-and-south-asia-1.867566.

63. Interview with Priyanka Sacheti, February 17, 2023.

64. Interview with Aathma Nirmala Dious, February 23, 2023.

65. https://www.instagram.com/p/B88iD6HJTXR/, posted February 24, 2020.

66. When I spoke to her, Priyanka was working on an essay on these topics, published soon after as "Home is a House in Oman," *The Markas Review*, March 5, 2023, https://themarkaz.org/home-is-a-house-in-oman/#_ftnref1.

67. Benedict Anderson, *Imagined Communities: Reflections on the Origin and Spread of Nationalism* (London: Verso Books, 1991).

68. Thomas Hylland Eriksen, "Nationalism and the Internet," *Nations and Nationalism* 13, 1 (2007): 1–17; Sabina Mihelj and César Jiménez-Martínez, "Digital Nationalism: Understanding the Role of Digital Media in the Rise of 'New' Nationalism," *Nations and Nationalism* 27, no. 2 (2021): 331–46.

69. I noted, however, that Ayesha had asked for Manju's permission to repost the image in the comments.

70. Interview with Manju Sara Rajan, February 27, 2023.

71. Email correspondence with Neetha Kurup, March 1, 2023 and December 13, 2024.

72. On the introduction of the requirement, see Huda Tabrez, "If You Don't Do These Classes, You Will Not Get Your Labour Card in the UAE," December 31, 2019, *Gulf News*. My employment visa described me as an "assistant teacher," and I was told in fall 2022 that the requirement was new, perhaps suggesting that the categories of workers involved had expanded.

73. For the larger context and history of the use of categories of "skill" in regulating migration in the Gulf, including its connection to colonial legal legacies, see Natasha Iskander, *Does Skill Make Us Human?: Migrant Workers in 21st-Century Qatar and Beyond* (Princeton: Princeton University Press, 2021).

74. Interview with Aathma Nirmala Dious, February 23, 2023; follow-up correspondence over email, January 6, 2025.

75. Ibid.

76. Interview with Ruth D'Souza, February 20, 2023.

## Conclusion: Uprooting History

1. I am particularly grateful for the conversations I had with Sergio Infante and Barbara Shi about their own experience researching and writing about their families in the context of taking this course.

# SELECT ARCHIVES, SPECIAL COLLECTIONS, AND DIGITAL RESOURCES

## ARKIB NEGARA MALAYSIA, KUALA LUMPUR (ANMKL)

Treasury, Public Works, Police, Survey, Lands, Klang, Selangor, Chinese Secretariat, Resident, and Kuala Lumpur Records

## NATIONAL ARCHIVES OF SINGAPORE (NAS)

Oral History Interviews
Maps and Building Plans

## NATIONAL LIBRARY OF SINGAPORE

NewspapersSG

## NATIONAL ARCHIVES, ZANZIBAR, TANZANIA (ZNA)

High Court Files
Probate

## GANDHI-LUTHULI DOCUMENTATION CENTRE, UNIVERSITY OF KWAZULU-NATAL, DURBAN, SOUTH AFRICA

Student Roots Projects
Ships List Spreadsheets

## NATIONAL ARCHIVES OF SOUTH AFRICA, KWAZULU-NATAL, PIETERMARITZBURG (NAB)

Indian Immigration Department
Surveyor General's Office

### THE NATIONAL ARCHIVES, KEW, UNITED KINGDOM (TNA)

Board of Trade, Home, Colonial, and Dominions Offices

### NATIONAL ARCHIVES OF INDIA, DELHI (NAI)

Revenue and Agriculture Department
Emigration Department

### BRITISH LIBRARY, LONDON (BL)

Privy Council Case Records, Social Science Collections
India Office Records, Asian and African Studies Collections (IOR)

### UNITED STATES CITIZENSHIP AND IMMIGRATION SERVICES, GENEALOGY PROGRAM

C-Files

### NATIONAL ARCHIVES AND RECORDS ADMINISTRATION, UNITED STATES (NARA)

(Naturalization) Litigation Case Files and Enclosures, General Records of the Department of Justice (Record Group 60, College Park, MD)
Records of District Courts of the United States (Record Group 21, Chicago, IL)

### NORTHWESTERN UNIVERSITY LIBRARIES, CHICAGO, IL, USA

The Humphrey Winterton Collection of East African Photographs

### UNIVERSITY OF IOWA SPECIAL COLLECTIONS, IOWA CITY, IA, USA

Redpath Chautauqua Collection

### TOWER HAMLETS LOCAL HISTORY LIBRARY & ARCHIVES, LONDON, UK

Oral Histories, Papers of Caroline Adams

PEABODY ESSEX MUSEUM, SALEM, MASSACHUSETTS, USA

LEIDEN UNIVERSITY LIBRARIES, NETHERLANDS

FLATEN ART MUSEUM, ST. OLAF COLLEGE, NORTHFIELD, MN, USA

SOUTH ASIAN AMERICAN DIGITAL ARCHIVES

NATIONAL MARITIME MUSEUM, GREENWICH, LONDON, UK

## MUSEUM EXHIBITIONS

Renluka Maharaj, "Bhumi's Daughters," Project for Empty Space, October 1, 2022–January 21, 2023, Newark, NJ, USA.

Suchitra Mattai, "Myth from Matter," National Museum of Women in the Arts, September 20, 2024–January 15, 2025, Washington, D.C., USA.

## DIGITAL GENEALOGY

Ancestry.com
MyHeritage.com
Findmypast.com
Familysearch.org
Geni.com
Familytreedna.com

## SOCIAL MEDIA

Malaysian Heritage and History Club, Facebook
Girmit Global, Facebook
Brown History, Instagram
Indian Memory Project, Instagram
Museum of Material Memory, Instagram
Gulf ⇄ South Asia, Instagram

# INDEX

Page numbers in italics refer to figures.